D1027476

Early encouragements for

Healing Your Financial Soul

David is on to something here with *Healing Your Financial Soul*. Carol and I are well aware of how the blessings of God's love can be blocked by the power of unforgiveness and judgments, but hadn't thought of the financial implications. **But the lights came on when I read this book.** Poverty is never a friend – this book will lead you deeper into the kindness of God, including financially.
John and Carol Arnott
Founding Pastors, Toronto Airport Christian Fellowship

This is a great book and it will help many people move into financial abundance. This book guides us in removing the conflicting beliefs we hold about money deep in our hearts. The result is that our hearts can now fully believe God's promises to us about financial blessing, and full faith paves the way for complete financial transformation in our lives.
Well done, David! I am going to personally work through all the exercises in this book and insure that my heart is completely free from all negative ideas concerning money.
Mark Virkler, President, Christian Leadership University
Founder, Communion with God Ministries

In late December of '06, I found that I had committed myself to reading four different manuscripts for endorsements and/or suggestions. One of them proved to be a good book and two of them turned out to be very good books, but "Healing Your Financial Soul" turned out be both **very good and very, very fun to read.** As I have taught quite a bit on finances from a Biblical standpoint, I was eager to read David's book. I can honestly say that not only is this book sound in Biblical truth re: money, it is also **truly fresh, even pioneering**, in the tools and perspectives it gives the reader.

I am excited to say this book delivers the goods to heal your financial soul and to help bring you to the place where you can both live and give, like our heavenly Father, out of abundance of soul and provision. Thanks, David, for a fresh and creative look at God's standards for our lives.
Marc A. Dupont
Mantle of Praise Ministries

Does God want you to be rich?

Hmmm...
I know he wants a lot more people to be wealthy so they can help save lives in Darfur, energize inner city outreaches, patronize the arts, kick start businesses, provide scholarships and feed & clothe the poor. Because money helps.

And I know he also wants more people to embrace a call to self-denial and be field agents for change among the deprived and neglected. Which may mean letting go of middling, financially stressful lifestyles.

I know he wants a lot people to stop all the financial hand-wringing and tackle their dreams, aspirations and callings – whether it's in business, art, ministry, sport, community life, media, politics, family, academics, or whatever.

Whichever scenario you go into – affluence, simplicity or somewhere in between – you won't do it well until your relationship with money is *healthy*.

You can flourish and thrive in a lot of ways that you only daydream about right now
But not until you're in a healthy place with money – *then* you can pursue and embrace your financial destiny, whether that's mobilizing an abundance of finances for good works, or answering a call to austerity.

So many people, perhaps including you, are blocked from any of the above by their lousy relationship with money. And not just in their surface thinking and opinions on the subject. Even the best teaching and most sensible strategies will be undone by your underlying beliefs and overriding impulses if we don't get to the roots of those frustrating and disappointing patterns.

Healing Your Financial Soul is a no-nonsense, warm, seriously irreverent, definitely iconoclastic, challenging yet fun, renovation of your programming, behaviour and experiences with finances, *i.e.* money itself, and the role it plays in how you live, work, play and share.

HEALING YOUR FINANCIAL SOUL

An Interactive Guide
to Restoring Your
Relationship with Money

David Hicks

To my friend, Brenda,

Here's to your abundance!

D.H.

P E N S A R I O Publishing

First Edition, April, 2007

HEALING YOUR FINANCIAL SOUL
An Interactive Guide to Restoring Your Relationship with Money

Cover design: Diesel Design Associates
Stratford, Ontario, Canada www.dieseldesign.ca

Notes:
*To get around the grammatical sticking point of having to use a
pronoun to generally address either a woman or man, I've often
used "they" and "their", rather than the traditional "he" and "his",
or the more clumsy "he/she" and "his/her".*
*I've also bent a number of rules for line breaks, tabbing and para-
graphs. I blame modern poetry.*
*Although I've considered the liberal use of italics, boldface and
underlining to support a writer's voice to be a sign of weak writing, I've succumbed. Frequently.*
*Bible references, when not my own paraphrase, tend to be from
the New International Version, for no better reason than that's the
version I usually reflect upon.*

P E N S A R I O Publishing
P.O. Box 5
Sebringville ON
N0K 1X0 Canada
www.pensariopublishing.com
www.healingyourfinancialsoul.com

Printed in Canada

Dedications

This book is for, and because of...

My fabulous wife, Charmaine, for a life of romance and adventure, and for being such an encourager and supporter of this project. "The cat lives!"

My parents, who modeled our Father's kindness, patience and generosity, consummately expressed in Jesus and his Holy Spirit.

Our many friends and loved ones around the world, whose names would overflow the covers of this book, for all you've shared. May this book serve you well.

And The Church. We all get to practice on each other and often learn at one another's expense – grace & humour to you all.

The preamble before we peramble

You can be wealthy and yet have a lousy relationship with money.
You can take a vow of poverty and still feel rich.
You can be middleclass and have the worst of both. Many do.

The fact that you've opened this book more than hints that your own relationship with money is not, shall we say, exactly what you're looking for. You might feel stuck. Or out of control. Or overburdened. Or maybe you're dismayed at the financial frustration, even schizophrenia and chaos, you see around you at home, work and church.
What ever it is, something's not working.

And it's not like you haven't heard enough about finances. There are more than enough opinions, counsel and messages on the subject to keep anyone confused and confounded for this lifetime and the next – all of it proffering 'successful strategies', 'practical steps' and of course God's expectations and frustrations. And such a variety!
Some of it helpful, much of it confusing, all of it debatable.

I say, let's set aside all that stress, strain and striving, just admit that, guilty or not, you're dissatisfied with your finances and decide that it's time to work on your relationship with money. Then, once you get some relief, clarity and direction, you can choose a fulfilling destination for you and your finances. Whether that's to be affluence, self-denial or something in between, you and your money can be healthy and happy together.

Healing Your Financial Soul is an interactive guide designed to walk you into, through and out the other side of the self-fulfilling prophecies, misconceptions, frustrations and disappointments that beset you and your money, and release you into a new direction that's encouraging, satisfying, even fun!

Round Up the Usual Answers
You might be thinking: "All it would take is just a bit more income. Not too much, just enough to relieve some of the pressures."
Wrong.

A mathematical increase in your income will simply produce a corresponding increase in your expenses and stresses. Your house might be bigger, but so will you're headaches. Your car might be faster, but so will its depreciation in value. You'll 'net out' at the same level you're at now. Guaranteed.

You can be stuck when you're rich. You can be stuck when you're poor. You might have a preference between the two, but either way you're still stuck.

"Then what do I need to do differently for my finances to improve?" Wrong question.

I hope you're ready to hear this (and if not, I hope you'll be back) but it won't matter what you do differently. Yes, change is necessary. But even if you pick up new insights and try doing something different, you'll soon be back on course to duplicating the same results you've created thus far.

In fact, you're on that track now. Trying to do something new will not make a difference because, in the same way that the law of gravity eventually prevails, sooner or later our old thinking will win out and we'll slip back and 'do' something from our old ways (in other words, what we've really believed all along) and derail whatever progress we've managed through the raw force of effort. When either pressure or enticement arrives, it's all too easy to default back to our old programming and be left scrambling to rationalize another goofy decision and disappointing result.

Yes, there are success stories out there about how discipline and sacrifice worked for individuals and families, and their specialness and rarity attest to how few make it by taking that course. Effort needs to be in the mix, but effort alone will not get you over the hump and into financial peace and health.

"Okay, so what about <u>thinking</u> differently about money?" That's a better question and it'll help. But we're going for deep change...

Your Inner Penguin
Simply finding a different idea or line of thinking to give mental assent is like a penguin atop an iceberg trying to change his destination by facing the other way – being on top helps him think he's in charge, the view changes a bit, a new breeze of doctrine promises change, but the 9/10[ths] of the iceberg below the surface continues to obey the ocean current's momentum. We need

to make our changes below the surface. More to the point, below our surface thinking.

We're waking to the realization that for our circumstances to be different, we need to not just do, or even think, differently – we need to be different. From the inside out. Change the undercurrents as well as the surface orientation. And that's what Healing Your Financial Soul is about.

Instead of selling you on
    yet another (doomed) investment scheme,
        or yoking you to a budget (aka, recipe for failure),
            or getting out the old cat'o'nine tithes,
                we're going to have some fun!

We'll sort through the clutter in your financial attic (what you think you know about money), help you with new ways of understanding and viewing money (because your current tangle of beliefs has gotten you where you are now) and give you some fun things to do so you'll start feeling, believing, thinking and living differently with your money.

Then I believe you'll see
    your finances improve,
        your money flourish,
            your bad history fade into the background,
            and a new horizon of financial fulfillment open up.

And as a result, money will stop being an obstacle and become an opportunity,
    finances will stop being a need and become an asset,
        "If only..." wishes will become "Hey, let's..." ventures,
            Kingdom frustration will give way to Kingdom adventure.

But it won't happen in our outer circumstances unless it first happens from within. That's why I've called this book, Healing Your Financial Soul. Because, to paraphrase Jesus, what's the point in amassing earthly wealth while your own soul is lost and suffering?[1]

I believe that one of the fruits of a healthy soul will be healthy finances, which can in turn enable you to participate in our Father's will being done in your life, and through you in the lives of oth-

ers, as it is in Heaven.
That is, with joy, gratitude and celebration.

Special note to engaged couples

I know you've got a lot to think about and pull together between now and the wedding. And I trust you're meeting with somebody in lieu of pre-marital counseling. This book can be a tremendously helpful pre-marriage course in itself.

I'll tell you up front, that if you go through this book together you'll learn a great deal about yourselves and each other, in more ways than just financial. If anything, you'll appreciate each other all the more.

But given the way marriages are affected by financial strain and differing values concerning money, earning, spending, the cost of living, and so forth, especially during the first year of marriage, this book can help you start your married life on a much more positive, resilient foundation.

Besides, the interactive qualities of the experiences in this book can be quite fun when done with your loved one, and easier to press through with a supportive partner when things get sticky.

One thing for sure, you'll have a lot to talk about!

Introduction

How We'll Do This

The book of James points out that one of the quirks of human thinking is how a man can look into a mirror at himself, then turn around and immediately 'forget' what he looks like.[1] This is the person who notices something about himself, acknowledges it, but then turns and lives as if he hadn't. Recognition alone does not change the way he lives.

This is why reading this book will not suffice to change your finances – you have to play.
So I've designed this book to be interactive and experiential:
   I'll ask you to participate,
      make what you discover stick,
         then face a new direction,
            set that course into motion,
            and generate momentum
               that will yield new experiences.

We'll do this by working on several different levels...

Reflect & decide

- I can give you lots to think about, but nothing different will happen until you purposefully decide to allow a new perspective to prove itself. So read each section with an open mind. And in particular, note any feelings that stir.
- Our experiences with money are inextricably linked to strong, often conflicting, emotions – some helpful, some hindering, some enjoyable, some unpleasant. And they're very real. In fact, they're mostly why you've gotten where you are now, whether that's good, bad or indifferent. Your feelings will always be a critical factor, so we'll take them seriously.
- As you read and venture into new ways, you may experience excitement, anticipation or nervousness. These are good signs – congratulate yourself and keep going.
- If your reactions are skepticism, scorn, sadness, resentment, guilt or embarrassment, don't be surprised and don't try to deny, ignore or suppress them. Just stop and tell your inner monologue...
I understand that this is how I have felt up to now, but I'm not satisfied. So I'm going to consider other options.
Repeat as needed. Don't worry, this is not weird – even King David had to issue directives to his own soul.[2] In fact, why

wait? Put your hand on your head (c'mon, it won't hurt) and make that statement out loud.
Not just in your head, out loud.
Here's why...

Write & verbalize
+ Part of how we'll deal with old thinking, untangle discrepancies, re-solve accumulated contradictions and set a new course, will be to pro-nounce and pro-claim the intention to try new and different ways. Little ever gets done without saying it first. (Creation, for instance.) So don't shy away from this. When we get to those points in the book, don't just nod, speak loudly! Think of this as the rallying fanfare for a new era – scripture points out that a trumpet call needs to be clear and distinct to effectively rally support.[3]
+ If it feels to you more like a voice crying in the wilderness, that'll still do as a starting point, just keep choosing to give it a chance. If you're not convinced by the sound of your own voice, just treat it as an experiment, use your will and try it anyway. That's not falseness or presumption, it's determination. James wrote that the tongue is a little rudder that directs an entire ship (and its crew and cargo)[4] and we often quote that in the context of causing trouble. But if the rudder works then it works – so in this context we're going to turn that rudder to your benefit.
+ Some things you'll want to share with a spouse or friend – sharing should generate excitement, agreement will give your decision more weight, and knowing that someone else knows what you're up to will encourage you to follow through. If it's your spouse, you'll need their support and I hope they'll participate as well. If it's a friend, make sure it's not a skeptical or ambivalent one – no sarcasm allowed!
+ As we go along, I'll give you some things to say and do immediately. Even if it doesn't seem convenient at the moment, do it anyway and don't delay – it's actually more inconvenient to have to retrace and do it later. And less likely to happen.
Most things are quick. Some things you'll need to spend a bit of time on, but I'll explain those.

Gestures & body language
+ Some insights need to be rooted, grafted, anchored, woven or otherwise secured into your thinking with physical motions and sensations. Body language and tactile memory. This is a

crucial aspect of what we'll do, and probably different from what you were expecting, so allow me to set the backdrop a few different ways...

+ Clinical communication studies at the University of California in Los Angeles (UCLA) studied how information is conveyed via print (content only), radio (content + tone of voice) and TV (content + tone of voice + body language). They found what actually registers with people comes 7% from content, 38% from tone of voice, and a whopping 55% from body language. Never scorn a song-and-dance man. So we'll use a lot of body language to heal your finances.

+ I know a consultant to law enforcement and intelligence agencies, immigration officials and corporations who detects genuine and misleading statements on video by using a catalogue of over 200 different facial movements and expressions – that's how articulate and subtle your face's body language is. So however you may like to think you're directing a conversation by choosing your words, your face is blabbing what you really feel and think.

Relevance? The monologue of words running through your head can be synced up and reinforced with the powerful (and inevitable) effect of your own body language. You can choose this to your own benefit.

+ **Here's your first exercise:** This week, every time you answer the phone, make sure you're smiling (even if you don't feel like it) and just see if your calls don't go better than usual. You could tape a reminder to smile onto your phone's handset. Although you may not say anything different and people can't see with their eyes that you're smiling, two things will happen:

1 - they can "hear" that you're smiling (remember: vocab is only 7%) and they'll respond to your sonic smile;

2 - your own attitude will follow your smile's lead and you'll be a more positive and constructive person to deal with. Just because you pushed your facial muscles in that position.

+ **Why is this?** Feelings, thoughts, actions and results flow in both directions. When you feel good, you smile. Also vice versa. When you smile, you aren't simply baring your fangs – profound emotional associations are set in motion: your facial muscles adopt a familiar and pleasing pose (you may notice your scalp, neck and shoulders soon follow suit); deliberately relaxing your mouth, throat, vocal and breathing affects your voice's sound quality; even your face's topogra-

phy affects how your voice projects; your own hearing associates that "smiling" sound in a familiar, pleasing way with
many other happy sensations; your internal Department of
Emotions responds, "Oh, is this what we're doing? That feels
better..." so your mood brightens, the tone of your thought-
life improves, you can make better decisions, and your circumstances bear better fruit.

* Alternatively, if you
   physically slump and look down > you start to feel down
      feel down > your thoughts head south
         downward thoughts > low-quality decisions
            negative choices > bad results and circumstances.
Anyone can put their personal downward spiral into motion.

* **The point:** This also applies to restoring your finances. You
can work the interconnectedness of your feelings, beliefs,
physical sensations and behaviours in either direction, and
leverage the whole system from different points – you were
created for unity and your many facets will naturally shift to
re-align to achieve that unity. But like I said before, tweaking
the slippery, fickle mind at the surface will not suffice – yes,
we need to take destructive thoughts captive, but that alone
won't effect lasting change.

* **A larger point:** Sometimes it's not easy to get a conscious
hold on the deeper beliefs that influence us so profoundly.
Since the mechanism runs in both directions, we'll actually
use body language and physical gestures to help articulate,
leverage and re-align our thoughts and deeper beliefs about
money, finances and wealth. Then your choices, and therefore your circumstances, will deliver the promise of unity:
success.

* **A cautionary point:** You know that internal monologue we
all have running through our heads? That narrator's voiceover
as you walk and work? That stream of words trickling across
the top of your thoughts? The stuff that your spouse catches
you muttering to yourself? Well, that region of your mind
thinks that he or she is the smartest person around, is the one
in charge, is the real you, tends to be dismissive of the other
facets, and presumes to speak for all other stakeholders (your
desires, needs, emotions, motives, instincts, intuitions and
automatic functions) and will try to act as the gatekeeper for
your soul. This imperious little autocrat will object to suggestions that he or she is not calling the shots and will debate,
argue, insist and protest in its own favour.

But consider this: when you do something you "know" is wrong, why do you do it anyway? When you "know" what's good for you, why is it hard to do? In all the times you've either gotten into trouble or accomplished something really great was it because the fickle little penguin atop your iceberg squawked and made it so, or was it a tsunami of passion, inspiration, need, loneliness, imagination, anger, bravery or fear that welled up and surfed you to your result?

Yup, the heart is king. Even in one's relationship with God, no one thinks their way into it. C.S. Lewis is a case in point. Those who like to think they intellectually responded are just jury-rigging logic and reason to accommodate a deeper emotional need to make it look like a rational, reasonable decision. Why? Likely for feelings of security and comfort (reassurance), control and power (the fear of not having power over reality) or pride (the appearance of enlightenment).

♦ **Okay, I know I'm rambling, but here it is:** That opinionated penguin congratulates itself on knowing the score. The reality is that the genius undercurrent (even tsunami[5]) of your imagination, passion, emotion and need will prevail. If your finances look like a natural disaster site, the dynamic that caused it lies at the ocean floor of your emotions, well below the surface of your opinions and last week's factoids. The good news is that the chain of body-emotion-mind-actions-results can be re-aligned, and we'll use body language and gestures to help sync up those deeper beliefs, feelings and impulses so they're more constructive and supportive of your goals. Eventually, even your inner penguin will be satisfied with the results.

♦ A new direction calls for motion which can begin with the smallest of gestures and body language. So we'll give it impetus with simple tasks, non-intimidating gestures – "a little leaven" or "thin edge of the wedge". (Those phrases also are often used negatively, but the dynamic is true and this time we'll make the dynamic work for you.) These tasks and gestures will begin working once you've set them in motion. You'll learn how it FEELS to do better, SEE that you can do something without solving everything at once, and OWN qualities you weren't sure you had. Most are simply fun, so enjoy them.

♦ Even if it feels a bit funny at first, do not be repressed by your own self-consciousness… unless you actually prefer what that self has gotten you thus far.

♦ And smile.

Instigation, practice & habit
+ Along with the body language and gestures, I'll give you some concrete, do-able tasks that will add momentum to the motion we've instigated.
+ Try them without prejudice.
+ No, really. Try them.

If you try just reading this book, you'll just add a new set of clutter to your own junk collection, and you don't need yet another handful of ideas to sprinkle around the back of your mind. And realistically, no one jumps from simply hearing to rock-solid practice, even if they feel momentarily inspired by what they read – inspirational books tend to be only temporary effect. If you expect that of yourself, you're setting yourself up for striving, frustration and failure.
Again.

Instead, we're going to tangibly, physically anchor in your body a new understanding of finances, grounded in the depths of your heart, to renew your mind and thought-life, adopt a new financial posture, nudge yourself out in that direction, and prime your momentum toward encouraging, successful results.

Keep a pen handy
Like I said, please don't just read this book. Part of the fun in the interactive, participatory nature of this book is that you'll jot down some key impressions, ideas and observations. Important ones. Surprising ones! Stuff you won't want to forget later. So keep a pen handy and by all means write in this book:
    questions that come to mind (we'll respect those),
    random thoughts (no such thing),
    quirky reminders (let's call them "innovative"),
    whatever.
If something seemingly oblique comes to mind (especially a name, place or anecdote) note it in the margins – it could make sense later as to why it popped up. You'll understand more when we get to the last few sections of the book.

Speaking of which
I have an admission to make. I'm the kind of guy who typically reads 2/3 of a book and then lets it languish. (Or I let Charmaine read it and give me a verbal executive summary later.) Don't do that with this book! It's designed as a participatory process that develops:

we lay some foundational understanding, then build some momentum and accelerate through transformational experiences.
You cannot win if you do not play.
Or finish.

So, ready for some fun? Let's get started...

1 James 3: 23-25
2 Psalms 42 & 43
3 I Corinthians 14:8
4 James 3
5 A tsunami wave begins as a seismic impulse at the ocean's floor and rolls unseen along the bottom until it lunges up and out of the shallows to overwhelm the shoreline, as we tragically witnessed in Southeast Asia. Its hiddenness makes it so surprising and its momentum so destructive.

Chapter 1
Thoughts & Feelings: Who's in charge here?

Our passions are more powerful than our opinions. As much as we like to think our thought-of-the-day or teaching-tape-of-the-week or doctrine-of-the-season will secure a new future for us, we are actually too deep, too complex, too intricately woven to fool ourselves about anything for very long. So your outer circumstances are already speaking volumes about your inner state – what you actually believe.

To illustrate
Way down deep, the molten magma of your fundamental needs is already convinced of whether it is well with your soul, or not: such as, "Ah, I'm loved..." or perhaps, "Ugh, I'm trapped..."
  ◆ These thoughts of satisfaction or dissatisfaction show up as a general outlook,
     "Woo-hoo, let's go..." or "What's the point..."
  ◆ which justifies its own presence by using beliefs,
     "Because I'm worth it..." or "I'm such a loser..."
  ◆ and reinforcing itself with related beliefs,
     "Better things always come..." or "I don't deserve..."
  ◆ and assumptions,
     "My boss will..." or "There's no time to..."
  ◆ by carefully selecting examples,
     "Like when I got upgraded..." or "When I spilled..."
  ◆ Then that emotionally laden momentum hip-checks your thoughts into formulating a brilliant vision to satisfy its own mood,
     "What if I try..." or "Just watch, he won't..."
  ◆ and those thoughts rationalize decisions,
     "I'll get an appointment..." or "I'll just have ice cream..."
  ◆ which eventually produce results that serve and confirm the root assumption you started out with,
     "See, they liked my idea. I'm loved!"
     or "See, it never changes. I'm trapped."

At this very moment, your beliefs, thoughts, feelings, decisions and experiences specifically about money are already operating in a similar loop, either...
    a) building upon positives toward success,

b) re-hashing "reasons" for failure,
c) some pattern of interference between the two.
Most likely c).

I'm not talking about moods

I mean our fundamental beliefs about our worth, our role, our identity and overall perspective about our value as people. Because your finances already illustrate what you really think about yourself:
   what you're capable of,
   what you mean to people around you,
   what strangers will accept or reject about you,
   what you deserve,
   how much you believe of what others say you deserve,
   who could be bothered with you,
   who would listen to you,
   who would trust you, and with how much.
And so on.

This is why we need to adjust our finances not by scraping and painting over your current situation, but by plumbing the depths of the soul for restoration and reconstruction. As clever as your surface thoughts are, including any bravado you can muster, your own emotional system cannot be masked for long by mental pep talks, sympathetic chat, adjustable moods or posturing.

Yes, we will need to make choices that are compatible with our goals, but denial or hype will eventually succumb to the gravity of emotional reality.[1] You can resist emotional gravity with inspirational speeches or intellectual fantasies for a little while, but gravity is patient. Before long something circumstantial will come along to bump you, start a bit of a wobble, build to a swerve, send you careening off course, and you'll once again be demonstrating its effect.

And why is this so powerful? The overall direction of your choices illustrates what actually feels 'right' to your emotions because then you get the ultimate, glorious, *sine qua non* of satisfactions:
                "See? I was right!"

Even if it's the most undesirable and unhappy outcome, there's an "I knew it" pay-out. Lousy circumstances, including poor finances, have a huge guardian "I told you so" posted as a bouncer to mind the door. Probably a whole squad of them.

At any particular moment, you are constantly selecting from what has produced pleasingly good (or self-confirmingly poor) results from some other time and place. For example, the real decision is not whether we're in favour of physical fitness in general, or specifically which fitness club to join or which flavour of ice cream is beckoning from the fridge – it's way back at what your root emotional outlook insists is true about your self:

worthy or unworthy,
      capable or clumsy,
            hopeful or doomed.

Money is emotional

As a financial example of the role of emotion, let's take the popularity of "retail therapy":

A woman sees a beaded pair of shoes and thinks, They're 1/3 off... I could use them... my black pumps are looking tired... the company dinner is this weekend... Therefore, I like them + I need them + it's a deal = I'll buy them... and save money!

Problem is, she's saved so much money this year that the credit card account is already at $3,000-below-zero. Her emotional 'facts' trump the mathematical evidence of her credit card statement. The disconnect is fairly obvious, so why is this scenario so familiar?

Answer: Her spending is not actually a financial decision, it's a manifestation of her emotional state: "I need." She doesn't have an available emotional state which could choose instead, "I'll feel better in the end if I hold off" to counterbalance her spending impulse. She's not a bad or silly person, she just doesn't have that emotional message hardwired into her shopping behaviour.

Similarly, how else can a guy get a $50 a week raise and figure that's a good time to buy a $3,000 TV system? On credit at extortionate interest! Because there's an emotional impulse inside that says, "This will help."
Help what? Essentially, he's saying something about how he feels: I need... I deserve... I look like... I have to... My home isn't... My spare time is...
All subjective emotional stuff.

Am I exaggerating? *USA Today* recently ran a six-week series called "Young & In Debt" which reported that 49% of American 20-some-things have "stopped paying a debt, forcing lenders to 'charge off' the debt and sell it to a collection agency, or had cars repossessed or sought bankruptcy protection."

That's half. That's huge.

Admittedly, a chunk of this relates to the cost of higher education in the US, but clearly, this isn't due to lack of clear data and helpful financial information – we're looking at a crazy mix of assumptions, beliefs, pressures and behaviour.

Emotions.

Money is spiritual

We'll get into this in more depth shortly, but for now let it suffice to point out that there are nearly 2,400 verses in the Bible directly mentioning money and possessions. Same with about 15% of what Jesus is quoted as saying – some of it literal and some of it allegorical, but he was obviously comfortable with working with the subject matter.

Now let's talk about you

If your finances aren't great, then you have programmed files of need, gratification and avoidance that are putting a disconnect between your heart's true ideals and your mind's surface ideas about long-term financial success. And not just in the area of spending, like the examples above, but also saving, investing, giving, recreation, planning and *particularly* your experience of God's generosity. Otherwise, you'd probably be rich by now. And not so stressed.

The good news is that rectifying this is not only possible, but can even be enjoyable and exciting. We'll clear up more of the clutter a little later, especially in the areas of family and religious conditioning, but for now let's install some of that needed, hardwired access to emotionally helpful beliefs and supportive messages that will serve our financial goals, not sabotage them.

Your First *Healing Your Financial Soul* Exercise: Re-calibrate your financial compass

We'll start the practical work by building into your thinking and beliefs a helpful, emotional, financial perspective – a kind of magnetic north pole and compass for your finances. The popular expression would be "the zone". Think of a golfer's concentration, the artist lost in her work, the race car driver's line, where a jazz musician 'goes' when her eyes are shut, how a chess player fore-

sees the board and the pieces' movements, a skipper so in tune with his boat he calls it "she"... Their physical prowess and artistry flow naturally, instinctively, almost automatically, synced up to their mental picture with verve, passion and clarity.
It's their joy.

We're now going to stake out a similar mental/emotional/physical vantage point you can work from regarding your finances. You can feel, think, decide and act in ways that are congruent, consistent and heading in the direction of your heart's true desires. Ready?

Get your pen, then pray with me:
Holy Spirit, please help me recognize my heart's true desires for finances.
Sit back, shrug your shoulders, take a deep breath, think of a favourite worship song or scripture, or mentally picture a place where you have found spiritual refreshment – something you relate to easily.
Let yourself re-experience it in detail.
Notice the lighting and colours, hear the way sound reaches you, and feel it for a moment or two.

Now ask yourself this question:
What characteristic describes my heart's desire specific to finances? What quality or word names it?

Notice the first thing that bobs to the surface of your thinking.
It should be a term you can apply money and financial well-being.

Got it? Great. It might be something like subjective like generosity, innovation, compassion, creativity, faith, abundance, opportunity, favour, blessing, surplus, overflow...
Or something more objective like cash, property, relationships, career options, inventions, contracts...
Or a combination like favourable contracts, generous relationships, creative options...
Or even better, something unexpected and surprising.
(If you need to, you can just go back, re-relax and ask & hear again.)

Write that term, that quality, in this blank:
"I am rich in _____!"

Don't just think about it – write it in by hand.

Now look at it. Consider it. Let it sink in.
Say it out aloud, so you hear your own voice stating it.
Speak it out loud, confidently.

Now think of an example of when you experienced that quality to some degree. The more dramatic the example, the better, such as...
 • you landed a great job,
 • you made a successful investment,
 • you won something,
 • you bought or sold something significant *with cash*,
 • you were unexpectedly given money (or an equivalent like airline tickets),
 • you cleared off a debt,
 • you were prompted you to give and you wrote the cheque because you knew you had the money in the bank (not "in faith", we'll get to that later).
It doesn't have to be a spectacular event, just one where you experienced that quality.2 Write a word here just as a prompt to remind you of it (*ex.* "suit", "Julie" or "Paris"): _____

Now, fix that scenario in your mind and...
 • clarify the visual impression in detail (physical surroundings, lighting, colours, significant objects or action);
 • focus on what you heard (what was said, ambient sound, or the thought you heard in your head);
 • feel that physical sense of "I'm there" (including any smells, tastes, temperature, and sensations like heartbeat, butterflies, goose bumps, *etc.*).
Allow the excitement, satisfaction, gratitude, anticipation, or other positive emotions to well up. Let that experience of the moment build until you think you're strongly in touch with it.

Then come back to the present and physically re-set: shrug, stretch, stand up, turn around, whatever.

Choose three simple things that you can easily remember to access:
 • Pick one **object** you can immediately picture in your mind's eye (a visual symbol or thing, like a light switch or your favourite chair)
 Note it here: _____

+ Choose one **sound or word** you can readily hear in your head (an auditory key like a favourite word, a hero's name, a phrase from a song)
  Note it here: _____
+ Now one small, fairly inconspicuous **gesture** you can make at pretty much any time (a kinesthetic key like squeezing a thumbnail or scratching an eyebrow)
  Note it here: _____

Keep those three and your "I am rich in _____!" statement at the ready.

Now go back and re-experience that amazing financial situation from a couple of minutes ago. Dial it back up so your recollection is vivid again, *especially for the way it made you feel*, and hold it.

Then just as the feelings are coming back to a peak, hold it in your mind and do all three...
   picture the object,
     hear the word/sound,
       make the gesture,
         say, *"I am rich in _____!"* With *oomph!*

Okay, re-set again (stretch, sigh, shake your arms, look out the window...) and think of something else.

Now test your keys: picture the object in your mind, hear the word or sound in your head, make the gesture, and say "I am rich in _____!"
Notice how these bring back the same feelings you associated with that positive financial experience. If the effect is not yet pronounced, do the same process again, using the same examples, and you'll find the connection will strengthen. (And it's okay to laugh.)

Finally, choose the one key (visual, auditory or kinesthetic) that works best with your "I am rich in _____!" statement. One will stand out morethan the others. You don't need all three – people tend to be naturally inclined to either visual or auditory or kinesthetic memory.

What have you just done?
You've just forged a direct access, link, switch or hotline to a constructive, helpful state of *feeling* associated with financial benefits (which your mind knows is rooted in reality) from which you can

now think and make choices specific to finances, spending, saving, earning, *etc.*.
It's a key to activate a positive financial perspective.

From this day forth
Every time anything good happens regarding money...
* you get paid, you give money away,
* your stocks go up, you deposit money into savings,
* you find a dime on the ground, a cheque arrives in the mail,
* you receive a gift, get a tax refund, pay a bill,
* someone pays for lunch... *an-y-thing good...*

activate your key and tell yourself, *"I am rich in _____!"*
This will establish and build a stable, positive vantage point for your finances.

Is this really okay?
We do this all the time to access a helpful state, sometimes deliberately, sometimes casually: "Bow your heads and close your eyes," hum a favourite song, recite a memory verse, day dream about the view at the cottage, keep your kids' photo on the fridge door, and so on.

In a similar way, we can intentionally secure a mental/emotional/physical vantage point, based on your heart's desire, from which to work out our financial life. You just created your own personal magnetic north pole with your *"I am rich in _____!"* statement and the visual/auditory/kinesthetic key.

In the same way that when you drive along a freeway you're mostly just making small adjustments to the steering to keep you in your lane, this will help keep you facing the right direction and on track to your heart's desire and vision for positive experiences with money and finances.

If this body-mind-emotion dynamic seems farfetched, let me ask, did you ever visit your old school and notice the smell? You also experienced something emotional, didn't you? Maybe something else physical, like in your stomach?
Or think of the sight of a dog – could be good or bad emotion there. Or the thought of your least favourite singer. Or the possibility of meeting someone who has deeply hurt you.
All you just did was think of them, but your internal reactions were

both emotional and physical. And it was immediate and "right there", wasn't it? For a few moments, any one of them could adversely affect your tennis serve or ability to do math in your head. Or your money decisions.

So what we're doing here is using your ability to re-experience positive, tangible experiences with their attending emotions to make them available whenever you're thinking about or doing anything financial, whether it's planning, spending, shopping, investing, saving, giving or whatever. Your "zone" is now immediately available as a footing from which you can operate financially. And it will grow over time in vividness and influence.

Future present

If you're unsure about saying, *"I am rich in _____!"* because you don't see it reflected numerically in your bank statements just yet, then view your proclamation as a seed. An acorn has the same DNA as a full-grown oak. Any seed already carries the same built-in, programmed, characteristics of a mature plant or creature.

  ✦   Perhaps more importantly, for every oak tree you see, at some point an acorn just had to "get on with it" despite lacking physical evidence of tree-ness, such as leaves and roots and bark.
  ✦   Further, for every oak tree that exists in the future, there's an acorn that exists now! You cannot have that future oak tree without this present acorn, the certainty of an oak tree in the future proves the existence of the acorn now – the determining factor is your accepting the acorn now.

The future is just as real as the present, and both are here. Stop restricting reality to what little you can see or grab.

So take heart and choose to believe for the financial restoration that has just begun, and is even here now!
And say with me, *"I am rich in _____!"*

---

1 This illustrates why our life in God is instigated by Him, and not we of ourselves.

2 If the quality for your "I am rich in _____!" statement is something you deeply desire but has so far eluded your own experience, think of a role model who possesses, or possessed, that quality – either someone you know or someone you've read about and inspires you, and imagine what it would be like to be in their shoes.

Chapter 2, part 1
As You Thunk, So You Is

The gift of choice

Our existence is driven by options and choices. And as believers in God, the degree to which we experience his kindness, optimism, favour and purpose in our lives is tied directly to how willing we are to line up our choices with his way of seeing things.

Transforming our perspective
by conforming it to his perspective.

So at one point, God said to his adopted people, the Hebrews, shortly after prying them loose from Egypt, "I set before you two ways..."[1] and went on to explain what his path of blessing would look like:

+ identity, security, opportunities, freedom, co-operation, success, fruitfulness and growth, along with regular celebration, care and maintenance of their relationship with him.

And then what the path apart from him would look like:

+ distortion, frustration, restriction, confusion, competition, failure, pain and avoidance, along with the wear and tear from living in self-imposed exile from his grace, *i.e.* the way of cursing.

Take five minutes to read it. It's been thousands of years since it was written, but it'll look and feel very current.

The point of that passage is not a threat, a do-it-my-way-or-else ultimatum. God is too secure to resort to threats. Rather, it's the most generous offer we could ever receive: *choice* – a gift we'll probably never fully appreciate, and the opportunity to thrive and flourish along the lines of his original design. The downside option is not vindictiveness, just a realistic picture of how things go for us when we opt for our own near-sightedness and knack for self-destruction. And the world is strewn with examples of that.

What's even more amazing is that God is so absolutely flexible for our sakes, in that he's willing to work with us from whatever starting point we'll give him. No entrance requirements except admitting that we're falling short, needing his help and willing to try things his way. God is the humblest, most accepting person I know.

For our part as believers, we are taught to understand that God's beauty and blessings surround us, the rain falls for us whether we're just or unjust, his love never changes. So why is it often such a struggle to see that way of blessing, that abundance, manifested in tangible terms? Including money?

( ) Is the problem God's delivery system?

( ) Or is it our receiving system?

(Check one.)

Put your hand on your head and say,

I deliberately, consciously choose to accept God's offer of the way of blessing and all of his benefits!

Put your hand over your heart and say,

I give you permission, Lord,
to show me where the impediments are
so I can receive your best,
and satisfy your desire to see me living in your kindness,
generosity and vision for my life.

Use your key and say, *"I am rich in _____!"*

Before we go any further, a quick check: How you feelin'?

As I explained in the beginning, simply introducing a few novel ideas, shuffling your vocabulary around, or nodding assent because this is "a book", will not create any lasting change for you. If you're complying on the outside but inside you're thinking, "Pffft...I doubt this..." or "These things don't work for me..." or "Well, we'll see..." then those thinly camouflaged beliefs and rejections will undermine and stymie your noble intentions.

The key to genuine change is your emotional state.

The one you choose. In fact, intentionally associating a positive emotional feeling with these prayers and activations is *crucial.*

One of the scarier verses in the Bible voices God's own similar frustration: *These people honour me with their lips but their hearts are far from me.*[2] Even if we're performing on the outside, it doesn't count if on the inside we're sulking or emotionally rejecting better ways. Why? Because our unspoken, unarticulated posture is, "Yeah, but I *know* better!" So you'll continue to generate what you (your ego) continues to prefer as, "Yeah, but..." It means you're still waiting and insisting that circumstances change so you don't have to. Until you surrender the rights to your "Yeah, but..." opinions, you will not see material change in your finances. You're already getting what you expect.

In my own case, I noticed something when a visiting speaker taught on finances in our church. What he taught "worked" for people who were open to being enthusiastic, excited and emotionally engaged with his message – they took his advice to heart and amazing financial miracles fell into place within days. And not for me. Oh, I *complied*. I decided to do the things he was advocating, and even out-did them, out-gave them, out-sacrificed them... in every way *except* emotionally and attitudinally. I was complying, and then upped the "Yeah, but..." ante and raised it with an "I'll show you..." My underlying attitude of detachment, even superiority, was all opinion and stubbornness, which was emotionally aggravated because I didn't care for the guy's heavy rings, heavy suit, heavy hair and heavy demeanour. My emotional posture was, "He's heavy, he ain't my brother."

But it wasn't really about him. I was emotionally churned up about my own finances, and not in a good way. I was actually over-giving, over-tithing and over-sacrificing while expending myself in ministry out of frustration and anxiety, despite my intellectual determination to *learn* the right things and *do* the right things.
I should have decided to *feel* the right things and change my heart – that set of opinions+emotions I was insisting upon.

In retrospect, I am convinced that parking my attitude and embracing encouragement would have brought better results. Not the least of which would have been less irritation and more peace in my own heart.

If you want real change, choose an optimistic feeling, dial up an enjoyable state of mind, find your sense of humour3 again – it makes all the difference.

So if you need to go back and do that little head & heart prayer again, take the time now. And this time lean forward, *SMILE*, use an encouraging tone of voice, and engage a positive emotional feeling, like hope, confidence, satisfaction or love as you speak it out. This is not corny, it's getting over your ego.

Inner and outer segregated
The disparity between God's kind intentions and our frustrating experiences has a lot to do with how we've partitioned our thinking between our spirituality and what we call "reality". Little by little, disappointment by disappointment, and mini-conclusion by

mini-conclusion, we've kinked the hose between spiritual cause & material effect.
Or rather, God's promises & our desired results.

We've all felt how outward circumstances impact us inwardly – lousy finances, hunger, sickness, isolation, heartache, or any other kind of deprivation, make it harder to live freely, fulfill our purpose and enjoy the adventure. Our external "reality" can create real hardship in one's spiritual life and over time cramp and smother one's internal life. We've all seen it and lived it to some extent.

Here's what we're not so clear on: the degree to which our inner landscape of beliefs, expectations and principles creates our outward experiences.
Okay, let's start with an easy, if negative, example:
 * Someone has a bad attitude and they're unhappy a lot
 * maybe that makes it harder to do their job well
 * which makes it harder to get along with people at work
 * which overshadows his good characteristics
 * business gets lean but people are relieved to see him go
 * his finances and personal circumstances suffer.

This person might say he didn't "do" anything to deserve being the first one laid off, yet his prevailing mental/emotional posture has...
 * set his own course (content, tone of voice & body language), gave off his own vibes, brought his dark cloud into work with him, *etc.*
 * taught everyone around him how to view him and trained them how to treat him (avoiding, criticizing, blaming, *etc.*)
We'd say he brought it on himself, created his own outcome, it caught up with him, and so on.

Furthermore, *hundreds* of small, minute-by-minute decisions in his communication's content, tone & body language were in play. *Thousands* of subtle, but influential, mini-choices contributed – even down to his facial micro-expressions, as I mentioned in the introduction.

Even further, a kind of cloud of nano-mannerisms was actually generating an incessant sort of aura around him. Ever noticed how some people just change the room when they walk in? We'd say it's intangible, but the tangible effect is very influential. For either good or bad effect.

Relevance: You've been doing the same with your finances – at all those levels
If your financial circumstances are disappointing, frustrating or failing, it's not because money is at fault. It isn't because money has refused to show up for you. Actually, you are the architect of your financial situation. You may think you want better finances, but in between you and financial success (whatever that looks like to you) you have entire sub-systems of contentious little beliefs, sub-beliefs, micro-behaviours and nano-traits adding up to a jumble of divided loyalties that get in your way, undermine and frustrate your efforts.

Zoom out for a minute
Your circumstances reflect the choices you've made based on your own inner beliefs. Like it or not, you are the world's finest showpiece for your own set of beliefs – the ones you've been living by.
* Who are you? How do you really view yourself? Treat yourself?
* What do you deserve? What is your worth? Is it good, bad, neutral or irrelevant if it's reflected in money?
* How well do you relate with others? Do you trust others? Can you choose to trust people who have let you down? Or are they still making that decision for you?
* What were you taught about the nature of money? Do you truly feel that you deserve wealth? Could you really handle more money?
* Can you make decisions even if you're not in the mood? Can you take action despite pressure, inconvenience or discomfort? How's your follow-through?

Your thinking, your opinions, your actual beliefs are already determining your degree of financial success. Read it in the book of Proverbs, because *this is critical*:
"As a man thinketh, so is he."[4]

You see, your brain is arguably the most amazing creation in the universe. You are a greater marvel than any geographic or man-made construct on the planet. The functions, systems, alerts, processing, storage and creativity of your brain makes it the most advanced 'computer' in the world. And 90-95% of it is unused capacity! *Plus* you have a spirit and will of your own. So the good news is that you are already brilliantly equipped for success in achieving your goals.

Unfortunately brilliant
The not-so-good news is that you've already been "brilliantly" juggling, balancing and accommodating conflicting ideas and beliefs about money and wealth for years! That's why you struggle. A lot of those learned, subconscious beliefs that you own don't stack up well with your goals. Some of them might sound like this:
"Money isn't that important."
"The rich are only out for themselves."
"Money doesn't buy happiness."
"You can't have it all."
"Don't expect too much."
"Money corrupts."
"They're only in it for the money."
"Spoiled rich kid."
"Money is the root of all evil."
"Filthy stinking rich."
"Can't buy me love."
"Freedom's just another word for nothing left to lose"[5]
And so on.

The problem is you've set out to prove *all of them* are true and now wonder why money seems to avoid you! You're cleverly, systematically and tenaciously proving your own jumbled theories (often conflicting ones) and now you're frustrated with your mixed results.

So on the one hand you can congratulate yourself for your thorough work and tireless devotion to your principles.
But on the other hand, maybe it's time to reconsider those assignments and get some new ones!

Now here's the awful truth:
If you struggle financially, it's because deep down,
you were taught,
and you agreed to believe,
and made countless decisions to prove,
that you're *supposed* to struggle.

Woah! How could this be? Wouldn't a few breaks, a reliable income or a modest inheritance end the struggle?

Sadly, no. If you'll pardon another negative example, let's take that cliché about lottery winners dribbling away their winnings –

sadly, it's true. Just the other night, while doing some background reading for this book, I came across this TV news report about a record lottery jackpot in one of the US state lotteries. As a follow-up, they also did a short piece on how lottery winners frequently wind up with little or none of the money shortly thereafter – this process seems to take one-to-two years.

A professional financial planner was interviewed about this phenomenon, and he said,

I wish some of them would just get the notion to at least put part of it somewhere they can't get at it for a while... I don't want to get too Freudian or whatever about this, but it's almost as if people feel like they have to get rid of the money because they don't really feel they deserve it.[6]

Bingo! This vividly illustrates the power of our beliefs to prove themselves "true" by compelling and rationalizing bad decisions and despising good decisions. In spite of their surface thoughts about finally hitting it big and all the things they can do now. So despite the euphoria of winning, and the huge sums involved, these lottery winners soon revert back to the economic level to which they are accustomed, feel prepared to handle, and believe they actually deserve.

Their internal programming about money, their innate financial capacity for what to expect, how to receive and what they can keep, is initially swamped by the deluge of cash, but the belief system soon re-asserts itself, takes over and goes about the business of systematically bringing everything back to the level they believe deep down is "right" for them: badly timed investments, unsupported business decisions, evaporating luxuries, guilt-driven personal loans... whatever it takes to drag things back down to "normal".[7]

Here's the relevance to your situation
You have the same kind of financial thermostat built into your mental system and your finances are set to "Auto". If you come into money, you'll similarly find ways of subconsciously making sure it's all gone before long. If you lose a bunch of money, you'll go about doing things to bring it back, until you level out at what you innately believe you should have. And then progress no further. Not based on your surface opinions, but on your driving beliefs and emotionally rooted messages about money.

This is why so many people feel stuck:
Their financial thermostats are stuck.

So if winning a huge load of money doesn't fix people's inability to hold onto it, work with it, or at least keep *some* of it, can you see why a raise won't fix things for you either? Or a better job? Or a winning pick on the stock market? Or a big, interest-free loan?

No matter what temporary outward gain you come into, or loss you sustain, your own internal programming about money will fulfill itself, just as it does with these instant multi-millionaires.

And the determining factor in where your thermostat is set is what you *feel* about money and what you *sense* is appropriate for you financially.

Here's another way of looking at why you don't have more money. Picture yourself on an oceanside beach, holding a cup when a big breaker rolls in: No matter how much water rolls over and swirls around you, when the wave recedes you'll only retain as much as the cup you brought. See, the problem isn't the supply or availability of money – the world is awash in money.
    Just like those instant millionaires,
    the problem is your capacity.

Alternatively...
Have you noticed how the opposite is true of successful self-made millionaires? They can make, then lose, then re-make millions of dollars in a remarkably short period of time. On average, they go broke three or four times before "making it". Why? Because of their internal makeup of belief, confidence, motivation, thinking big, planning and action. They've created their own size XXL capacity to hold and handle money. And their capacity gets filled.
It's as if the money finds them.

And doesn't it seem to be more about who they are than whatever line of business catches their fancy this time around? Okay, maybe you don't like his hair, or her decorating ideas, but they assume success, devote themselves to it, live as if it's their right, and success moves right in with them.
Remember, *As a man thinketh, so is he.*[8]

Haven't you ever looked at those guys and thought, "I could've done that. How come I don't get these breaks?" "Why can't I find that kind of seed capital?" "Where's my angel-investor?" It's your capacity.

Even if you have an insightful idea,
    your sub-ideas are small capacity,
    your questions are small capacity,
    your beliefs are small capacity,
    your contacts are small capacity,
    your actions are small capacity,
    your risks are small capacity,
    your results are small capacity.

So the real issues aren't finding and getting more money, they're
  ⬧ dismantling your thermostat and re-setting it to the level of success you aspire to;
  ⬧ increasing your financial capacity to suit your true potential, which is huge but underutilized.

How you thunk, so you is
  ⬧ Have you ever blown your budget? Sabotaged your financial plan? Your relationships? Your work projects? Your job? Your career?
  ⬧ Can you see there's a part of your mind that booby traps your positive intentions? Lays landmines of judgements, holds hostage your ability to commit, burns bridges with resentment, ambushes you with self-fulfilling I-told-you-so's?
  ⬧ Has your inner moaning manifested as an emptied bank account or bloated credit card balance? You have an internal whisper campaign spreading lies about yourself and to some extent you have agreed with the accuser of your soul.

We've all done it. Thank God, once we have turned over our spiritual, mental, emotional and physical citizenship to Jesus, we can begin to change it all as his Holy Spirit helps us. But it usually doesn't happen instantaneously – those saboteurs are rogue forces, guerillas and squatters who need to be identified and supplanted by life-giving beliefs, helpful thought patterns, uplifting emotions and constructive habits. Some of it happens quickly, most of it takes time. Sometimes it takes a crisis.
(Which is why crises can be your friends, if you think them through, stick close to the Lord, and learn from them.)

The reason it takes time is that every attitude, opinion, debilitating thought, unhelpful conclusion and negative prediction is one that you've agreed to (at some level) and is consuming precious time, space and energy in your mental world. So you must choose your beliefs wisely. But remember, those *detri*-mental thoughts are not "you": They may be old baggage and "stuff" among your possessions (like contraband idols from an old, former life[9]) but they can be shed without losing your genuine re-born self.

And fortunately, we can choose to substitute better beliefs and understanding that will move you closer to your heart's desires, toward your happiness and fulfillment. Actually you must, because just as nature abhors a vacuum, you need to be deliberate about supplanting obstructions with constructive beliefs and thoughts.

So, interim review:
+ Your actual thought-life and beliefs are already being demonstrated in your finances
+ Those beliefs determine your "capacity" for how much wealth you can generate, handle and retain
+ Your unhelpful old assumptions and negatively-charged directives can be swapped out for encouraging and constructive ones.

Your memory is better than your realize
Let's get back to your Inner Penguin again, your vocal thought-life, your opinions, protestations, theories, preferences, current interests, good intentions and distractions. A pioneer of modern brain surgery, a Canadian named Dr. Wilder Penfield, inadvertently discovered during an operation that physically poking the brain stimulated and triggered long-idle memories in a patient (the brain has no pain-sensing nerves, so it was an open-head surgery).

Ensuing research verifies that you have stored *way* more than you realize of what you've read, the things you've said, faces you've seen, the smell of the corridor on the first day of school, the colour of your mother's hair, your father's tone of voice, the feel of your favourite gym shoes, the grade six math test you forgot to study for... even names and phone numbers you've convinced yourself you're not good with. And as far as the physical activity in your brain is concerned, it's just as real as anything else registering with it right now.

So, you don't have a bad memory. Your memory is excellent. It's your recall system that's unreliable.[10]

Brain wave scans have also demonstrated that the vast majority of your brain activity occurs below the conscious level. If you can hum a tune, picture the face of a loved one and drive at the same time, then you have a glimpse of how multi-layered activities could also be going on below your surface consciousness... at this very moment! In any given second, your nervous system is processing about *20 million* bits of stimuli – your conscious mind constitutes a dribble of about 40 bits per second. (You thought I was overstating about the penguin?)

It's like operating a car: using your foot to accelerate doesn't take much conscious thought; the pedal doesn't make you move, it's just a linkage to the devices under the hood that control the flow of fuel. Also, you don't have to give separate instructions to the car's electrical or cooling systems – they're just working, supporting whatever's happening behind the wheel. In the brain, there are innumerable sub-routines simultaneously supporting any conscious action, and countless others at the ready. Including emotional ones, with their linkages into your financial behaviour and results.

Likewise, negative, critical, despairing beliefs and pronouncements that you've heard, accepted and reiterated (especially the ones wired to strong emotions like sorrow, shock, joy, delight, love, bitterness, *etc.*) are also under there, idling, ticking over, taking up space, accumulating evidence, fattening their files, building their cases as "truth" and "fact".

So, to paraphrase Jesus again, if a lily is clothed more splendidly than Solomon, without the striving and conniving, how uncomplicated, natural and effortless should it be to meet your needs? And, assuming you're more important than a sparrow, how much more does your Heavenly Father want you to have your needs and wants met without consuming anxiety?

Hooray for the good guys
The other good news is that just as there are self-defeating routines, programs and entire "departments" working in the background, in other areas and at other levels, there are parts of your mind that are even more dissatisfied with your money situation than you realize. And even more frustrated with the grip of those rationalizations

over your heart and spirit. And in sequestered workshops of your brain you already have in-house mini-taskforces problemsolving like crazy to find ways of getting better results.[11]

The frustration is how to consciously access their findings, 'cause it seems the memos hardly ever surface. Let alone get acted on. It's the same kind of internal politics and bureaucracy we see in corporations and institutions, but on a micro level. We're going to cut through the red tape and open up that communication.

Plus you have access to God's own thoughts linked into your own – which we refer to as having the mind of Christ.[12] It's amazing to me how people can have selfish thoughts and be okay with the idea that the devil is behind the temptation, and yet they don't think they're spiritually sensitive enough to hear God's voice as loving, encouraging, constructive thoughts. *Harumph.* For now let it stand that where the enemy of your soul is out to steal, kill and destroy[13], your Father's desire is to see you blessed, thriving and advancing.
Including in your finances.

Therefore...
   ◆ God's generous, optimistic offer of "I set before you two paths," and "As a man thinketh, so is he," will be a fascinating and fulfilling opportunity, not a depressing life sentence
   ◆ You are a living wonder, already subconsciously generating better ideas and strategies for better financial results – we just need to cut through the red tape and coax them to the surface of your thinking
   ◆ You have the ability to jettison your faulty internal arguments and habits (hey, let's just call it "sin"!) and adopt constructive beliefs and practices that have made others wealthy, or otherwise fulfilled

So smile, take a deep breath, put your hand on your head and say,
   My inner landscape also shapes my outer circumstances.
   And I admit that some of my beliefs and opinions have not given me the best map of reality.
   I will admit to, and ditch, the frustrating and destructive thoughts and beliefs
   and replace them with helpful, constructive ones.
   Thank-you Jesus for making this possible for me.

Put your hand over the middle of your chest and say,
I respect the fact that I need more input from my subcon-
scious, my spirit and my emotions.
I choose to be open to the wisdom of my own heart, my own
spirit and the Spirit of God who fills me.
I invite those great ideas to surface in my thinking!
"I am rich in _____!"

Your next activation: Honey, I shrank my "but"
We're going to do an exercise to kick your personal, internal problem-solving taskforce into gear. It's a bit of a mini-drama to give
you vision for how your problem-solving creativity can begin revo-
lutionizing your relationship with money from the inside out, from
this point forward.

• Put this book where you can read it easily, you'll need both
hands free as you follow this one – a bookstand would be
handy, and you'll need a pen. (Even better, get your partner
to read you through the instructions.)

• Get into a relaxed position and eliminate distracting sights
and sounds around you.

• Think of a financial paradox you are currently facing, specifically:
a) a good thing your heart desires,
b) and the main reason it's not happening.
Make sure this is about yourself, for example,
a) I should be saving for retirement,
b) but I have to take care of this big debt first.
Or perhaps,
a) I'd love a vacation,
b) but there's no block of time when I'm not busy.
Or maybe,
a) A second income would be great,
b) but I don't have time to spare.

Write it in here:
It'd be great to _____,
but _____.

• Sit back, shrug your shoulders and take a deep breath.
If you tend to be visually oriented, take a moment to picture
something pleasing, like a pet, or a favourite beach.
If you're auditory, run a musical passage through your head,
like the chorus of a song.

If you're kinesthetically inclined, think about something pleasing like a hot shower or the smell of baking.
Let your chosen sensation become vivid.

+ Place your hands palms-up on your lap.

Look to your left hand and picture a miniature version of you, 2 or 3 inches tall (like they do in movies and on TV). Let this represent your creative side, your optimism, the part of you that wants to see good things happen.
'Thank' them for being here. (Go ahead, no one's watching.)

+ In your right hand, imagine another tiny version of you that represents your practical self, the sensible side of you that knows why things do or don't work. It's important to thank them for coming realizing that they're really looking out for you.

+ Pray with me:
Lord, you said to let the peace of Christ be the arbiter in my heart[14] - Jesus, please join us for this discussion. Thanks.

+ Turn and address the 'you' in your left hand and inquire,
*I'd like to hear more about why "It'd be great to _____."
Please explain.*

Now just quietly listen for a minute to the flow of your own thoughts as they surface - don't analyze or edit. And you don't have to remember them, just say 'thanks' when you sense the flow finishes.

+ Turn to your right, and ask,
Okay, what do you think? Why do you say, "But _____?"
Quietly listen and acknowledge any reasons that come up. Don't debate or object, just let it flow. Thank them when they're done.

+ Say to them both,
Jesus, the master creator is here and his Holy Spirit is willing to work with you both. Knowing that all of your concerns will be satisfied, would you be willing to work together with him to come up with creative solutions you can both embrace?

+ Turn your attention to each hand to let each 'answer' in turn. Wait until you 'hear' both parties agree - the sign will be a sense of peace settling in.

+ When you feel that peace come, thank them, and suggest,
*Okay, why don't you both get with the Holy Spirit now and start working on this?
I want you to come up with dozens, even hundreds, of fan-*

tastic ideas about how this can work.
And I invite you to bring the best ones to my conscious atten-
tion over the next days and weeks.
* Now gently fold your hands.

Now, rather than being "doubleminded"[15] over the issue, your innate creativity will unify to work on the issue, in the background, below the surface of your conscious thought, submitted to the Holy Spirit, on how you can have what you desire without despising your own legitimate concerns and getting bogged down with internal infighting and contradiction.

As the ideas come to you over the next few days and weeks, come back and write them here. They don't have to be fully formed, but neither should you tell yourself, "That's okay, I'll remember later..." Committing them to paper is an important element of lending recognition and legitimizing your own creativity, so use this space:

_____

_____

_____

_____

_____

_____

And each time you do, finish with your key and say,
"I am rich in _____!"

1 Deuteronomy 30
2 Isaiah 29:13 The Pharisees being the classic example of "right idea, wrong heart."
3 Humour, not sarcasm.
4 Proverbs 23:7.
5 Apologies to Lennon & McCartney and Kris Kristofferson.
6 The italics are my emphasis.
7 A lot of them die, too.
8 Here's another variation on the same theme. You might know a wealthy person who has a large net worth because he does everything on the cheap and penny-pinched his way

to owning cheap apartments, tatty blocks of downtown retail space, plus a sizable savings account earning miniscule rates of interest. Or has wads of cash stashed in weird places at home. And you look at it and think, "Wow, what potential. Why doesn't he do something with that?" Because although he's rich, he's still cheap. A cheapskate millionaire. As a man thinketh, so is he.

9 Joshua 7, the story of Achan.

10 Even "forgetting" requires memory. Maybe you can't recall who's bringing dessert, but you recall that you asked someone and they said, "Yes."

11 As a negative example, have you noticed that no matter how elaborately you consciously rationalize a lie to yourself, it still seems to take on a life of its own, and your own personal Department of Guilt is loathe to drop the case until it's resolved. This inner conflict will surface, even if it's forced to manifest physically. Perhaps as sickness. This is why confession feels so good (after) and long-term guilt cripples. More on this later...

12 I Corinthians 2:16

13 John 10:10

14 Colossians 3:15

15 James 1:7&8

Chapter 2, part 2

Turn Up the Thunk

By now, you may be a little, shall we say, churned up about money. Now would be a good time to share your desire to restore your finances from the inside out. If you're married, get with your spouse for this. If you're single, choose a friend who would be encouraging about your pursuit of financial mental health – make sure it's someone who won't tease you or discourage you with a "more realistic" perspective – you don't need someone else's opinions added to the mix.

If you are committed to seeing your financial mindset changed (and by changed I don't mean suddenly what you've been doing up to now magically starts working) then sit with your partner and get them to hold this book so you can read this page; put one hand in their hand (guys, you can do this!) and the other hand either over your heart or your fingertips on your temple, and read this out loud:

> *Starting today, I am committed to changing my understanding about money – my feelings and thoughts, my subconscious beliefs and my behaviour. I'm tired of the way my finances are and I'm now changing them.*
> *I am willing to let go of my fears, resentments, negative expectations and internal contradictions about money. I will admit to my illusions and false beliefs and replace them with healthy, constructive ones. I will press through, even when it gets uncomfortable or inconvenient.*
> *I am committed to mastery over my money. I am committed to achieving my financial potential and flourishing. I want prosperity, I want generosity, I want wisdom, I want fun!*
> *And I give you, (name), permission to ask me about my progress, remind me of what I am learning, and encourage me to keep my attitude on track.*

And your partner looks you in the eye and replies:
> *Yes, I believe it for you!*

If they're into it, trade places and do likewise.

There's energy in the spoken word, power in agreement and encouragement in knowing someone is aware of your goals.

Now, let's talk about the kind of thinking that makes rich people so different that they're financially better off than you.

So what is it about the rich?
It's not as if the wealthy are inherently better people. But they are richer.

Are they happier? Not necessarily. But they are richer.

Are the wealthy more intelligent? No. Let's face it, we're all under-achievers using a fraction of our brain capacities. But they do view and handle money *differently* from people who struggle financially.

And when it comes to making the most of life, financial wellbeing is usually more conducive than financial frustration.
As a friend used to say, "I've been rich, I've been poor. I like rich better."[1]

Show me (more than just) the money
This isn't just about money. There are many noble, significant and successful people with less money than you, and yet they're rich in other ways. They desire, believe, think and act in ways that cultivate and produce other kinds of riches, such as
  spiritual depth, healthy families, social reform, success in
  ministry, academic achievement, artistry, athleticism and
  political influence.
But the same dynamics of enabling/disabling thoughts and beliefs are in play.

They excel, and find exultation, according to how clear, unfettered and well-developed their desires, beliefs and thoughts are, so...
  * although everyone is creative in some way,
       a few become artists;
  * many are popular,
       a small number become celebrities;
  * some are socially active,
       but some are called reformers;
  * everyone can and should do good works,
       but miracle workers are rare;

- we're all given a measure of faith,
  some become giants of faith;
- we all have money,
  some become wealthy.

The difference in degree stems from their foundational desires and beliefs.

Are you beginning to see how there's more to "the joy of the Lord is my strength" than just being in a good mood? Joy is a kind of clarity that generates strength which produces change, achievement and satisfaction. Including financially.

So if we can agree that rich people aren't better or simply lucky, why not adopt some of their attitudes, beliefs, thoughts and habits that produce better, even exceptional, finances? The job will be to identify your *un*helpful beliefs, interrupt them and swap in more helpful thinking.

Put your hand on your head, *smile* to yourself and say:
Okay, okay! I'll try something different, including what has worked for other successful, even rich, people.
Put your hand on your heart, and say:
For everyone's sake, I open my heart and invite inspection of my deep beliefs and expectations about money.
Jesus, I invite you to sift through my files and records.
I am rich in _____!

Well, here's where it starts
I'll be blunt. Before you get anywhere with this, you'll need to come to a place of being able to admit something: specifically that *you* are responsible for the state your finances are in. You cannot attribute this to
the soft economy, your ungrateful boss, your lazy business partner, your unmotivated staff, the heartless bank, the fickle stock market, your inept broker, your imperfect parents, the Illuminati.
You're not going to get anywhere until you can accept responsibility for the financial struggles you have.

Now notice that I said to accept "responsibility", not "blame". There are huge differences between casting blame and simply identifying where responsibility lies.
- Blame looks backward and generates condemnation, shame,

discouragement, resentment, helplessness and a wasteful, consuming anger that does nothing but glue defeat into place. Don't go there!

+ Responsibility, while acknowledging what is past, is also forward-looking, objective, compassionate, empowering, and encourages solutions.

Responsibility is not a ball and chain, it's authority. It frees you to confidently do what's needed with vision and energy. It's a starting point for a new experience that you can cheer about!

So, think about responsibility for a minute:
Who went into business with your partner?
Who bought and sold those stocks at a loss?
Who blew your savings?
Who stayed in that job too long?
Who turned down the transfer? Or the training course?
Who married the spendthrift? Or the penny pincher?
Who didn't finish their education?
Who got behind in their payments?
Who made all those decisions?
Nine times out of 10, the answer is *you did*.
Either that or you accepted and settled for what you already had, and that was your decision too.

I realize that you may also have faced circumstantial obstacles regarding your age, sex, race, class, faith, culture, health and upbringing – my wife and I have lived in the US twice, we've seen how those factors change the odds. Factors sometimes beyond your immediate control. So when I suggest that you accept responsibility for your struggles, I'm not denying or dismissing challenges, problems, setbacks or disappointments you've faced. Or perhaps ways you've been financially taken advantage of. Even ripped off or abused. I'm saying that there are ways to get beyond those things, there are people who have proved it, and you haven't succeeded in surmounting them just yet.
Is that objectively true enough?

Can we also agree with this assessment: that for every mistake, disadvantage or offense stacked against you, there were also possibilities, options and solutions that you did not make use of? Again, I'm not talking about shame, blame, condemnation, guilt or even second-guessing, I just mean to ask, "Can you accept responsibil-

ity for the position you are now in?"
Because if you don't, who do you expect will do it for you?

What about God?
We'll get into this more deeply in a later chapter, but regarding the "here & now" responsibility and current struggles, let's start here: God is your Father, and however your natural father may have done things, can we put your earthly Dad's ways aside just for the moment? From Heaven's perspective, our Father could snap his fingers and change a lot of things for you; he could sneeze and you'd be overwhelmed with an abundance of money and material comforts. But as a wise and humble Dad, he may well be waiting for you to make changes of your own, from where you are now, so that he can encourage and support you in bigger and better things to come.

Also, if your Father waved a hand and made you rich, then he could say, "See what I did for my kid." But God isn't much into bragging about himself.

Instead, what if he could say, as the Universal Proud Papa, "Look at what my daughter has done! Isn't she fantastic? I'm going to reward her with even more, add my blessing and give her my favour to accomplish even greater things!"
It's what got King Solomon off to such a great start.[2]

So if you've been passively waiting for God to legitimize what hasn't worked thus far, could it be that he's just waiting to see you do some preparatory work?
    Opinions repented of?
    Beliefs changed?
    Thinking re-directed?
    Capacity increased?

Hand on head:
    Lord, I admit that my financial struggles have been my own doing. I have shaped my own finances. I choose "respon-sibility" and I will stop blaming myself, blaming others, or blaming you.
    I accept responsibility for my current and future financial results and I'm ready to move forward. Please help me to learn a better way that pleases you.
    I want that increased capacity!

Hand on heart:
My heart is now open to examining and surrendering my incorrect, even painful, misunderstandings about money and wealth, and to clearing out that interfering clutter.
More importantly, we're about to replace them with helpful, en-JOY-able beliefs, thoughts, sensations and practices.
This is going to be great!
I am rich in _____!

Now, let's delve more deeply into cause-and-effect
We habitually live as if anything "real" is limited to what is grabable, what we experience sensually through our physical senses. And there's no shortage of painful negative experiences to dominate our attention – you don't often hear someone say, "Nine of my fingers *don't* have splinters!"

One of the effects of these distracting, demanding, up-front negatives is that the positive causes and effects get pushed further and further into the background, eventually to the point where hopes, aspirations and desires for other good things become relegated to becoming distant wishes or "ideals" only glimpsed from afar, in our thoughts, imaginations and emotions. And you can't eat or spend ideals and dreams, right? So we partition those desirables off as subjective yearning – theoretical, detached, nice ideas perhaps, but "unreal". We reinforce their removal as, "Get real." And we either file them as wishful thinking, or consign them to the "spiritual" category, *i.e.* hope. (Though I wonder if we don't really mean "wish".) The gradual effect we don't notice, is that little by little, example by example, degree by degree, we're eventually left with the spiritual realm of possibilities consisting of everything that's out of reach. Above our heads. Meanwhile we're down here glued to the ground, settling for whatever we can force into working. No wonder it's such a struggle here, with the spiritual dimension so far removed, just because it's not within the grasp of our physical senses.[3]

So,
    external = tangible = natural, practical, somewhat predictable, but characterized by struggle;
and
    internal = theoretical = spiritual, idealistic and beneficial, but tenuous and elusive. [4]
That's our inner/outer, spiritual/material paradigm. Although you

may have noticed how Jesus incessantly messed with this system and said we should too, how many people do you see living that way and seeing tangible results?

Rationalists Anonymous
Unfortunately, a watered down reading of Greek philosophers helped our culture to buy into this lowest of common denominators. As westerners, we have settled for this gap between those outer and inner realms, based for the most part on our ability to detect light, sound, pressure (touch) and chemical changes (taste and smell) – "reality" is constrained to what we can apprehend physically. Don't get me wrong, these normal functions are even more wondrous than we're able to scientifically understand, but they're still of limited use for scrutinizing reality. Yet we tend to live as if there's a gulf between reality and spirituality which begins pretty much at the surface of our skin.

Thankfully, we are awakening to the prospect that God's idea of reality, including our experience of it, is actually all a continuum,
from lumpen to ethereal,
from sub-atomic to cosmic,
from energy to matter,
from mechanical to miraculous.
It's all on a scale that runs in both (or many) directions way-ay-ay beyond our ability to touch, hear or even see. Or even picture in our imaginations. And that the limits of our senses aren't necessarily reliable interpreters or predictors of reality. When we say God's ways are above our ways, and his thoughts above our thoughts,[5] it isn't because he's already read everything in the Christian book store. Can we begin to trust that around, within and throughout our experience, or even concept of reality, there already exists even greater reality? His reality? Even more certain, and even less distorted by our egos and limitations? Not for the sweet bye'n'bye, but surrounding you right now?

It's not easy. This is why we are so intimidated when Jesus says that by his spirit we'll be able to tell a mountain to throw itself into the ocean. Or that we'll perform greater miracles than he did. We read these things and nod outwardly because it's in black & white in the Bible, but inwardly we cannot grasp it and it goes into the "spiritual/hope" or "denial" file. Including your desires regarding money and financial freedom to participate in works of compassion and vision.

The point: Your inner landscape, that set of beliefs and opinions shaped by experiences (or often lack of good experiences) has played a starring role in shaping your current, outward circumstances through your actions, words and thoughts. Right down to the micro, or even quantum, level. Your carnal, inner life is self-fulfilling, and your spirituality has been held hostage.
That's why your finances stink.

"Ouch! But I believe! I am spiritual!" you protest. Saying you're spiritual is like saying you breathe oxygen – it's true of everyone, but who's seeing a difference? Elijah's own personal servant believed in God, was following Elijah's lead, but needed his eyes opened to the spiritual presence of the angelic army already arrayed around him.[6]

Okay, so we're at the point of having accepted responsibility for the lacklustre finances we've been living with. And maybe there's a whole lot more to reality, including financial reality, than the eye can see and the ear hear. In fact, we need to tap into that pervasive reality by changing our selves. Including in our understanding of the nature of money.

Your assignment: Get thee behind me, Moaner!
Here's something that's almost as bad for you as blaming: complaining.
I wish I had said this first, but I need to quote T. Harv Eker because he said it so well:
Complaining makes me a living, breathing crap magnet! [7]

Blaming is bad enough, because it keeps you stuck in the past. But complaining starts with blame and then spreads to defile everyone within earshot. Its only purpose is to co-opt people into agreeing and pull others down to that miserable level.[8]

Part of the problem is that complaining often starts with a credible glimpse of perspective or shred of information. It can *seem* true enough. But an irritated sense of right & wrong, plus a strong shot of victim mentality, twists it into a self-righteous emphasis on flaws with the resulting heaviness of conversation, the sourness in the voice, the hope-sucking pull for sympathy, the swirling vortex of criticism... um, I should stop.

The tragic thing is that "like usually attracts like"[9], so complainers will never be satisfied with simply identifying something to be solved. They'd rather drag others down by magnifying the flaws, filling their vision and thought-life with them, and projecting them into generalizations:

The government never...   Our industries don't...

Trucks these days are just...   People nowadays are so...

And they're relying on you to affirm their misery, or at least win your polite nod of acknowledgment.

Stop encouraging them!

If you stop and think about it, you'll notice that complainers get more than their fair share of disappointments and shabby treatment. That's because they're actually attracting disappointments with the *Law of Sowing & Reaping*:

Sow corn, you reap corn.

Sow dandelion seed, you get dandelions.

Sow gossip, you reap gossip.

Sow complaints, you get...

... something else to complain about.

Another paraphrase: There's no avoiding it, God has ingeniously designed the universe so that a man will get what he gives.[10]

Also in play is the *Law of Increase*: What you sow doesn't come back one-for-one, it increases 5-fold, 10-fold, even 100-fold. So if you're breathing out complaints and criticism, you'll reap... even more to be unhappy about.

Ergo, crap magnet!

Here's the relevance: Complainers rarely succeed

If you want to get out of whatever financial bind you're in and reach your financial goals and God-assigned potential, you need to root out and starve out this family of weeds from your own mindset. If you even suspect you have the tendency to complain (and if not, ask the guy in the mirror) here are a few things to do:

1 – Break your own complaint pattern

Complaining is a habit, so let's break it. For the next two weeks, every time you catch yourself complaining about how someone did something, why something doesn't measure up, what's "probably" going to happen... *thwack* yourself on the wrist and re-state it as a positive anticipation or an occasion for gratitude. You can thwack your wrist using your fingernail – a rubber band around your wrist is better. But make sure it smarts! It might sound like this...

• "Boy, our defensive line is lousy... *thwack!*"

"The offense is good, now we can focus on the defence!"

- "What crummy weather... *thwack!*"
"Curling up with a coffee and a magazine sounds like a relaxing morning to me!"
- "Savings account interest is a joke... *thwack!*"
"All the easier to beat it with mutual funds!"
Or, "Loan rates must be low too!"
- "Man, I can't stand salesmen... *thwack!*"
"These guys need some encouragement!"
- "I hate cheesy promotion... *thwack!*"
"People have to know about this!"
- "They're just after my money... *thwack!*"
"I wonder what it is they really need!"
- "But that sounds so *co-mer-shull... thwack!*"
"Get it out there! The more, the merrier!"
Get the idea?

Be ruthless. Don't justify, who cares if you're "right"? No one's that impressed. Complaining is sabotaging your goal of financial restoration.

Do this for two full weeks – switch wrists if you have to. It takes that long to break a negative mental habit.

I hope this isn't getting too corny for you. If it is, then you *really* need this.
Decide now:
    You can be "right", or you can be happy.
    You can be cool and aloof, or you can be wealthy.
    You can think you're entitled to maintain your distance,
        or you can be successful and fulfilled.
I'm serious. Decide you're going to have a sense of humour about all this (even a laugh at your own expense) because the world doesn't need another gloomy rich person.
Choose now, "right" or "rich", because you won't have it both ways.

2 – Remove chronic complainers from your life
Sounds harsh, but you are actually making them worse by giving them the audience they need to perform. And they will sour you before you sweeten them. After all, from their perspective, why would they want you to 'help' them when they're just being insightful about what's "right"? Your attempts will only help them feel hurt, angry and misunderstood. The best thing you can do is

get yourself out of range of their crap-magnetic field. If you can't get away from them entirely, do what you can to minimize their presence.

3 – Don't complain to them about their complaining
Lord knows I've tried. But do you think they'd listen? No way. I barely get started in explaining when they start in about how nobody really listens, change is hard for people, and then they just go right back to... um, *thwack!*

"I am rich in _____!"

1 Obviously "rich" is relative – if you have running water, hot water even, central heat and/or air conditioning, more than one room to live in, and expect to eat several times today, and tomorrow, you're already wealthy compared with the vast sea of humanity, past and present. Gratitude is an essential part of any healthy vision for financial restoration and growth.

2 I Kings 3

3 This is what Jesus was going up against when he repeatedly said, "The Kingdom is among you."

4 This is a resignation and misrepresentation of Platonic thought: that above and beyond our carnal experience is a realm of the ideal – Plato meant it as an inspirational horizon for seekers of truth in a stubborn world, but we misuse it as a pessimistic resignation, i.e. an unattainable ideal, a reason to "Be realistic."

5 Isaiah 55:9

6 II Kings 6:17

7 "Secrets of the Millionaire Mind". With apologies to you Brits!

8 I'm talking about a chronic attitudinal condition. For instance, a consumer "complaint" is different if you have to work something out in order to be satisfied with the value of what you've received – they might not improve what they do if you don't point it out.

9 Forget the "opposites attract" thing – bitterness doesn't attract hope, cheapness doesn't attract generosity, laziness doesn't attract motivation, boredom doesn't attract excitement. It's just that sometimes the virtuous attract the needy.

10 Galatians 6:7 "God is not mocked" is not about baiting God, this is a way of saying that you can't make God look foolish by getting away with something through trickery or force.

Chapter 3, part 1
Money & I Made Up

Augh! We get so twisted into knots about money!
We want it. We distrust it.
We need it. We resent it.
We feel better when we have it,
    then we feel guilty for wanting more.
We glibly fantasize about being generous,
    but we worry it'll corrupt us.
We're relieved when it comes in,
    but we're embarrassed about asking for it.
It's okay to talk about finances, gifts, cheques, and
    buh-lessings,
    just don't call it 'money'.
It's acceptable, even assumed, you'll struggle financially
    if you're in The Ministry.
You get blessed with money occasionally,
    just enough to keep you struggling.
It's okay to want to be successful,
    but you shouldn't want to be rich.
It's impolite to talk about money.
No wonder money doesn't like being around you.

Of *course* you struggle.
    You can't create or gather what you despise.
      You won't attract or keep what embarrasses you.
      You won't prosper by what you distrust.
        Your ambivalence toward money
          is the biggest reason you don't have much of it.

Isn't it ironic that we are comfortable, or even pleased, to admire people's accomplishments in the forms of
    sports prowess,   academic achievement,
      artistic reputation,   public recognition,
      technical knowledge,   career advancement...
but making money, creating wealth and getting rich are met with varying levels of discomfort, distaste, suspicion and even resentment?

Now, tell me which of the accomplishments just listed were specifically *commended* by Jesus? (Hint: "good and faithful".) Ironic, indeed. We'll get into Jesus & money in a later chapter but isn't it interesting how we prefer a partition between achievement and money? It's ironic because those who excel in those areas usually get rich too. So we'll cheer their scoring ability, applaud their wins and congratulate them on their awards, but we'd rather overlook the money. Especially their marketing savvy.

The belief we have bought into is that money might be okay as a side effect, a secondary reward, but not as a goal. And beware of mingling your money and your spiritual progress!

There is so much confusion and inner conflict surrounding money, its nature and its effects. And this kind of uncertainty won't help your finances improve. In order to restore your financial soul, we need a healthy, growing relationship with money.

As you might with any relationship, let's start by taking a fresh look at the nature of your counterpart – let's focus on and re-evaluate our opinions about the nature of money itself.

MONEY = ENERGY + TIME
That's all money is. It's just a way of quantifying increase in value because of somebody's effort + the time they took. (Materials usually shrink in significance.)

To illustrate: Whatever it is that you're sitting on right now required a direct input of TIME+ENERGY: design, a bit of gathered material, manufacturing, shipping, stocking, sales, purchase and delivery. That's a lot of invested TIME+ENERGY, *i.e.*, thought, motivation, effort and cooperation. And at every stage, more and more people joined in and added value in the form of improvements and availability. Every person's contribution of effort and time was recognized in units of money.

Money is just how we "store" our TIME+ENERGY.
Money is how we move (give and receive) that TIME+ENERGY.
    Time is not dirty, is it?
        Energy is not evil, is it?
           Neither is TIME+ENERGY: money.

So, is it selfish to want more time?
    Is it unhealthy to want more energy?

So should we be embarrassed about having
abundant TIME+ENERGY?

Could you do good things with more time?
 Can you do spiritual things with extra energy?
 So why shouldn't you celebrate having
   more and more TIME+ENERGY at your disposal?

Yes, we need to have a healthy respect for money's influence and
effect, like we do with electricity. Large amounts of uncontrolled
electricity is dangerous (*i.e.* lightning) but where would our communities be without high voltage systems to generate, harness,
direct and deliver electrical power? So if having ample electricity
is beneficial, why shouldn't we see having ample money as beneficial too? Yet we short circuit the flow of our own finances with
random flaws in our mental wiring.

For instance, have you told yourself, and others, that the world would
be a better place without money? Maybe you meant that money
should be *distributed* better, but money itself got blamed.
  Are there aberrations? Sure.
   Are there abuses? Yes.
    Is it money's fault? No.
     Re-pent, *re*-think, *re*-thwack!

Money is *good* for you
And the degree to which that statement makes you hiccup, squirm
or fidget hints at how much your relationship with money needs
to be healed, for your sake and the sake of others. Here are some
more things to consider about money...

Money is constructive in nature, not destructive. We add thought,
time and effort to wood to make a table, so our appreciation for
the wood's value increases, and that's measured in money. And if
it becomes an antique, then time is *really* on its side.

Money is cooperative in nature, not divisive. It's a form of consensus and agreement, especially now that we aren't using the
gold standard. Billions of minds have to agree on the value every
dollar holds. Yes, there's competition for it, but that makes us do
things better. For more people.

Money is positive and affirming, not depressing and cruel. Strong ideas are affirmed with more money, weak ideas attract less money – this inspires, even forces, improvement. And that's why...

Money highlights the truth, it is not deceptive. People can temporarily insulate themselves from the truth with money, but if something's really amiss the symptoms often manifest in the form of money. And adjustments, even justice, *will* follow.

Money is a tool that simply makes contributing TIME+ENERGY easier.

Money is a reward, it takes a selfish heart to turn it into a trap.

Money is abundant, not scarce. The flow of capital and commerce is a virtual torrent around you and your community. But it slips past you because you're ambivalent toward it or anxious about it – and who enjoys ambivalent or anxious company?

Therefore, money is not a problem after all. It never is. A lack of money is just how some of your *real* problems are showing up. It means you're believing, feeling and doing something wrong with your energy and your time. Fix *those* problems and you remove obstructions to the flow money in your life.

So let's disable your belief that "money is a problem"
If you've told yourself that money is a problem, or talked about "money problems", then you've believed and/or agreed to that proposition. And that is where your perception got stuck. It's now a self-fulfilling prophecy in your thinking, observations and beliefs. And it will continue to play out in your relationship with money until you supplant it with something better, something more positive, something more attractive.

Take a minute and think about how you would have said it (you might even have a specific example or favourite expression) including any reinforcing physical reactions such as groans or heavy sighs; or body language like frustrated gestures (head in hand, banging a fist, rubbing eyes), picture to whom you would have expressed it, and write what you said or thought here:

_____

_____

Now read it out loud and immediately *thwack!* it, hard enough that it smarts, and immediately speak out the first *positive* thing that pops into your head in response to counter it. (Like, "No, no, the money I did have helped." or "No, no, I just need *more* money." or "It's okay, it all worked out.")
It's fine to make it up, as long as it is affirming of money's positive role.
Then write that encouraging truth about money here:

_____

_____

That *thwack!* is what's called a "pattern interrupt" – an intentional distraction can deliberately break a chain of thought, the way a small wire can short out and disable a whole electrical circuit. So when you notice a bad line of thought, a bad circuit of belief, if you identify and interrupt it, you create an opportunity to replace the debilitating belief with a helpful belief of your choosing. After all, you chose to put the bad message in place – no reason why you can't replace it with a better one.

But make sure you swap in a positive, helpful truth about money itself. The physicality drives the point deeper than your surface thoughts – the sharper your *thwack!*, the more pronounced the change in your thinking.

Can't I just think the happy thoughts and not worry about the bad ones?
No, for at least two reasons.
1 – A bad belief is a form of self-comfort and usually based on a lie. A credible-sounding one, but a lie nonetheless. Such as...
    "There, there, we can't all be the best."
    "Oh well, money isn't that important."
    "Just be happy with what you have."
    "I don't need much."
    "If I get ahead, it might be at someone else's expense."
Those are common, debilitating lies about money & you.
They're designed for temporary consolation and soothing.
They're pseudo-logical "reasons" coating your emotions (not resolving and healing them) and this "learning" cements negative experiences into place.

And they're lies that stand between you & money.
Damned lies.

Any lie can become a belief when it's disguised as believable evidence. Once you acknowledge, accept and take it on board as being true, you give that lie a place of legitimacy, so it will continue to occupy space in your mental makeup, have a voice in your decisions and demand to be defended within your belief system. As I noted earlier, have you noticed how much mental energy it takes to maintain a lie?
Think of them as parasites.

2 – Lies thwart truth. It's automatic. Whenever relevant circumstances arise, they will run interference against new, constructive, helpful ideas or beliefs. In fact, they'll kick in before your conscious stream of thoughts has time to analyze and formulate a response – you'll feel something negative almost immediately, and you'll be frustrated by reasonable-sounding lies just because they're (still) there.
Some things you can let lie, but not lies.

So use the *thwack!*,
    swap in a good, helpful belief
        and declare, *"I am rich in _____!"*

In fact, now it would be a good time to go back and do the same with, "The world would be a better place without money."
Thwack! it, replace it, and declare, *"I am rich in _____!"*

The energy behind, in & around money
Because money is an expression of energy, it also has unique properties. You might even say a life of its own – at the very least in the sense that we'd also say an electrical wire is 'live'.

I trust you can now see how behind every coin and bill there is stored ENERGY+TIME. And like electricity, wealth has its generators, conductors, resistors and consumers where it's either converted into activity or stored.

And it goes further. Have you ever held a lot of money in your hand? It feels very different from holding other paper products such as a book, stack of newspapers or pile of greeting cards. And it gives you that sensation not just because of the central bank's taste in paper products. I'd go at least as far as saying it is ener-gized – the potency of money is actually tangible.

It takes tremendous common purpose and concerted effort for a country to create money – it is invested and imbued with your nation's collective energy. Just try to imagine the prayer, desire, talk, anxiety, ambition and political power brought to bear on the money you hold and the channels it follows. When you visit a large corporation's offices, or your nation's capital buildings, or an old stately home, you can tangibly sense the aura of power and wealth generated and conveyed by all that money.

And through common purpose and continued circulation, that aura of wealth draws and mobilizes more wealth. Like attracts like.

Money as magnetism
Here's another important thing to have in your relationship with money: *attraction*. You can increase your capacity for money by making yourself actually attractive to its inherent ENERGY+TIME. In fact, you can be a kind of magnet for money. Whatever your explana-tion for the way money has avoided you so far, the following will help to reverse that phenomenon.

If you'll pardon yet another physics analogy, anyone can turn an ordinary rod or bar of iron into a magnet. You probably did this in science class:
♦   In one hand hold the plain rod of iron, in the other a magnet.
♦   Then you stroke the iron rod with one end of the magnet, repeat-edly, always in the same direction.
♦   The action of the magnet's magnetic field repeatedly passed across and through the bar will actually re-align the jumbled, irreg-ular molecules in the plain iron until they line up and develop their own magnetic field.[1]

Money's energy can have the same effect on the financial aspect of our soul, if we can just get our inner chaos about money to line up in a common direction by consistently applying it in an inten-tional, helpful direction. So let's start working with a couple of ways to get money's inherent energy, its magnetism, working to attract more money into your life. How?

Talk nice, talk often
Every relationship thrives on attraction and a sense of anticipa-

tion, optimism, appreciation and respect, right? The same holds for your relationship with money.

In any relationship that has become dull, confused and lame, you're dealing with a complex web of perceptions, interpretations, evaluations, attractions & repulsions, actions & avoidances, and all of the decisions, speech, body language, mini-gestures and nano-tics that reflect your actual feelings about the relationship. You cannot hide the way you really feel without an elaborate and determined effort.

And if you want to keep such a relationship, whether a friendship, romance, marriage, working relationship or social acquaintance, you'd need to make some intentional decisions and deliberate changes to re-kindle it. That, or keep doing exactly what you're doing now and lose it. And since you have a will to choose, it's up to you to make the first move. (Interestingly, Charmaine and I attended a marriage communication workshop early in our marriage, and one of their credos was, "Love is a choice.")

Your financial situation will not change until you choose to *at least* talk about it differently. So here's one of the first things you can do:
   **Deliberately, intentionally, consistently change
   the way you talk about money to yourself.**
Even if it seems awkward at first, you need to say it, to hear your own voice saying it, and verbally register your renewed commitment to your relationship with money.[2]

This might feel a bit awkward and forced at first, like squinting to see something in the distance, but that's okay. The point is you're being intentional. And, as you would hope in a human relationship, you will see money respond.

Now, this might feel funny, but go with it for now and we'll talk after...
Repeat the following after me,
   line-by-line,
      out loud,
         with *oomph!* ...

I LIKE MONEY!

Money is good for me, money is useful and helps me.
I like money, I like having it, I like using it.
I want more money to work with, play with and share.

I appreciate money. I respect money's energy and
 its effect.
My money is "live" and has "a life of its own" –
 it's a kind of seed that grows and multiplies for me.
Because I have lots of money, I have lots of this ENERGY+TIME
 to work with, play with and share.

I attract money.
 I attract money in every form and fashion.
I am attracting more money all the time,
 around the clock, even as I sleep.
There's more money coming to me now
 than I've ever seen before.
Today I am expanding my capacity to receive, create
 and give money.

I enjoy money. I'm glad I have it.
Money is abundant around me – there's more
 than enough for me, my loved ones and others.
I like the feeling of money in my hand, in my wallet
 and in my accounts.

I like money, I attract money and money responds.
My Heavenly Father will supply my every need
 and he'll be generous with the desires of my heart.
The Lord has already prepared accomplishments for my
 life,
 including the necessary money.
I can accumulate money, use money and enjoy money
 with a clear conscience, gratitude and enthusiasm.

"I am rich in _____!"

How was that? Feels strange? Kinda self-conscious? A bit over-board? That's good!

We're not trying to "be balanced". We're pushing against and through the current state of your finances, and the harder you push the sooner you'll grow into freedom. After all, if you remain perfectly balanced all the time, you will never walk – you need to be willing to over-balance your weight on one foot in order to pick up and move the other. So if some of these statements feel like we're over-emphasizing finances and money, that's okay, it's just us learning to walk.

Times and seasons will come and go when the Lord asks you to de-emphasize money, but you won't be able to do that either if you don't have any! You cannot give, share and distribute what you do not possess because you were too self-conscious to have much of it. Please don't water these statements down – get aggressive, press on and press through.

For the next month, recite this declaration at least once a day. Twice is better: once in the morning and once before you go to sleep.

Re-write, re-type or photocopy this proclamation and put it some-where you'll see it, read it aloud and deliberately re-apply it. Maybe at your desk, in your bathroom, by your nightstand. But like the iron rod and magnet, the trick is to do this repeatedly and con-sistently, and with an expectant heart. And you will notice posi-tive changes in your own regard for money and comfort level with having it around.

As I write, I'm recovering from a broken leg. (Don't ask!) To get my leg back to its natural flexibility and strength, I have to delib-erately stretch out my tendons and muscles. It's awkward, uncom-fortable and actually feels quite unnatural. *But for now I must force this stretching if I ever want to walk normally again.* So it is with your view and self-talk about money. We need to force our self-talk into being positive about money, stretch out our view of money as a positive, active agent in our lives, and push past the self-conscious discomfort.

Here's why
You've spent years hearing, thinking, reading, saying and believ-ing crummy things about money. By taking a deliberate stand,

declaring a different thought-life about money, and hearing yourself affirm that money is beneficial, your feelings about money will improve, your subconscious routines of thinking will start lining up, your capacity will stretch and increase, you'll gather and retain more of that great swirl of money around you, and your finances *will* improve.

If you were an athlete trying to get on top of your game, you'd be doing the same sorts of things: mentally psyching yourself into better and better performance with self-encouragement, breaking bad playing habits, working on specific muscle groups, fixing your mind on what a winning shot looks like, building awareness of dynamics on the playing field, and so on. Just today, I heard a radio interview with a National Hockey League player, Ted Nolan, who was hired to coach the Buffalo Sabres in 1996. Up until then he had no coaching experience, but after he was hired he started turning over plays and strategies in his mind before he began the job. He said, "I must have played two or three hundred games in my mind before I coached a single game." And he took the Sabres to the Stanley Cup finals that year.

This is important. We're working on your inner financial fitness and your relationship with money, and part of that process is helping you to be comfortable with the fact that *money has to be more important to you now than it has been in the past.* You need to treat it that way, you need to talk about it that way, you need to think and feel about it that way. More important than TV, more important than cutting your lawn, more than joke e-mails, more than playing games.

So if that proclamation about money rankled, I suggest you go back again and read it aloud right now, *oomph*ily. After a few times, you'll notice positive changes in your comfort level with the declaration. And with money itself.
And money's comfort level with *you*.

Next... Healing Your Financial Soul field trip #1
Time to take it outside and have a bit of fun. This weekend, instead of going to your usual café or coffee shop, dress *nicely* and go alone to the nicest, posh-est, most expensive hotel in your area, the place where the wealthy people go. (If you figure you shouldn't have to dress up a bit, then that's part of your problem.)
Sit in the lobby lounge and order a coffee or pot of tea. Nothing more.

Do not balk at the price! You've wasted more on worse things. Do not offer excuses to the staff as to why you're there or why a drink will do. Do not order food – you don't have to justify your presence by ordering more.

If you live in a smaller community, either drive to a city or look up a country inn on the internet and drive there. We're looking for *upscale* – if there's a TV within sight, leave. We want no Boston ferns and brass foot rails, thank-you. Spider plants are the worst.

Do not bring a newspaper or work with you.

And for pity's sake, turn off your mobile phone.

Just enjoy your drink and watch the people – people who accept that they belong there and routinely pay to stay in places of this calibre. Allow yourself to feel a part of that scene.

Observe who comes and goes, discretely take note of the dynamics of their conversations, take a reading of their personal state (facial and body language, tone of voice, dress, *etc.*).

Accept no pressure, especially from yourself, to do any more than just smile, be there and be comfortable in the moment, because at this moment you *belong* there.

As you feel this realization sinking in, use your key and affirm,

"*I am rich in _____!*"

And leave a good tip based on how well you were served, not a mathematical derivative of the price of coffee.

I'm quite serious about this one

This is not just cute. We're acclimating your active mental state, subconscious, emotions and now body language to be at ease around wealth. The vast majority of people hang around with people who earn the same income, plus or minus 10% – they have no upside influences, expectations or encouragement.

You'll learn just by being there – if you just get the feeling.

If you're going through this book with your spouse or fiancé, you can go back a second time with them. But go on your own first. No excuses.

Do it because "*I am rich in _____!*"

---

1 You could also apply this analogy to scripture. Stroking your mind with the Bible by reading, reflecting and memorizing scripture will line up your thoughts and ways with God's thoughts and ways. It's the power of the Holy Spirit that does this.

2 If this is sounding too much like "the love of money" of evil root fame, stick with me and we'll get to that one too.

Chapter 3, part 2
More About Your Money Make-up

If you're anything like me, you'll notice a direct relationship between your level of intent & enthusiasm and the degree of change you're seeing as you go through these exercises, prayers and activations. Remember, *"As* a man sows..."
The more willingness you sow or invest, the more generous and expansive your attitude and your feelings...
    the more you will notice, experience and even attract
    God's willingness, generosity and expansiveness.

And I don't mean pretending on the one hand and on the other striving and straining to force something into happening. That's how we got into the messes we're in. I mean deliberately taking pleasure in the process. Yes, you can choose that. Remember what I said at the outset about leveraging your own emotional state simply by smiling? I wasn't just being corny – you're grabbing your emotional state by the handle and deliberately hoisting it into a more enjoyable, helpful posture.
Just because you can, just because it feels better.

You might object, "But I can't just 'feel good' when this-and-that are happening around me."
Yes, you can.

If you took out a credit card from your wallet right now, and laughed at yourself for something silly you've done with it, would the numbers on your statement suddenly, magically change?
    Probably not.
If you got in touch with what a drag it is to get behind on paying off your balance, would someone else then get your bill in the mail instead of you?
    Still no change.
How have you done with changing your spending behaviour with the card so far?
    Not so great?
Hmm, then perhaps the *easiest* thing to change is your feelings.

You decide who's in charge of your emotional state: you or your circumstances.

So allow me to repeat:
The more willingness you invest,
the more generous and expansive your outlook
and feelings,
the more you will notice, experience and even attract
God's willingness, generosity and expansiveness.

This is about choosing your emotional state:
specifically, thankfulness, celebration and joy.
And yes, you can choose them.
There's always something to be thankful for, and anything you're thankful for is worth celebrating and finding the joy in it.
The key is your decision to turn in that direction.

Rather than depending on other people, or circumstances, to shift in order to accommodate you and provide you with joy, *you* choose joy. Why wait for the rest of the world to get around to giving it to you?

When I get into a downward emotional pattern, such as the morning after a lousy night's sleep, I will stop and remind myself, "Choose your state, David." And I can choose to feel and function as if my sleep had been normal.[1] It's my choice to respond to the occasion with disappointment, resignation or pessimism – I can use the same will to change the direction of my feelings and thoughts to anticipate something better. My choice. Your choice.

Nodding in
If you like the content of our "I Like Money" declaration, and you can see merit in the ideas, and you wish you could embrace it more fully, we can send that message another level deeper into your belief system by incorporating your body language.

Remember how we talked about the linkage between your mind and your physical body? And how we can leverage that system from any point on the cognitive / emotional / spiritual / physical spectrum? And how we anchored your "I am rich in _____!" statement with a visual, auditory or kinesthetic association and gesture? We can also make the words and ideas in "I Like Money" permeate a deeper level of your thinking, and eventually your financial experience, with physical gestures.

To illustrate, you've noticed during election campaigns how newspapers not only publicly endorse particular candidates in editorials but their coverage syncs up in a lot of ways. And depending on your own views, you've been either pleased or irritated by the sorts of coverage they dole out – how the headlines are phrased, the 'news angle' taken, the inclusion or exclusion of opposing views, the flattering or unflattering photo selections, and so on. There have been scads of media studies examining the effects of this subjective, sub-surface messaging, substantiated by polling and voting statistics. So, there's the obvious surface content and then there's the subtle, even subliminal, stuff as well. You're getting an intentional blend of body language (via photos), tone of voice and choice of words even though it's a print medium and supposedly objective and unbiased.

And much has been debated about how far people's political convictions can be nudged by the time they get to the polling booth – they don't need to turn far-left voters into far-right voters, just sway enough of a percentage of the voters in the middle a few degrees one way or the other. It's safe to say deeper levels of communication are at work on your thinking and beliefs as well, even despite surface assumptions and objections.

Funny thing is, you can actually shape your own deeper convictions and shape your own views and thoughts. Malcolm Gladwell, in his book, *The Tipping Point,* cites a clinical study where university students were recruited ostensibly to evaluate the sound quality of earphones. They were all given music to listen to and then an audio editorial coincidentally arguing for a 25% hike in tuition fees. One third were instructed to keep their heads still while listening, one third to shake their heads from side to side throughout the material, and one third to nod their heads vigorously, supposedly to find out if the sound quality was affected. At the end of the evaluation interview, the students were incidentally asked their thoughts on tuition costs:
  + the motionless control group were neutral about the editorial and estimated a fair tuition within $5 of what they currently were;
  + the head shakers strongly disagreed and felt fees should drop, on average, by $120;
  + the nodders found the arguments rather convincing and believed tuition should rise an average of $60.
This is not coincidence. It seems that physical motions (in this case, body language strongly associated with yes and no) actually rein-

forced or undermined the content of the argument, and shaped their own convictions about their own money.[2] (Note also that the downside was easier to generate than the upside.)

So, let's use this same dynamic to your own advantage. If you can see the benefits in the "I Like Money" manifesto, and you want to feel better about what it's saying, and want to see that kind of fruit in your own life, then go back and re-declare it while nodding your head – the more pronounced and kinesthetic, the better. Okay, it might seem awkward at first, but how small a price is this to pay for real change in your financial mentality? You may notice a pronounced emotional shift in how you relate to the content right away, as I did even though I'd already been working with it for months. Or it may be subtle. But it's a simple choice you can make for yourself and your finances.

There's perception and then there's perception
NASA, the United States' space agency, did this experiment where they put specialized goggles on their trainees. The goggles contained mirrors that flipped everything they saw upside down and they had to wear them continuously, with no relief. It was disorienting, they were dizzy, they stumbled about, they threw up... it was driving them mad. And then something surprising happened.

After a couple of weeks of suffering, their brains suddenly flipped everything back right-side-up, re-inverting their vision so they could work again with what they saw and feel re-oriented. And it was sudden, not a gradual slide. Some switch in their heads suddenly got flicked, their perception went 'bink', and *everything normalized despite the goggles*. Each subject experienced the same. It took each of their cognitive processes about the same time to work out the problem, re-route their visual processing and re-orient – their Internal Department of Equilibrium re-routed the information along new neural pathways in their brains, without specific rational guidance or cognitive direction.

By the way, your eye lenses invert everything you see on your retinas – the top of this page is actually registering light at the bottom of the backs of your eyeballs, the bottom of this page is projected on the tops of your retinas; the type is imprinting from right to left and the letters are all backward. But your brain learned how to work with that when you were a baby. So, if a baby can do this, let's work with your brain's ability to perceive, and even invert, disoriented input to better effect, deliberately choose to look at things differently and change your perception for the better. If your brain can do this with your physical sense of vision via your optic nerves, how much more your choices about attitudes and perceptions of logic?

For instance, bills are great!
Does it feel good to pay your electricity bill? It should.
   Are you thankful to pay taxes? You could be.
      Do you feel grateful in advance that your mortgage
      is paid off every time you make a payment? You can.

We're going to start re-wiring your perception and perspective about bills and taxes. Here's how...

You'll need three things for this exercise:
   1. Your current, outstanding bills (utilities, taxes, credit cards *if you clear the balance each month*).
   2. Your file of already-paid bills and loan payment receipts (car loans, mortgage payments, lines of credit) and charitable donation receipts. If your bank returns your used cheques grab those too.
   3. Balance statements for ongoing credit and loans (mortgage schedule, credit card statements if you are running a balance and carrying it from month to month at interest, a blank income tax form for your next tax deadline (if available), charitable appeals you expect to respond to... basically the things you expect to pay in the future).
   Oh, and a bit of floor space.

(This one might be a bit easier if you have someone else to read the steps to you, or you can do it on your own starting with this book in your left hand. Allow 10 or 15 minutes and make sure you won't be interrupted.)

   • Flip through that stack of old statements, receipts and cheques, and notice all the numbers that you've gone through, by the hundreds and thousands, the dates that have gone by, the places you've been, the things you've done and bought, and so on.
   • Arrange your papers on the floor in front of you in three piles like so, from left to right:
      past bills & statements : current bills : future payments.[3]

* Stand back, facing the three piles, and pray with me:
Lord, please give me your eternal perspective
on all these bills.
Use your visual/auditory/kinesthetic key and remind yourself,
"I am rich in _____!"

Briefly, but firmly, press your thumb nails into the tips of your ring fingers on each hand – just once each. You'll do this again shortly.

* Take a deep breath and look down at the middle pile of current bills and pause to consider how it makes you feel to know you need to pay every one of them. Is there any apprehension? Pay attention to any negative words or expressions you "hear", any physical sensations in your body, any visual images that come to mind, and especially any negative emotions.
* Step onto that middle pile and stand on it long enough to allow yourself to strongly engage those negative feelings and emotions. When you feel them reach a peak, firmly press your *right* thumbnail into your *right* ring-fingertip once.
* Step back off the pile and reset by shrugging, sighing, wiggling your toes, whatever. (Move this book to your right hand.)
* Now look at the left pile of receipts and proofs of payment and consider that you used to feel the same way about all of those past bills. But the fact is they're old news. Allow yourself to feel good about the satisfaction, gratitude and encouragement that all those payments are *behind you and in the past*, and afterward more money came to replace it. They're paid, they're done, that's fact![4]
* Also consider that they represent things you got to do, have or give – you heated your home, you wore clothes, you drove, you walked on a paved sidewalk, you contributed... Each one means you and others benefited somehow. Notice any positive realizations and feelings that come, along with good memories or pleasing sensations.
* Step onto that left pile, stand on it and allow those same good feelings to become vivid – what words would you put to them? Satisfaction? Relief? Thankfulness? Lightness? Fun? Contentment? Freedom? When you're strongly engaged with those positive feelings, press your *left* thumbnail into the fingertip of your *left* ring finger.
* Step back and reset again.

+ Fix your gaze again on that middle pile in front of you, consider that every 'paid' receipt on your left used to belong in this middle pile, and it is a fact that these current bills will join them very soon.
So smile, take a breath, and *as you step onto those current bills* again, simultaneously press *both* thumbnails into *both* ring-fingertips.
+ Your negative feelings about the current bills should be neutralized while the positive ones linger. (The internal shift you feel may be pronounced or subtle. Once is usually enough, but it's okay if you need to step back and re-do the step with both thumbnails.)
+ Remain standing on the middle pile, turn to face your future payments on your right. Consider that every payment ahead of you is just as surely on its way to the 'paid' pile now behind you; that ahead of you are even more benefits, experiences, freedoms, purchases, *etc., and* the money to pay for them. All three piles are real, all three piles are paid, the only difference is the date.
+ *As you step forward onto the future pile,* press your *left* thumbnail again to anchor your positive, optimistic state to the completion of those future payments. Allow yourself to stand there, gazing forward for a few moments to absorb the fact that when your financial future arrives and both the time and money pass behind you, you will remain as the constant. Deep breath.
+ You now have a positive emotional state relevant to your financial future and a reason to step into your future with faith, confidence and strength.
Feel free to express your gratitude and declare, *"I am rich in* _____*!"* With *oomph!*

Now you can legitimately feel *good* about paying for all the hot showers, phone conversations, shared meals, the books, tickets and visits you enjoy; the country and community you live in; the help you give others... And you can feel *good* about your mortgage being paid off, your credit card balance cleared, your tuitions paid and your medical bills finished.

Nowadays, every time I get a bill, I hold it up and thank God that it's as good as paid because Jesus said, "Your father knows you hath need of these things."[5]

Whenever I pay bills online I use my key and say, *"I am rich in _____!"*

Apply faith & gratitude.
   Always faith & gratitude.
      Abundant faith & gratitude.
Flip the "normal" perception of bills and payments on its head to the positive and appreciative.

And if it feels odd (even ridiculous) at first, keep at it and, like those inverting glasses that they experimented with at NASA, your brain will flip your perception and you'll be capable of perceiving and operating from that perspective. If you're deliberate, consistent and persistent, your mind will accommodate you and normalize this constructive, encouraging point of view for you and you'll be oriented toward abundance.
Is it okay if that takes a couple of weeks?

By now, you may have been asking yourself,
"Is all of this leading to the dreaded love of money?"
I was going to tackle that one later. But why not? Let's do it now.

Hopefully, you're becoming accustomed to your own need to at least *like* money – as in, recognize it for what it is, be comfortable around it, enjoy it, actually look forward to more involvement with it and the opportunities it can help put within your grasp. The question is, how much is too much? Where can it go wrong? Will working with money compromise or taint your love relationship with God? Your apprehension, even discomfort, as we get closer to this issue is understandable because of the number of times we've all been threatened, intimidated and discouraged with "the root of all evil."

First of all, the Bible does not say, "Money is the root of all evil." That's a misquote. Which makes it a lie.
If there's a part of you that still wants to be accommodating and not dismiss that false cliché entirely, then we've just found another snag in your money mindset. Feel free to *thwack!* and replace that now.

Secondly, there is plenty of evil out there which is not rooted in money. And although it might be somewhat covered off under "Thou shalt not steal" and "Thou shalt not covet", money doesn't even get mentioned in the Ten Commandments.

Thirdly, what Paul wrote was,
"The *love* of money
is *a* root
of *all sorts of* evil."[6]
The Bible is reliable, so it's true. But there is a context here.

The flow of the conversation Paul is having is advice to his disciple Timothy, about how to live a healthy spiritual life as a leader. He was contrasting against men who have an agenda to use wonky teaching and controversy as a way to make a name for themselves and use the novelty to take people's money – wolves in shepherd's clothing. And how some of them had taken it so far that they lost their faith and spun out. And taken out well-meaning followers as well.

If we stick with the intent of what Paul was addressing, a renewed rendering of Paul's statement could be,
"That thirst for money,
is a cause of
all sorts of compromise, strife and regret."
It's not the money – it's the deliberate empire-building, the pride and ambition to create a personal following at the expense of friction, division and woundedness among the followers. These men were not creating anything of value by which to prosper – they were just gathering followers around themselves with novel "teaching" to syphon off people's money. You've probably seen fringe-y little churches get weird like this. And big ones.

Which brings us to a couple of points:
 • You don't have to have any money to suffer from that thirst for personal profile and people's giving – poor people can be just as petty, territorial and grasping about money and followers as rich people. I've seen it in all kinds of places: Africa, Central America, the Caribbean and North America.
 • It still comes back to the state of the self-styled leader's heart, motivations and the emotions that coat their relationship with money.
Paul was not saying money is voodoo. But again, the energy of money was magnifying what was in those men's hearts.

A few verses later, Paul switches topics to a healthy scenario and gives this advice for wealthy believers:

Command those who are rich in this present world
not to be arrogant
nor to put their hope in wealth
but to put their hope in God,
who richly provides us with everything
for our enjoyment.
Command them to do good,
to be rich in good deeds,
and to be generous and willing to share.
In this way they will lay up treasure for themselves
as a firm foundation for the coming age,
so that they may take hold of the life that is truly life.

Does that appeal to you? Think it'd be worth going for?
So is it okay to be rich?
Is being rich the same as having a personal power agenda and
ambition to take money?
I strongly suggest you read that passage over again, and under-
line and circle the words which stand out for you. It'll only take
two minutes, and it's good medicine.

So now we can shake off the glib and careless use of the "love of
money" clause, which refers not to the rich, but to ambitious con-
troversialists.

Otherwise, every time someone earns, uses or gives evil-root,
they're risking an evil-root transplant.

More love
This should make it clearer as we tackle another negatively skewed
verse. This one was written as counsel in a book for believers
with a Jewish background (*Hebrews*) and needs to be untangled
as well:
    Keep yourself free from the love of money
    And be content with what you have[7]
And then goes on about how God will neither abandon nor forsake
us where it comes to our material needs.

It never ceases to amaze me how we can take positive, encouraging advice meant to build our confidence and turn it into a dour
threat and financial put-down.

Paul says elsewhere that his ideal state is having a flexible and cooperative outlook which can be "content" with both plenty and little[8] – plenty is not the ideal, little is not the ideal, being content is the ideal.

+ Can you have a lot of money and be content with what you have, free of guilt or an unhealthy, anxious thirst for money? Sure.

+ Can you have very little money and still be content, not suffering from resentment or anxiety for more money? Yes, again.

So the contrast that the writer of *Hebrews* is drawing is between that "being content" versus the "love of money", *i.e.* that conniving itch for cash. It's the emotional state associated, the state of the heart, not the net worth. (As we've said elsewhere, if you could afford to buy, and are able to read, this book, you're already "rich" compared with most people, living and dead.)

+ The key to that verse is the word, "free". Not affluent. Not broke. Not middling.

+ Then the comparison is "free" with "content" – not nervous or grasping.

+ "Be content" is not the same as "Settle for whatever." It means to be at ease and trust.

+ Do not take "be content with what you have" out of context to make it mean "abandon any hopes for better".

+ Then, if being healthy and peacefully confident is the goal, rather than grasping or worried, then neither abundance nor simplicity is the issue. We need to be anxiety-free and energized in *either* case, and not craving or being preoccupied. (How many ways can I find to describe that shifty, nervous thirst for income?)

+ Funny how double-mindedness about this leads people to say things like, "It's okay for God's people to prosper, but not to be rich."

Wanting to prosper and thrive, even to be rich,
    is not the same as "the love of money".
Separate and *thwack!* the false equation and self-defeating bond between them.
Go ahead, *thwack!* it now, and write here the first thing that springs to mind to replace it:

_____

_____

Okay, one more section for this much-needed re-examination and re-evaluation of old perspectives.

Love and Mammon

These preceding misuses of "the love of money" as a grumpy, finger-wagging financial put-down to keep people from getting too uppity also gets used as fake evidence to scare people away from "Mammon". As if Mammon was the same as money. It's a false threat.

Jesus said that you cannot "serve" both God and Mammon.[9] Mammon is not simply a synonym for cash any more than God is just a substitute term for "niceness" – Mammon is something much bigger that is antithetical to God and his ways. If he was using the term mammon to simply mean cold, hard cash, Jesus would be a hypocrite for having a treasurer. Jesus is drawing a line and saying you must choose: God's side or this other thing that opposes him. The questions are, who is being served, and what does it mean to serve either?

In the Old Testament (the only scripture Jesus ever referred to) God repeatedly likened his own relationship with Israel to a marriage, and during their degenerate years he kept calling his 'bride' back to faithfulness and away from their 'adultery' – an analogy for the violences, lusts and obscenities of occult religions. Now, this is a bit antique to our 21st Century minds, but until very recently part of a bride's traditional vows to her groom was to serve him. And you only have to dip back a few hundred years to see social conventions where a wife would address her husband as her master, even lord. (Shakespeare, for instance, and look how weirded out we get over *The Taming of the Shrew* these days.) So, faithful marriage involved serving one's lord and master.

But as modern, independent, democratic people, we have NO CONCEPT of what it's like to "serve" a "master". None. Don't kid yourself just because you have a boss at work – you *don't* understand. In Jesus' time (actually until only very recently in the broad course of human history) to serve was not just to work for someone. It meant devotion, commitment, being legally bonded to, identified with and attached to the master's household. It was a legal relationship, not just agreeing to show up for work and leaving to go back to your own home and life. This *was* your life, identity and foreseeable future to a binding degree that we rarely see nowadays. Unless you've been an addict.

A Study in God, Mammon and the Rich

William Wilberforce was a son of a wealthy merchant and English Parliamentarian. Elected in 1780, he had a born-again experience in 1785 and agreed in 1787 to head up the Quakers' campaign to abolish the British slave trade. (The Quakers refused participation in politics, so they needed a front man.)

Two years later, he introduced the topic in Parliament, met opposition, but succeeded in creating a select committee to study the matter for a year. His first bill was blown out of the water in 1791, 163 votes to 88. It's important to get this: it's not just that he didn't get enough votes – it's that twice as many well-respected people voted *against* abolition. The educated class, let alone anyone else, could not conceive of a world, or economy, without slave labour.

Over the ensuing years, Wilberforce repeatedly campaigned and re-introduced motions while the Quakers ran the first modern PR campaign in history to generate public support. In 1806 he strategically succeeded in slapping a ban on foreign slave trade, mostly American ships with British crews, which appealed to the government because it cramped the economies of the French Caribbean colonies. In 1807 he got corresponding legislation passed. But that was just the slave *trading* business – not ownership. Assaulting slavery was still an uphill battle.

It wasn't until another 26 years later, on July 26, 1833, while sick in bed with influenza, that he heard British Parliament had passed *The Slavery Abolition Act*. Wilberforce died three days later.

So that was a 46-year quest which took a heavy toll on his family fortune. Wilberforce and other members of the British aristocracy and establishment sponsoring the campaign were privileged and rich, but who were they serving? God.

And who was the opposition? Who, or what, kept slapping them down? The debate in Great Britain had little to do with racial prejudice (though there were ignorant stereotypes). This was a battle over business and economics. Slavery was common to almost every "civilized" culture, economy and nation in the world. In history, really. And frankly, few people could imagine a world without it. Most economies ran on either physical slavery or the financial bondage of indentured farmers. It kept profit margins and import/export markets healthy.

Abolition was held back largely because of fears that the loss of slave labour would mean the loss of competitive prices for traded commodities such as sugar, indigo and cotton. So...

What financial interest fought to protect slavery? Mammon.

Who repeatedly voted against abolition? Mammon.

Who also kept children out of school and working in the mines? Mammon.

Who broke heads over decent pay and factory conditions? Mammon.

What resisted women's suffrage? Mammon.

Who now drives the child sex tourist trade in Bangkok? Mammon.

Who's behind the flood of pornography and trafficking of women through Sarajevo? Mammon.

So what's the force among the world's economic interests that enslaves? Mammon.

Now do you see why Jesus said you'll need to choose? In each of these scenarios of breakthrough, you'll find devoted Christians at the frontline, battling Mammon. And that often takes money.

Mammon is the inertia and power structure, not the cash. The desire for money was a catalyst for injustice, indifference and sin against fellow humans – and anxiousness about losing it. And Wilberforce, out of Christian compassion and conviction, fuelled his cause with money, energy and time (in fact, the better part of his lifetime) to beat back Mammon in a protracted battle against slavery. [11]

Wilberforce was devoted to God. And God spent Wilberforce's fortune on justice and righteousness in a 46-year campaign that revolutionized the world's economies and the histories of nations and races. [12]

Does that appeal to you?
Because it may well be God's plan for you and your money. To spend it on mercy, justice and freedom. If you've got any.

So, your national currency is not the bad guy. Whether or not you want to have more money is a different issue and a different decision from whether you'll serve God.

Some rich people serve God,
    other rich people serve Mammon.

Some poor people serve God,
  other poor people serve Mammon.
The antagonism of God vs. Mammon
  is freedom vs. bondage,
    and love vs. self.
      But money gets used as a weapon.

Resolution
You can be wealthy and righteous – plenty of biblical, historical and contemporary examples. But you cannot devote yourself to, and serve, both God and that Mammon. Like any good husband, God is looking for good faith and unity. Including getting past anxiety, fear and preoccupation with money.

So let's deal with Mammon
If you have been held back by the fear that...
  actively cultivating wealth = 'the love of money'
Or...
  wanting to be wealthy = 'serving Mammon'
Or some other maxim along those lines, get your pen ready.

And then pray with your hand on your head:
  Jesus, I want to see and understand money
    the way you do.
  I submit my beliefs about the nature of money to you,
    and I'm open to learn from your Holy Spirit
    the truth about money.
Hand on your heart:
  Lord, I renounce the lie that building wealth,
  even the enjoyment of money,
  is the same as 'the love of money', as in spiritual adultery
  and rejecting you.
  I'm sorry for believing it,
  for all the opportunities, time and energy I forfeited by
  believing it,
  and for how this lie has frustrated me, my loved ones and
  my role in your will being done on Earth.
  Would you please forgive me? Thank-you.

  Holy Spirit, if the lie was '_____ = the love of money',
  then what is the truth? (Write the first thing you hear...)

Thanks, Lord, I choose to believe that.

And Lord, I renounce the lie that wanting more money to work with, play with and share is the same as 'serving Mammon.'
I renounce Mammon and every form of financial bondage that I've inherited from my family background and culture,
that I've bought into and created for myself,
and that I've wrongly encouraged in others.
Both in my thought-life and in my finances.
I choose the freedom you offer, God, and I serve you.
Thanks for making it possible.

Holy Spirit, if the lie was '_____ = serving Mammon', then what's the truth?

_____

_____

Thanks again, Lord, I choose to believe you.
And thanks to you, "I am rich in _____!"

That should feel better
Okay, we'll do more work on religious clutter in an upcoming chapter, but for the next few days, you know what to do when old clichés and criticisms surface in your thinking:
- identify the lie / conflict,
- renounce it,
- listen for the truth,
- choose that,
- thank him for a better way.

For your own encouragement, I suggest you record your new, helpful beliefs here as they surface and you process them out of your beliefs – it'll encourage you later to come back and read them over again:

_____

_____

Looking forward: money is your friend
There's so much that money can help put into action. So let's think about the positive possibilities.

As we did earlier, put this book aside for a minute and
- roll your shoulders a couple of times,
- picture the face of a loved one who makes you smile,
- hear the sound of wind in the trees when seasons change,
- remember what it feels like to sit in your favourite summer place.

Finish with your key and *"I am rich in _____!"*
Stay in that state of relaxed openness and pray with me:
  Lord, would you like to join me?
  Let's talk again about the desires you have placed in my heart...
Now stay relaxed and without hesitating to analyse and cogitate, fill in the left column below – don't stop to edit, don't second-guess, don't worry about being noble, sensible or profound.
Just smile and quickly write about this...
  If I could accomplish ANY 5 things over the next 10 years,
  without worrying about how I'd support myself,
  I'd love to...

		t	e	m
1				
2				
3				
4				
5				

Great! Now, look them over and rank them in the first right-hand column, under "t", according to *how much of your time* you'd spend making them happen (1 = the most time required, 5 = the least).

Then, consider for a minute *how much of your personal physical and mental energy* you'd invest while making each happen, and rank them in the "e" column.

Some things might take a lot of time, but not so much energy – like growing a bonsai tree. Some might take a lot of energy but happen fairly quickly - such as learning how to build websites.

Now let's put money back into the picture. Given the amounts of time and energy you're looking at, take a minute for each of the five scenarios and think about whether a consistent source of cash would affect each pursuit, in terms of completion and/or your experience. What would change?
    Speed? Location? Excitement? Quality? Volume? Personnel? Intensity? Longevity? Level of satisfaction? Responsibility?

Rank them under "m" according to how *pronounced* the effect of money would be – 1 for the most affected by the availability of money, 5 for the least money-dependent. And don't be ashamed to smile about the possibilities.

Observe...
+   First, did you notice how, when it came to your own TIME+ENERGY, you were fine with me using the words 'spend' and 'invest'? Financial terms.
+   In the "m" column, did the differences involve accessing other people's TIME+ENERGY (including their time, money and resources such as equipment, skills, connections or effort)?
+   Also, did the presence or absence of money affect those goals equally? Or how differently?

This is crucial to understand:
    When money is important, it tends to be very important.
    When money is unimportant, it tends to be
      practically irrelevant.

Consider what money can and cannot do
    Money can pay for experiences,
      it cannot make you wise.

Money can free you to pursue your dreams,
  it cannot tell you what your calling is.
Money can make others notice you,
  it cannot make them respect you.
Money can allow you to communicate,
  it will not make people understand you.
Money can help reduce distractions,
  it will not make your ideas better.
Money can pay for the best care,
  it will not heal you physically, emotionally or spiritually.
Money can quickly attract thanks,
  it will not buy genuine friendship.
If you rely on money to please people,
  they'll be even less pleased with you when it's gone.

So, in some respects money is very effective,
and in others it's practically inert.

Money just amplifies whatever's already in your heart
Money is a catalyst. An accelerant. Which is great.
In a lot of cases, adding money to the scenario can add energy to
whatever is already in play.

On the downside:
  If you're greedy, money will only fuel your appetite.
  If you're irresponsible, you'll simply waste larger
  amounts.
  If you have lousy people skills, wealth will generate conflict.
  If you don't trust people, money will make you paranoid.
  If you're a spender, you'll spend faster, not smarter.
  If you're insecure, money will attract flatterers.
  If you're boring... money won't help that either.

On the upside:
  If you're flexible, money opens up more options.
  If you're secure, money helps you relax and have fun.
  If you're visionary, money moves your ideas within reach.
  If you're ambitious, money underwrites greater pursuits.
  If you're generous, you'll be all the more giving.
  If you're creative, money will alleviate some distractions.
  If you're hardworking, you'll afford better tools.
  If you're humble... you'll find wealth requires more
    prudence and creativity.

So you see, money is a magnifier of what's already in your heart. In that sense, money is not neutral.

However, money is not moral – it simply affords you TIME+ENERGY for more of what your morals already tell you is right or wrong, acceptable or not acceptable.

So can we start treating money like an opportunity and help, and not such a 'guilty necessity'?

And finally, money is culturally relevant

I know, that statement looks like an open invitation for derision, so let me quickly get to my point. Most of the people who will read this book are living in a western or western-influenced culture. (If you aren't, I'd love to hear what you think about all this!) And one of the dominant characteristics shared by our cultures is the unprecedented availability of money, and the opportunities available to generate even more of the stuff. In some cases, *ridiculous* amounts of it. The possible negative that could result is vapid and garish materialism (stupid vehicles, stupid houses, stupid junk, stupid stunts), but let's stick to the opportunity.

If the generation of money is a cultural strong suit, it makes sense to play to your culture's strengths, learn how to work with it and leverage it for the benefit of others. Since our culture is fueled by capital (money), and you live within that culture, it makes more sense to understand money and be skillful with it than try to ignore it and get run over by it. Too many people spend their lives under the tires.

Am I advocating resignation to materialism and complacency? Only if that's what's already in your heart – you can also plan to live differently within your culture and money will be very helpful in making that possible.

Also, our financial culture should benefit others. Consider how third-world church leaders are adopting the "stay home, send money" philosophy of missions. Why spend 10^s and 100^s of thousands of dollars shipping, equipping, housing and educating missionary families to prop up their first-world comforts while the local pastors struggle? For the cost of one missionary family's SUV, you could put bicycles and motorcycles under hundreds and hundreds of local pastors and evangelists and mobilize *them* to exponential effect.[13]

So let's make lots of money here in our culture, where it's relatively easy, so we're in a position to send lots of money to people in other cultures who are motivated and committed to serve locally.

And don't be embarrassed to say, *"I am rich in _____!"*

Assignment: Get used to having money around
This is going to be fun!
* Go to your bank and take out $300. Don't settle for $200. You probably don't need $400... but you can if you like.
I suggest three $100 bills, but six 50ˢ will feel pretty good too. If you're British or European or living somewhere else, just make them three *substantial* bills.
* Put the money in your wallet and *just leave it there* for a full week as you go about your normal life.
Do not spend it. Just keep it in there all week.
If you're a couple working through this book and the amount will tap you out if you both take out $300 at once, then you can alternate weeks.
(If you're really worried that it'll be swept into being spent, it's okay to keep it in a separate compartment, but *only* if you'll still see it there every time you open your wallet.)

If you're a guy... In the morning, you probably take your wallet from the top of your dresser or a drawer. Notice the way having that much money in your wallet changes how it feels in your hand when you pick it up and put it in your pocket. Especially how it makes you feel. Observe how it feels different in your pocket at various points during the day. Pay attention to the sensation you get every time you take it out to pay for something, big or small, and you see that money in there. And then again at the end of the day when you empty your pockets and put it back in its place for the night.

If you're a woman... I have it on good authority (my wife's) that this will be more about purse-consciousness than wallet-consciousness.[14] No matter. You will still find your awareness – morning, noon and night – affected by the mere presence of the cash. Allow yourself the sensation, do not push it away.

I repeat: The $300 is solely for the sensation of having it with you – not for spending.
After a full week... deposit the money back into your account.

The point of this one
If you don't like shopping because you don't like paying for things, I'll bet it's largely because you don't like the looks of the inside of your wallet. Kind of like that apprehension when you go to the cashier wondering if you've brought enough money with you. Or worse, wondering if your credit card limit can bear the added strain.[15]

What we're doing with the $300 is re-educating your emotions, your subconscious mind and your muscle memory with the physical presence of *ample* money. We're stretching your capacity by learning how it feels to be comfortable with *having* money on you, and what a positive feeling it is to know you have enough with you. (And what it feels like to not-worry about having enough with you.)

If this exercise concerns you for security reasons because of where you live, work or shop, then pause to assess the risk. I am not telling you to be careless, so you might need to be creative – maybe do this on a series of day-trips or a couple of weekends away. The point is to practice having the feeling of having ample money. If you want your financial soul to be healed, you need to learn to feel natural with having it.

If you're a spender by nature and concerned you'll use the money "because it's there", then put it in one of those back compartments of your wallet so it's visible but separate from your usual cash-on-hand. If that's not good enough, put an elastic band around it. The point is to be aware of its presence with you.

So go get the cash out, live with it for a week, and remember you have it because, *"I am rich in _____!"*

You might want to record your impressions here:

_____

_____

_____

_____

1 Don't rely on this to avoid dealing with an ongoing problem though, such as illness, chronic pain, ongoing lifestyle compromises, etc..

2 This made me think of the anecdote where a Chinese pastor who experienced miracles in his ministry explained to a western pastor that it was because he read the Bible up-and-down, not side-to-side.

3 If some of these are not at hand, write them on separate pieces of paper.

4 If these led to a point of decision like personal bankruptcy, or re-possession, that's okay – you're on the other side of that point of decision too and you're moving further and further away from it.

5 Matthew 6:32

6 I Timothy 6:10

7 Hebrews 13

8 Philipians 4

9 Matthew 6, Luke 16

11 Read "Bury the Chains: Prophets and Rebels in the Fight to Free an Empire's Slaves", by Arnold Hochschild, which focuses on Thomas Clarkson, the Cambridge divinity grad who recruited Wilberforce and spearheaded the Quaker abolitionist movement in Britain.

12 The United States' Emancipation Proclamation followed 30 years later in 1863. Russia freed its serfs two years earlier in 1861. Canada transitioned out 1793-1810. France, in 1794-1802. Spain, not until 1880 in their colonies. Japan abolished slavery way back in 1588 (although heavy serfdom persisted into the 20th Century). Slavery persisted in some countries into the last century (China for one), and still exists in some African countries.

13 I don't mean to diss all missionaries, they can also be very effective if they're mobilizing local believers to do the work of the ministry. The point is, where's the leverage?

14 Personally, I am seized with apprehension whenever she says, "Honey, would you go into my purse..." Most men will have no trouble empathizing with me on this one.

15 Although nothing touches the anxiety of being left in the grocery store checkout line and hearing, "Stay here in line while I just go grab one more thing..."

Chapter 4

Asking Is Not Optional, It's Critical

Feeling challenged yet? Maybe a bit provoked? A little out of your comfort zone? Great, but I hope you're having fun as well.

How was it, living with a wallet full of money? Until I thought of trying this, I didn't realize just how discouraging my own wallet was to me. I always carried less than $60 with me thinking I was being careful and would spend less money this way. Actually, the effect was that every time I took out my wallet, I saw, thought and was reminded, "I don't have much money," "I only have a few dollars," "I'm just about broke," "I'm nearly out of money," "I need money again," and so on. Just think what a relentless, discouraging put-down, disappointment, warning, distortion and lie I faced every time I opened it. My own wallet had been incessantly berating me, "No money... No money... No money..."

The truth was that I had no more or less, whether it was in my wallet, in my accounts or hidden under a mattress. But it sure looked and felt marginal.

When I carried the $300 around I noticed a pronounced difference in my self-confidence, optimism, even my posture! Whatever dramatizations I had assembled in my mental files of what it would look like when the inevitable happened and I was stuck somewhere with no cash and not a banking machine in sight, it felt like they didn't matter any more. What was even more noticeable however was how it felt after I put it back in the bank. I still posessed just as much money, but I felt "skint" again.

I've gone back to carrying the cash. If something ever happens to the cash, that'd be a small loss compared with the kind of self-induced mockery I used to live with. I strongly suggest you do the same for yourself as a permanent practice. And seriously, how much savings account interest do you really think you'll forfeit?

Are you consistently using your key and *"I am rich in _____!"*? Remember to do one or the other, or both, whenever you do *anything* financial – spending, saving, paying, receiving, finding or giving money. It all counts.

How's the thwacking?
I went through two rounds of thwacking: the first time I smartly flicked my wrist with a fingernail. The second time I used a good stiff rubber band. It helped me complain a lot less. Make sure you immediately listen for, and accept, the blessings, compliments and encouragements, and choose them to supplant your old, unhelpful beliefs.

What about the Creative Taskforce working on that dilemna? Any shifts in how you think or feel about that particular matter? New ideas coming to mind? Have circumstances around it changed? Does it even matter any more? Make sure you go back and note relevant insights and sensations on page 43 – trust and acknowledgment are *very* important, including for yourself. If you haven't really noticed, stop and check how you feel about it now... If you're still not sure, it's coming. In fact, you could also call a quick meeting for an update – don't be surprised if it occurs to you that there's a related issue blocking the progress – take that one to the Committee too.

Back in the '80s, scientists using brain scans (MRIs) discovered that before a conscious decision to act is even consciously contemplated, brain activity related to that activity had already begun stirring, before the conscious mind (that trickle of logic, your inner monologue, your inner penguin) recognized and addressed the task. So, backing up...
before the motor command to *tap* a finger,
before the decision of *when* to tap,
before the decision *yes* to tap,
before consciously *thinking* through to tap or not to tap,
the subconscious had already been rallying and assembling data relating to tapping in the lead-up to conscious thought.

So if a seed of an idea is being sown, then our subconscious minds are actually tilling the ground while the seed is still in midair. (Or alternatively, filling the pool before we think about diving.)

This illustrates there's a lot of activity mobilized before and below your conscious choices, and why we can't settle for a change of mind – we need a change of heart. Including in your finances. What we're cultivating here is the notion that we can also be proactive about this and be intentional about marshalling those resources with positive, problemsolving activity as well. Soon, we'll get into bumping that even further forward to tease out vision from our mental, emotional and experiential bric-a-brac and keepsakes.

And the "I LIKE MONEY!" proclamation? Are you more free now to talk about money? Keep applying it, like sunscreen or moisturizer. Smile when you speak it out, even laugh. Dial it up, engage your positive emotions, let vision percolate through your thinking! Hearing it, hearing your own voice saying it, will help open you up and connect with the possibilities.

It's important to grasp this concept: you are verbally pro-claiming (reaching forward and claiming) the place of money in your life. The manner in which you vocalize your intentions is very important. Work that tone of voice!

If you simply mutter, how engaged are you really?

If you rush through it, what is that really saying?

If you aren't willing to at least *sound* like these are your convictions, then what kind of response or change can you expect of yourself?

It's not just, "*What* you sow, you will reap."

There's also a sense of, "*As*, or *how* you sow, you will reap."

Sow generously, reap generously.

Sow feebly, reap feebly.

And really, what does it cost you to vocalize your desires with some enthusiasm? Someone might hear? I'd rather celebrate a financial turnaround and sound a little unusual, than be mousy and embarrassed and stay stuck. *Oomph!* counts.

Make your requests known

Here's another dynamic in vocalizing the desires of your heart which you're going to need for increased financial capacity: *asking.*

Unfortunately, many of us aren't very good at asking. We were taught it's impolite, it's pushy, it's presumptuous, you're not supposed to be greedy, or put people on the spot, or expect too much, you should be considerate, and so on. Sound familiar? Do you believe those things too? *Thwack!*

Here's the problem. By not asking, you are unfairly setting up a barrier of expectation and deliberately putting it outside of your control – trick pre-conditions – and putting others in the position of having to read your mind to participate in whatever's on your

mental terrain.
    And then deduce what you really want.
        And then guess how to respond.
You're doing that to other people, to God and to the rest of the universe. So, how "considerate" are you actually being?

And think about why you do this. Maybe so you don't have to discomfit yourself with the risk of asking and being rejected?
But that's abdicating, giving away your role, your initiative, your direction, your responsibility. It leaves your desires held hostage in limbo, with no chance of being modified to make it workable.

Or maybe it's your way of testing the love and perceptiveness of others. A kind of emotional secret quizz.
Now *that*'s selfish.

And it's unfair. I'd wager that the people around you would be happy to help you, give you what you need and see you achieve your goals (if you've thought them through). And they'd probably enjoy taking part in your success.

If you like the feeling you get when you help someone,
    then help someone else get that feeling by asking.
If you like being generous,
    then give others the chance to be generous by asking.

Same thing with God
His ambition is not to be your Divine Shipping & Receiving Department. His agenda is for you to *know* him. And how do you get to know someone? By doing stuff together. Building a personal history together. Far too many people dig in their heels and complain that they're "waiting on God" to give them direction, not realizing that they're actually sulking. God, like a good parent, often chooses not to respond to that.

Don't you want your friends to suggest something to do with you? I love hearing, "Hey David, do you want to go... ?" God loves that too. Stop treating him like a celestial government bureaucracy handing out contracts, and *suggest* something.

God already knows your heart even better than you do, so the problem is not whether he can figure out what's on your mind.
    Rather, part of what asking does is turn your attention toward

him and something you can work on together (which any good father enjoys).
It puts yourself back in touch with the knowledge that he is your ultimate source.
And his love finds another outlet to touch your life (which all love needs and responds to).

So a great way for you to have closer and closer relationship with him is to...
stop withholding
   open your heart
      step out of your comfort zone
         and ask.
            Expecting to receive.

Why? Because asking requires us to be vulnerable and self-revealing. So since God's love is pure, faithful and kind, we can learn to trust him and get used to opening our hearts to him. The problem is not whether he can afford what you're asking, the issue is how willing are you to risk being vulnerable?
Sow trust, you reap trust.

Articulating what you desire also leads to being honest with yourself about the merits of what you really want, and that's harder to avoid when you know you're asking someone who already knows your heart better than you do.

Activation: Unbottling with God and yourself
We're going to unbottle, uncork, unroll and shake out your requests before God.
   This will help get your desires unstuck,
   notify yourself, God and his creation what's on the table,
   take a step of vulnerability toward your Father,
   and initiate the process of seeing your dreams fulfilled.

I know this: your desires are very unlikely to be fulfilled if you're not even willing to articulate them. In detail. So let's have some fun!

This one will take a bit of time, so allow yourself an hour, or put the book down and come back to this when you can take the time.

Once again, have a pen handy, but you'll need a separate piece of paper (preferably your journal, or other note paper you'll keep).

Get into a comfortable position, stretch, roll your head around. Picture a favourite vacation spot. Notice the details, the sounds and sensations that surround you. Wait until you're vividly connected with that scene, dial in with *"I am rich in _____!"*

The tradition of Solomon's wisdom says,
"The purposes of a man's heart are deep waters,
but a wise man draws them out."[1]
So pray with me,
*Holy Spirit, please join me and help me draw out
the desires of my heart.*

Then just start writing a *l-o-n-g* list of your requests: Go crazy.
Everything you want to have or experience in your life:
big or small, noble or mundane,
practical or fanciful, mild or wild,
with *no* financial minimums or constraints.
Just write, write, write without judging or editing.
Spend at least 15 minutes - then return to these instructions.
. . .

Back? Count up the number of items on your list and go back and add more until you have a nice, long list of one hundred and one items. (Yes, I avoided writing the numeral because your eye would have jumped to it and your inner skeptic would squawk and cut in with objections and inhibitions.) Just take the plunge, and when the flow of ideas starts to wane, take a breath, roll your shoulders and dive back in again – you'll find the flow will rise and fall like waves, but there's always more.
Go back now, and come back to this spot when you're done.
. . .

Okay, if you didn't make it to the end, that's alright, either take another plunge now or come back to it later. Preferably today. Tomorrow at the latest. And don't stop until you have the full number filled in. (It took me four sittings because I'd bought into "I don't like to ask." So I wasn't very good at it. Still working on it, if you ask my wife.) Again, don't tweak, moralize, entertain objections or judge whether these things are selfish or silly.

When you have a complete list, look it over and notice the mix of material possessions and subjective experiences, things for others and things for yourself, small and large, quick and slow. There should be a good variety, a healthy mix.

Now use your key, say *"I am rich in _____!"* and go back over the list to sketch in some details for each item: size, colour, location, people, texture, and so on. The clearer the scenario, the better.

Important:
+ Make sure these are *your* requests. Not your kids', not your spouse's, not your clan's, not your ministry's, not your company's.
+ Make them positive statements of what *you* want, as opposed to what you don't want – instead of "Not be in debt," make it "Financially free in two years." The word "not" is unhelpful, so avoid it.
+ Avoid vague, general statements, like, "Be a better husband." Describe what would be different – what it will look like, sound like, feel like.
+ Some requests should be way-ay-ay beyond your current reach – things that are provocative and challenging and will require dramatic change.

Most importantly, stop at each one, read it out loud and allow yourself to *feel good about it!* Let yourself feel what it must be like to be, have or do that. Maybe lightness in your chest, clarity around your head, butterflies in your stomach, sureness underfoot, a weight off your shoulders... and mentally embrace what you found in your heart to add to your life.

As you finish contemplating each one, affirm it with *"I am rich in _____!"*

Keep this list somewhere so you can go back and re-visit it periodically. Check off and date the items as they come into your life. It's an important kind of encouragement and acknowledgement.

It's all in motion now
The barn doors are open, the horses are out. You've given yourself permission to experience your heart's desires, your sub-surface thought-life now has a number of missions to be on watch for and work on, your generous Heavenly Father has received your requests, and his creation will now shift to accommodate you with them.

Watch for the signs. You will see them take shape, move within reach and fall into place. Yes, you'll have to respond to opportunities and take some initiative (even risks), but you're no longer the only one who knows and cares about these things. They will begin to happen.

Why? Because you asked. And no word, no thought, no desire, no love goes without effect. In physics, energy is never destroyed – sometimes dissipated, sometimes stored up, sometimes converted to another form, but never destroyed. So why not set in motion the energy of your dreams? Including your financial dreams?

Even if you ask for the wrong thing?
Yes! Because the Holy Spirit, like any good teacher, can recognize the legitimate need in the background when a student asks "the wrong question". Let him teach you, it's what he loves to do. As an example, your list of 101 probably didn't include someone coming to harm, but even if you did, that harboured thought (which was already there anyway) would now be out on the table where God can sort through it with you and bring it to resolution. That would count as your answer, and you'd be happier and healthier for it.

It has been clinically demonstrated that prayer works over distance, between unfamiliar people, even about unspecified illnesses. But there are corresponding increases when the person praying has a name. More again if they have a photo. More yet when they have a description of the situation. Your mental energy focuses into a thought, the thought re-focuses into a prayer, your speech amplifies those prayers with more physical energy, your spoken prayers can be amplified again with emotional energy and conviction. So don't settle for passivity, ask with passion!

A quantum diversion and conversion
As solid as the chair may seem underneath you, it's actually just an arrangement of empty space and energy. The molecules making up the materials are not solid, but packets of empty space bound together with energy, with atoms way-ay-ay down in the centres. Each atom contains proportionately vast amounts of space, held together by the energy between the electrons and the nucleus. If, for example, we drew a single hydrogen atom (1 proton at the centre with 1 electron orbiting it) to scale and made the proton 1 centimeter in diameter, like a good-sized pea, then its electron would be smaller than the diameter of a hair. The freaky part is that the radius of the hair's-width electron's orbit around that pro-

ton-pea would be about 30 football fields away! If the proton was the size of a basketball, its electron would be hurtling around it about 20 miles away. 99.999999999999% of any atom's volume is empty space.

If you're hoping that the basketball-proton is solid, I'm afraid it's more like an empty soap bubble. With no soap. It's almost entirely empty space defined by energy as well. Within that bubbleless bubble, the proton is made up of three sub-atomic specks called quarks and leptons which are rolling and whirling around each other as a unit.[2]

So, are at least the subatomic quarks and leptons solid? We don't know, but we don't think so. At their core, they may be simply geometrical points with no substance whatsoever, just the energy that indicates their location. They're more like stains than objects.[3]

So picture your chair as just a bunch of virtually empty, soap-less bubbles, each with another practically empty soap-less bubble at the centre, and in the centre of that bubble is... another seemingly empty bubble. Why are you still sitting up? You're being supported by the strength of the *energy* that holds the bubbles together and in place. The same goes for the floor under your chair. That binding energy is strong enough to repel approaching light energy so you can detect (see) the light rejected by it. When you knock on it, that's the sound of the chair's surface energy rejecting the surface energy of your knuckles and some of the motion's energy spinning off and distorting into sound waves.

It's a very different view of physical "reality" to recognize that solids are not solid at all, just fields of space, energy and attraction that are stronger or weaker relative to each other. As Albert Einstein said, "Reality is merely an illusion, although a very persistent one."

Everything around you is made of energy. And so are you. That's quantum physics. It gets weirder, but if that glimpse doesn't unsettle you too much, maybe you can begin to see why the indestructible energy of your prayers can be "stored up" in Heaven[4]; how your thoughts, your words and your actions can reverberate beyond you? If everything is energy, can you glimpse that miracles are energy being rearranged? Water molecules rearranged into wine molecules? Or how about water supporting the walking weight of a man? "I felt power leave me."[5] A resurrected body? The power of life and death in the tongue? A prayer of impartation by the laying on of hands? A tangible, graphic movement of the Holy Spirit?

This helps explain why prayer is powerful – especially passionate, feeling prayer. It's not because you shouted loud enough for God to concentrate on something he's been overlooking. It's not because you clambered to the top of his to-do list. Or convinced him that you're really, really serious. Bearing in mind the Lord's prerogative to say 'no', or 'wait', or answer creatively, your requests can be set into motion by stating your intentions with conviction. It's so important to line up, focus and clarify what the energy of your beliefs, thoughts, feelings and actions are leading to. Also why they are effective.[6]

Here's an even more mind-bending observation from the world of particle accelerators: entanglement. In 1977, particle physicists separated pairs of 'entangled' electrons (each began in direct contact and physical relationship with each other) and shot them down separate fibre-optic cables to locations six miles apart. When they arrived, one of the electrons was tipped into a particular quantum state (analogous to a physical spin) *which automatically forced its twin electron miles away into the opposite spin.* No other input, it just happened. Strange enough, but it responded less than five-trillionths of a second later. Whatever the communication between the two particles was, it would have to be moving nearly 7 million times faster than the speed of light (as the crow flies). This has been demonstrated repeatedly but has not been satisfactorily explained – if we hang onto Einstein's theory that nothing goes faster than light, this forces the question of how the entangled objects are so inextricably related even when miles apart. One theory is that the phenomenon transfers cause & effect in a way that moves backward in time.

Interesting... but useful?
This phenomenon, although inexplicable, is the direction that large-scale computing is taking, perhaps you've heard the term 'quantum computing', beginning with the transfer of large loads of financial data. So yes, entanglement will have a direct influence on your personal finances in the very near future. (Whenever that was.)

But on a more quotidian level, given that this phenomenon happens between subatomic particles, does this begin to open your understanding of the complexity and beauty of your heart-to-heart interconnection with others? Our entanglement with the lives of people? How your prayers for them, or by them, can transcend distance? Even time?[7] How the great mystics of Christian faith always speak of personal intimacy with God? You might want to re-read the 17th chapter of John's gospel with this in mind.

Or consider that when God created everything, he spoke.
   That his creation is still entangled with him.
      Everything, everywhere, always.
         That Adam was created by hand.
            That "in him we live and move and have our being."[8]

The reality around you can be (and usually is) affected by your thoughts, intentions and beliefs, and amplified by the energy of your emotions. We don't "create" reality, but we are entangled with it, which also helps explain that we can input to rearrange it, shape it, direct it, and give it order, focus and attraction (vs. disorder, chaos and confusion) via our actions, words and prayers. "Thy kingdom come."

So thank-you for sticking with me and reading, speaking and asking all this stuff out loud in the exercises. And remember, passion and *oomph* count in shaping your financial reality. Not bland behaviour.

Ready for one more?
Your mere presence also affects the nature of reality around you. In 1927, German physicist Werner Heisenberg started bumping into problems in his experiments with subatomic particles and light. What he found was that depending on the circumstances, light would behave as either a set of waves or a stream of particles – they changed with the act of being measured. When left unattended and unobserved, the light behaved in wave fashion. When observation and measurement were added to the scenario, the light waves morphed and behaved like particles. It seemed that the act of consciously observing light caused the light to respond and behave differently. Reality shifted with the presence of an observer. Theoretical physicists have a knack for learning to live with this sort of dichotomy, but it raises the issue of just how far we can take the notion of how our tangible future is formed out of the liquid possibility of the present. And how possibilities can be influenced by our observation and intention. Perhaps how "faith

is the *substance* of things unseen"?[9]

So what's the relevance to money?

Think about the terminology surrounding money, like cash*flow*, *liquid*ity, *solvent*-cy, *current*-cy, investment *pool*, income *stream*, and so on. Money has properties that remind us of the behaviour of liquids. Money is real, but it's a very *malleable* form of reality. A paper bill is tangible but it merely serves as a representation of the more intangible, abstract perceptions of ENERGY+TIME being utilized elsewhere. And as such, the motion and behaviour of money and finances is more easily entangled and influenced by our perceptions and intentions than, say, bricks and mortar. Money is fluid. Start cobbling together conundrums like solidity, entanglement and observation, and be open to the physical (as in physics) possibilities of belief, faith and prayer creating better scenarios for you and your money. Because money is a fluid current of values, consensus, energy and time, its behaviour can be more easily guided, attracted or repelled than you've thought before.[10]

Application: Your Money Entanglement Jar

+ Get a jar, bottle or bowl, put it on your bedroom dresser and get a piece of money – a pound coin, a loonie, a dollar bill, a denarius, whatever is local – hold it up and declare out loud:
  Thank-you for your blessings, Father – all good things come out of your abundance.
  I am creating a future of financial abundance
  and I ask for your grace, blessing and favour.
  And I invite your creation to rise up and support me in this purpose.
+ Drop the cash in. (Canadian loonies, two-nies and British one-pound coins are good for this because of the sensory drama of the sound they make.)
+ Add something to the jar every day. Even if it's just your pocket change. Even if you only have a 5-, 10- or 20-dollar bill on you. If you have to, check under the sofa pillows to find something to put in, but do it. Consistency is crucial.

This will...

+ remind and refocus your own attention on the energy of money;
+ keep your request and purpose before God;
+ act as an entangled money-beacon, attracting abundance to your purpose.

Every three months – you'll empty the jar, but I'll tell you what to do with the money a few chapters from now. If you did this when you were a kid, don't reject it as juvenile – you could say the same about ice cream, but that's still workin', isn't it?

Seek, ask, knock

You'll probably find more and more of Jesus' teaching and actions coming into a different light as we go through these activations and exercises. And it only gets better. We're learning that the visible world is actually shaped almost entirely by what we cannot see, hear or feel.

On the cosmic level, where we used to think space was just empty void (except C.S. Lewis in *The Silent Planet*) astrophysicists are contending with evidence that the universe is only 5% stuff that we can see and identify (stars, planets, *etc.*) – the other 95% is 'dark matter' we can't find or define.

At the personal level, your circumstances in the world are basically just a printout of what you have been thinking, believing and expressing.

In our carnal nature, we put more stock in experience than belief. It's our flesh's insistence and habit. But if you think about God's reality prior to Creation, he was living in a complete spiritual reality of his thoughts, love, and spirit – the physical came last. And the fact that the physical was all "good" was a printout of the goodness of God's own thoughts, feelings and constancy. And in our particular case as humans, it was "very good" in Eden until we broke the continuity between God's spiritual thought-life & emotions and ourselves, his physical creation.

The extent to which we do not live spiritually – as in, "I have to see it to believe it" rather than "I have to believe it in order to see it" – is the extent to which we experience life as one of those swimming-through-chocolate-pudding dreams. Anxious, mired, straining, ineffective. We have to turn that around and understand, "If I want to see it, I have to first believe it."
Like a certain Roman centurion.[11]

The good news is that the way was opened up again through the unprecedented resurrection of Jesus. Now anyone can learn to live out of that reality. Faith is an intense, emotional thought. Not a

religious recipe ingredient, but a heart-felt, certain anticipation of what is already taking shape until it arrives.
And we must stop feeling guilty for the advantages we have. We must stop despising our inheritance which was hard-earned by previous generations. Success is still relative. A Wall Street investor can be just as happy or miserable as a goat herder on the fringes of the Gobi Desert, and the difference can't be measured by comparing incomes. The key is gratitude.
   And the more you ask,
      the more opportunity you'll have to express gratitude.

That's it for now, set up your jar, and now would be a good time to go back and flesh out some of the details of your 101 requests. Finishing, of course, with *"I am rich in _____!"*

1 Proverbs 20:5

2 There are 12 chief kinds of sub-atomic particles and their relationships are complicated, but there are about 200 identified types.

3 If you want to peer deeper into this stuff, check out PBS's program on String Theory, The Elegant Universe, online at www.pbs.org/wgbh/nova/elegant/program.html

4 Revelation 5:8, 8:3

5 Mark 5:3

6 And why the prayers of a righteous (God-focused) man availeth much (James 5:16). One of my favourite concert video shots is from a U2 concert in Mexico City – an aerial shot of the crowd where the fans flick their lighters as they hear the beat. You can see the sonic delay indicated visually as sound waves move out from the stage and pass across tens of thousands of people. Waves of lighters illuminating each bass drum "whomp". A nice metaphor for prayer.

7 Ever pray for someone, like a remote missionary, about a situation when the lag in communication meant that you were praying after the actual occurrence? If you're feeling adventurous, look into a scenario known as Schrödinger's Cat.

8 Acts 17:28

9 Hebrews 11:1

10 Next time you're in a really old house with old panes of glass in the windows, look at the ripples and how the glass is thicker at the bottom than the top. That's because natural glass is actually a liquid, not a solid, and it's slowly flowing downward due to gravity. Modern production methods now stabilize this liquid to hold it in place.

11 Matthew 8

Chapter 5

Are You Receiving?

Having started to work on your general mindset about finances, your comfort level with money, and getting over the fear of asking, here's the next important concept to lay hold of, cultivate and live out:

God's creation is inherently, fundamentally abundant, flourishing and growing.

And you were created to partake in that abundance, to enjoy it with him and help others do the same.

Specks in your eyes

Imagine that you could be on the outside looking into our universe, which apparently out at the edges is expanding at the speed of light. From innumerable swirling galaxies down to stars to planets and moons all spinning, burning, growing, exploding and imploding exactly as they were meant to do... there's just this one blue-green ball of water and rock, circling a minor star on the underside of an unexceptional galaxy off in an unimpressive corner where there's this pocket of resistance to God's design and will.

And even down there, things mostly adhere to his blueprint of goodness, from rain clouds to coral reefs to soil formation to molten magma beneath the surface – except where it's being tampered with. And most of the creatures there live as he intended, from bird migration to dolphin antics to snail trails.

There's just this one single species that interferes and actively resists. And thereby creates its own miseries. But otherwise the universe works beautifully, flourishes and expands. In the grand scheme, human deprivations are infinitesimally small and pretty much self-inflicted.

Does that put your electricity bill into perspective?

And the Bible states that within an entirely 'Good' creation, humans were the only part to receive God's coveted 'Very Good' rating. We even bear his very image and (in our better moments) exhibit his traits. Now we all know by experience how far we've deviated from that perfect image and become disconnected from him, but the whole point of Jesus' life, death and re-life was to re-open the connection with God's widespread abundance and generosity.

Our mission is to live out of that reality, and to help others back into it.

With all this abundance, where is the shortfall?

Probably in your circumstances, which as we've said are the printout of flawed thoughts, feelings and beliefs. Not surprisingly, some aspects of that shortage are measured in money. Granted, some of your difficulties are printouts of other people's thoughts, feelings and beliefs, but the way to extricate yourself is to determinedly break the grip of their patterns and intentionally think and believe for other possibilities for yourself. Like Paul said, do not be conformed to this world, but be transformed by the re-*new*-ing of your mind.[1] Get your mind back to the newness of the abundance and generosity God originally intended.

So God said to his people, "Draw near to me and I will draw near to you."[2] That's how generous, humble and responsive he is – he's just looking for willingness.

Likewise, his creation reflects his character: you reach out into his creation and creation will respond and reach back to you.

The question is, what kind of reception will you have waiting for that response?[3]

Now here's another key to re-gaining your rightful access to the possibilities of our inherently flourishing and 'Good' universe, full of growth and abundance:
     You must become a 'Very Good' receiver.

Creation was set up to support and encourage you

The life, health and purpose of the human race was a gift from the beginning – our difficulty with receiving is an outcome of our fallen state. It makes receiving feel to us about as awkward as asking. A lot of us are conditioned to believe that it is somehow more noble to deflect good things offered to us. Either we've taken on this veneer of erzatz humility or we really believe we are not worthy of good things. Or worry that by desiring something good we'll cause some sort of shortage elsewhere. But that doesn't make sense. Just about anything that is intended for me,
     as a blessing, an opportunity, a gift, a calling,
     a cheque, a meal, a compliment, an award or reward,
is quite unlikely to suit you, be useful to you, or even be attractive to you. My idea of a good time or great art or a good cause may

not be at all to your tastes.

Remember:
All of creation is abundant, obedient and
   made up of energy,
      and by deflecting and rejecting good things
         you are actually training a living, responsive universe
            to pass you over.

It's like setting up detour signs all around yourself.
   And when abundance dutifully avoids you,
      then you've 'won' in some way.
         There's some kind of 'I told you so' being satisfied.
Your reality is not just what you've gathered around yourself,
it's also what you've pushed away.

Of course, we get religious about it
There's the "It is better to give than to receive" thing. Yes, Jesus said
that,[4] but let's fill in that picture a bit. Paul was quoting him in the
context of sending financial aid to struggling believers. Should the
more needy churches by the same token have declined to receive
because it's better to give? What an insult! Paul was prodding the
givers to follow through, not to put down people who needed to
receive – he wrote to encourage integrity and generosity of heart,
not to denigrate receiving.

Both are crucial but I've observed this tendency among people
(me, for instance) that makes receiving awkward, rather than pleasurable. There's an emotional need to reject rather than embrace
what comes.
Funny, sometimes if someone is good at receiving, we say they're
'secure'.

Every giver, and every gift, needs a corresponding receiver,
   and if you aren't a good receiver yet,
      then you aren't doing your part.
If the intended receiver refuses the gift, the giver is stymied. Stuck.
Unfulfilled. And in the absence of free exchange (freely giving and
freely receiving), giving becomes self-conscious, awkward, unnatural and forced.

We glibly plaster pen holders and fridge magnets with the Bible
verse, "Hope deferred makes the heart sick..." assuming it's all

about us. Have you ever considered it might have the same effect on the heart of The Giver?

Let me put that even more strongly:
Given the magnitude of God's generosity,
    and the enormity of his creation's abundance,
        any desire on your part for humility (*i.e.* perspective)
        demands that you become better at receiving
            than you are at giving.
Stop and think about that.

Imagining that your ability to give could ever exceed your capacity to receive is pretense and folly.
  True humility, when it comes to giving and receiving, will
  stipulate that we submit our finite ability to give
  to God's limitless ability to give.
  To accept (even celebrate) that our generosity and concern
  will always be dwarfed by his.
  And that increasing our capacity to give depends on our
  first learning to expand our capacity to receive.
This is why I've been pushing this notion of expanding your capacity for money.

Consider:
  • You've perhaps heard the cliché that "You can't out-give God," but a lot of us are gamely, subconsciously trying to wrest control and take over by under-receiving.
  • Perhaps the reason the Bible says the Lord loves a cheerful giver[5] is that he knows how much *fun* it is.
  • Perhaps the nicest thing you could do for him today is do whatever you need to do to make yourself more receptive to his hilarious generosity (or figure out what's getting in the way of it).

In fact, I would work on your ability to say, 'Yes!' and 'Thank-you!' and get good at receiving generosity first, before you presume to be a generous giver.

I'm told that in Korean culture, it is impolite to accept something the first time it's offered, so people understand that if they really want you to have a cookie they'll offer a second time. That's a very polite and formal convention (if everyone understands), but the universe is not like that – decline, and it might be a long, long

time before it comes back around again.
So learn to stay in a mental posture of receiving.

Thou shalt not be coy
Receive graciously and wholeheartedly. Imagine if I was at your table and you offered me salt and pepper, and then I shook it on your potatoes because "I'm trying to cut down on salt." Or "I want your potatoes to taste better than mine." How soon would you offer the salt again? Or invite me over?

Or if you passed me a roll and I tore off and handed back a portion because "I shouldn't expect too much"? Would you offer that hunk to one of the other guests? Would you want that piece? Wouldn't I be the last one to get the butter after that?

Or what if I tipped my waitress $10 and she gave me back a dollar, humbly explaining, "Oh, I don't need that much. What if this lady with you needs it more than me?" What would she be saying about my estimation of her work? How impressed would my wife be?

But we do this. We deflect, we decline, we reject, we downplay, as if we're being humble or noble.

Or we like to placate our pride by immediately offering something back in return:
"Okay, but next time I'll buy/host/drive."
"Alright, but I owe you one."
"Well, I didn't mean for you to go to the trouble..."
How disparaging is that of someone else's generosity? I suspect it's often so we don't feel out-done. Yet we do this so frequently to people, to God and to his universe.

Another favourite is to "humbly" position ourselves to not-expect and not-receive blessings. Could it be that your finances are bunged up because at some point you decided it was more virtuous or pious to not-receive? And now you have exactly what you decided on in your heart. Let me hear that *thwack!*

Some people are testing. They believe if they back away, then they hope God, other people or the universe in general will notice and rush after them to seek them out. Then they'll *really* know they're included, wanted or loved. They do this with blessings, they do it socially, they do it professionally, they do it with their creativity,

they do it spiritually. That's not humble, that's coy.
The universe does not do coy.

And God may not continue to enable that sort of dishonest, manipulative, passive insistence. If you do this so you "won't be in the
way" or "take up too much time" or whatever, then you need to
examine if that's what you really want, or is it just an inverted,
inside-out plea? In which case, you're due for a thwacking and
need to ask Jesus for some truths to swap in.

Receive unpretentiously
Compliments are another example. When was the last time you
received a compliment without feeling like you had to even the
score and restore balance to the universe by immediately
re-paying with a counter-compliment?
 "I like what you did with your hair."
 "Thanks, I like your jacket!"
 [Huh?]
... or you devalued their opinion?
 "I really enjoyed that song you played!"
 "Oh, I made so many mistakes."
 [Implied: "But you wouldn't have noticed, would you?"]
... or refused to accept credit?
 "You're a really good cook."
 "Well, my mother taught me."
 [So it's her fault?]
Someone wants to encourage you, acknowledge you, and you bat
it away like a filthy housefly.

One of the kindest things you can do is accept a compliment just
because the person's opinion is valuable.

Optional assignment
Want to amuse yourself at others' expense? Compliment them.
Make it genuine, but watch the reactions and contortions they go
through to either...
 • ignore, or even contradict, what you're saying,
 • diminish your observation,
 • hijack the conversation from the point you're making, or
 • immediately volley a spare courtesy-compliment back to you.

Notice how often they'll do this without even stopping long enough
to simply thank you.

Next, when you are complimented or acknowledged in some way, try simply receiving it:
+ Pause, blink, take a breath, *literally inhale the compliment* and really let it settle into your heart and thinking.
+ As a separate response (not a knee-jerk reaction) look them in the eye and simply thank the person with just a bit more expression than they used. Don't shrug, don't explain, don't spread the credit to others – just thank them.
+ Notice how that feels to you.
+ *More importantly, observe how it affects the other person* – you'll also see a seed of gratitude sown into their thinking.

Without willingness to receive, gratitude is impossible
As I noted earlier, gratitude is essential to any restoration, financial, emotional, spiritual or otherwise.
Until you have gratitude in your heart,
　　you cannot respect what you possess;
until you have gratitude in your heart,
　　you cannot cultivate what you have;
until you have gratitude in your heart,
　　you cannot share your best;
until you have gratitude in your heart,
　　you cannot have confidence;
until you have gratitude in your heart,
　　you cannot be ready for more.

Gratitude is not just saying thank-you
**　for something good that we had no choice in.**
Yet we reduce it to that by deliberately practicing being embarrassed, reluctant or unenthusiastic when something good comes our way.

Instead, let's practice being enthusiastically grateful
Pray with me now, hand on heart:
Lord, you are SO good – you just can't help but be generous, can you?
And I'm sorry for downplaying or blocking you
*　with my false humility. Or even resentment and spite.*
I surrender that pattern to you now – please forgive me.
Thanks.
Now, I deliberately choose to receive your blessings – what's more, I invite them!
I embrace the abundance of your creation,

and receive the people you send through my life.
In fact, I choose to enthusiastically anticipate good things,
and even outdo everyone else in expressing
my appreciation.
Thank-you, thank-you, THANK-YOU!
You've made me rich in _____!

A possible objection
"But I don't want to look like I think I deserve it!"
Ooh, I could just parse out that objection all day – starting with the three occurrences of "I".
Actually, that's just your pride trying to use reverse psychology – your heart actually needs to receive love, to be cared for and be blessed, but there's a kink in the receiving line which your mind is bending over backwards to rationalize with a pretense of
"deprivation = humility".
Or "deprivation = faith".
Think about that.
Then *thwack!* it and replace it.

No one has to be told it's a virtuous thing to give. The issue here is the necessity of working on our ability to receive. Expand that capacity. And learn to bless the generous intentions of God, bless the fruitfulness of his creation, and bless others by helping them give to you. By both asking and receiving.

True, we are to live in such a way that we have fun trying to outdo each other with generosity, but that is not the same as declining-to-receive – that's a counterfeit, a pose and a block. To everyone.
So stop it.

Not-receiving also deprives others
Until you receive, you have nothing to give – so you must receive first. Then, when abundance comes to you, everyone around you benefits. You, your loved ones, your community, the causes you care about, the businesses you'll support, the employees that work for them, the communities where they live, and everyone else that stands to benefit by your decision to be a loving conduit of money. Choking off yourself chokes off others too.

If you want to be a channel of God's mercy and blessing, then money is a very liquid and flexible means. So choose to become a *very good* receiver. Specifically of money.

Practice receiving
So how does one become expert at receiving?
1 – *Gratitude* is key, both for what you have and as you receive more. Including not being embarrassed to tell others about it – it's not bragging to recognize it, but failing to acknowledge the blessing (and perhaps its source) is sure to dry up the flow.
2 – *Enthusiasm*, even extravagant celebration, in expressing your gratitude will amplify your attractiveness to further blessing and abundance. Ever notice how popularity tends to snowball? How wealth expands in the hands of the rich? How busy people wind up with even more to do? How creative people tap into greater inspiration? There's a dynamic in play:
It's fun to give to people who respond and appreciate it!
It's motivating to givers.
Importantly: gratitude & enthusiasm attract more of the same.

So when something good comes your way, celebrate!
Be over-the-top! Overdo it! Have a blast!
 ◆ When you find a coin, hold it up and exclaim, "Thank-you, thank-you, THANK-YOU!"
 ◆ When you get something for free, or a great deal, even a refund, hoot and clap and say, "Thank-you, thank-you, THANK-YOU!"
 ◆ When you enjoy a simple, earthly comfort or pleasure, like a hot shower, clean clothes, or cream in your coffee, make sure you say, "Thank-you, thank-you, THANK-YOU!"
 ◆ With *oomph!*

Bible quiz: fill in the blanks
 I will enter his gates with _____ in my heart;
 I will enter his courts with _____.[6]
There it is. That's expectation, that's anticipation, that's choice, that's gratitude, that's acknowledgement, that's enthusiasm, that's celebration... That's your ticket into God's presence.
And into his abundance. **With certainty.** I don't see anything tentative there – it's NOW. So try it and just see if that isn't what opens the floodgates of Heaven for you.

Now a two-part assignment:
1 - **Expectancy:** I don't have a sound etymological argument to support this, but I think of expectancy as the expanded capacity of your heart and mind to be *certain* in the here-and-

now, to already accept what you already have coming from God's abundance. Not in a grasping or presumptuous way, but confidently, for what *already exists now* in response to your stated desires (the asking).

♦ Take 15 minutes to go back to your 101 requests and read them out loud as "My..." statements. Make it personal.

♦ So instead of "A MINI Cooper Convertible..." say, "*My* MINI Cooper Convertible..." (Colour, rims and options should be in there by now.)

♦ Re-state "A university degree..." as "*My* Master of Arts degree from St. Stephen's University." (Add your goal if you know it.)

♦ As you go through them, anchor each one by using your visual, auditory or kinesthetic key.

Do this before you read on to the next exercise.

...

2 - Anticipation: I think of this as going beyond outlook and becomes dynamic in what you do with yourself. Because it's ingrained into your identity, anticipation feels both futuristic and experiential, both future-present and eternal, and moves you to imagine, plan, arrange for, decide about and act on that confidence. Every basketball player expects the ball to rebound, but the great ones anticipate it and are already reaching for it before it happens.

♦ Take another 15 minutes to go back over your 101 requests (yes, *again!*) and re-restate them as "I am..." statements.

Briefly picture yourself in that scenario and just blurt out details as they dawn on you, ex., you've just gone from "A trip to Italy" to "*My* trip to Venice in spring." Now make it "*I am* buying a piece of art in Venice." Or some action relevant to your passions.

Or, take your original "More money for charity" which you've re-stated as "*My* double-donation to the food bank." Make it, "*I am* writing a cheque for $5,000 and giving it to Cheryl, the food bank director."

What started as "Quit smoking." and you re-wrote as "*My* freedom from cigarettes." now can be re-stated as, "*I am* completely free of cravings and *I am* clean, inside and out."

♦ After each one, pause to say, "*I am rich in _____!*"

As you do these assignments, I expect you will see financial implications emerge – especially for financial healing in your life.

List Maintenance 101
Of course you'll need to respond and take action as the opportunities come around – make the phone call, watch the classifieds, pay a visit, speak up, invest in the course tuition, buy the tools. By making preparations, acting on the certainty of their arrival, you will hasten them. Like attracts like, so jumpstart that dynamic. I guarantee it'll be a lot more fun this way.

As the items on your list of 101 requests are fulfilled, make sure you check them off and date them. I keep my list on my computer's desktop where I'll see the file icon every morning that I sit down to work. About once a month, I'll open it, review it, read it aloud with conviction and allow myself to feel the joy and gratitude in anticipation of each item's meaning in my life. When they happen, I note the date and who was involved.

By the way, you can edit the list – time will change your priorities, so the items on your list should change with you.

Make sure there are some smaller items on there too, so you can practice and learn the feeling of receiving as you check them off.

And don't worry about overtaxing the generosity of such a creative and openhanded Father and his abundant creation. The shortage is almost always in your mind, in the form of limiting beliefs, or a product of them.

Remember, you are rich in _____!
And receive it!

Healing Your Financial Soul Field Trip #2: Taste & See
Make a date with your favourite person, or just by yourself, to go to a *very* nice restaurant – better than what you'd normally go to. In this exercise, your opponent is the menu's right-hand column. The one with all the numbers.

Your task: order with *complete disregard* for the items' prices. If there's a "market price" item, order that and be deliberate about not presaging the cost; if not, cover the right-hand column while you decide. Or have your companion order for you (heh-heh). If you're by yourself, ask your server for their recommendation and have that. Under *no* circumstance are you allowed to order "the chicken" or "the pasta" because it's less expensive! You may share an appetizer if ordering your own would be too much food. If you drink wine, use the same approach – ask the sommelier which wine they'd recommend with what you're eating. And better a glass of fine wine than a carafe of passable house wine. Again, I wager you've wasted or lost bigger amounts on much less satisfying things.

Let your entire focus be on the food, the moment, your company, the blessing of being there when so many cannot. But be grateful for the enjoyment, not maudlin. Reflect on the experience that you are gaining. Not on the end tally - the bill only supports what you are *re-ceiv-ing*. Receive the moment. Smile and express your gratitude, both to your date and your Father.

If you're a couple reading this and one of you finds this particularly difficult to take on, he or she should probably go out and do this on their own. They've probably been hiding behind the confidence of the other, deferring and taking the low road by trying to spend or expect less. Actually, it's a form of enabling behaviour disguised as thoughtfulness or selflessness – it's compensating for something and we need to kick out that crutch they've been using. If this is no challenge to you – send your partner alone.

If you're already a restaurant habitué and this wouldn't be a stretch for you, or you have health issues that don't allow this, choose a different outing: a spa treatment, rent a boat or cottage, spring for great theatre or concert tickets… if the impediment to doing this for yourself has been that you'd rather lower your expectations, or deprive yourself entirely, because you "don't want to spend the money", storm that barricade!

If that's you, then it may be due to feelings of…
unworthiness ("Oh no, I really couldn't. That sort of thing isn't for me.")
guilt ("It will help others if I have less.")
fear ("But what if it's too much?")
anger ("Nobody should spend like this on themselves!")
resentment ("No one else is this nice to me, why should I be?")
rejection ("I'm supposed to miss out.").

If you're already pretty secure about spending money on yourself, try doing something where you don't think you can afford the *time*. Money can be replaced, time cannot. But unless you have a cri-

sis to put you in touch with that fact, such as an illness, then you might not be in touch with how you're being miserly with yourself with time and doling it out to others as if you have an endless supply – mothers are particularly susceptible to this. So take off an entire day, delegate all of your responsibilities for a full 24 hours, and spend it on yourself, doing or having something that you just never get around to.
I dare you!

Two points to this one
Point 1: Capacity again. Like the coffee-in-the-lobby field trip you took a while ago, we're using a new experience to educate your emotions, beliefs and even body language. This is a concrete experience in becoming accustomed to
money serving you vs. *you serving your money inhibitions.*
It's defusing the unanswerable question, "Can I afford this?"; loosening the grip of your poverty mentality; stretching your financial comfort zone to acquire the feeling of belonging in a wealthy atmosphere.[7]
I'm not saying you have to *live* there, but you should be confident and at ease when and while you're in that context.
So relax. Smile. This is supposed to feel like a stretch.
You cannot give what you haven't received. How can you practice hospitality if you can't practice on yourself? If you can't, hospitality will remain either a duty or a fantasy.

Point 2: A friend once told me, "Money is the easiest thing in the world to replace. You cannot replace time, and you cannot replace people."[8] So drop-kick the poverty mentality that would put one or two hundred bucks ahead of treasured, memorable times and worthwhile people. I'm not teaching you to be careless with your credit card, I'm saying that money will always come, and will always go, no matter what you do. And it can always come back. Your time and your people deserve your being intentional.

Tangential point (but a good one)
You already know what it's like to do something out of habit, either good or bad. What you might not realize is that your life is also full of dark-matter habits of what you do *not* do. Just as nature abhors a vacuum, so does your life and behaviour. In an area of your life where you have neither a good habit nor a bad habit, you have a "not-habit". If you're an artist, designer or architect, you'll understand the concept of negative space: defining an object by the

boundaries of its immediate surroundings (where it isn't).

So for example, you can like exercise and sports and still be out of shape if you are in a not-habit of not-exercising because you rationalize that you're too busy with other things (working, computer gaming, commuting, socializing, committee meetings, *etc.*). Your physique demonstrates a not-habit of not-exercising.

Or, if you don't spoil your wife or husband once in a while, it might not be because you prefer to ignore them – it might be because you have the not-habit of not-paying attention to their need to feel special and you're spending hours on TV re-runs instead. Bleah!

Or if you're single, the not-habit of not-caring for yourself because you've packed your life with activity and busy-ness. Or unhealthy self-comfort like excess food or empty on-line chats or texting.

Your not-habits are just as much part of your life as your habits. Replace that not-habit with the habit of getting out, doing something special, something different, something very personal, at least once a month. Preferrably once a week.

One last question
Are you thinking you can't do this restaurant thing because you can't afford it?
Tempted to skip it?
If so, that means that you're already programmed to expect that you'll sink and drown before your finances will ever turn around. And your expectation is fulfilling itself:
   As you're thinking in your heart now, so you're going to be later.
Ditto if it's because you're thinking this is "too rich for my blood" – it is because you say it is, and that's the only real reason.
In either case, I hope you're seeing how much you need to make your financial changes from the inside out.

If you're thinking this is a bad idea because you've already dug yourself into a credit trap by indulging in too much of exactly this kind of thing...
Or that depriving you and yours of a bit of indulgence is your way of resisting the spirit of greed or poverty...
Then you *really* need to press through the rest of this book to cure your financial diarrhea or constipation.
So instead of the restaurant, find a low-cost (not cheap) pleasure

to share for an evening or weekend afternoon, like window-shopping the art gallery district, or go to a pay-what-you-can fringe theatre production, or an outdoor community concert. And teach your financial soul that money is only one aspect of wealth – not even the main ingredient.

And remind yourself, *"I am rich in _____!"*

1 Romans 2

2 James 4:8

3 Luke 18:8

4 Acts 20:35

5 II Corinthians 9:7

6 "thanksgiving" which we know simply means giving thanks, and "praise" which means to outwardly express appreciation, Psalm 100:4.

7 Paul said he'd learned to be content in both plenty and want (Philippians 4) – might as well get familiar with the "plenty" part, the "want" scenario doesn't need your invitation.

8 We've lost contact with our friend Tony, who taught me this one – Tony, if you read this, please get in touch!

Chapter 6

Clearing the Clutter, part I

Pruning the Family Money Tree

Your problems and limitations will always be bigger than you until you deal with your limiting beliefs, thoughts, "proofs" and the decisions on which you base them. Including in the area of money.

Same goes for the limits they impose on your faith, relationships, and more. The good news is that not only can you outgrow those, you'll grow faster and easier when you have clarity, lightness and joy working in your favour.

So we're going to have some fun clearing out a bunch of the broken junk, outdated gadgets, worn-out devices and ill-fitting hand-me-downs that you've accumulated during years of absorbing mixed messages and half-truths about money. We'll do this in three parts: first, your family junk; then your religious clap-trap, then your own souvenirs of sorrow.

From the time you were fed as a baby, clothed as a child, celebrated birthdays and Christmases, attended school and church, participated in clubs or sports, and entered the work force, you've been incessantly shaped by other people's ideas of what you can or cannot expect. Particularly what you should or shouldn't expect. Which does two things:
  * It's a negative way of learning...
    Q: How do you find out you should or shouldn't if you don't know?
    A: By getting it wrong!
  * It often charges messages about behaviour with the weight of moral authority and loyalty,
    (obedience & position *vs.* costs & benefits).

Most people in those positions of authority intend well and are doing the best they know to do, but everyone gets to experience bad examples (and I would not for a minute downplay their impact on your life). However, we were created with a kind of innate durability, resilience and grace that on balance serves us and sees us through such scenarios. Including our capacity to detect and find nourishment in the love of flawed people in less-than-optimal circumstances. So maybe you've come through well, maybe you've always struggled, probably it's been a mixed bag. However, we aren't looking to assign blame, just to recognize what's not helping now and choose something better from here on.

Our focus is on finances, but you'll likely discover how this section applies to other areas of your life as well.

Your family money tree
Every family has its own little culture: food rituals, conversation patterns, level of tidiness, preferred styles of confrontation, daily and weekly routines, expressions of love, seasonal traditions, sense of humour, and so on. Same with their money and finances: cash inside birthday cards, money from the Tooth Fairy, an allowance, money for good report cards, encouragement to baby-sit or get a newspaper route, summer jobs, advice about education for a job or career, and so forth. You were groomed verbally, by example, and by experience as to what to expect in life regarding money. Those handed-down beliefs, sayings, teachings and the attending emotions formed the foundation of your experience and you've been influenced by them ever since, even if (*especially* if) your response was to reject them.

So let's take a couple of minutes to sketch out what the money influences were around you as you were growing up.

We're going to do some serious work here, and this might take a bit of time, even a couple of sittings, so get a pen and your journal, or use the spaces provided below, and make yourself comfortable.
Then pray with me:
> *Lord, I thank you for every person you've brought through my life, and for all I can learn by them, directly and indirectly. Both the positive and the negative ones.*
> *Holy Spirit, would you please lift to the surface of my memory, the guiding words and influential events that have shaped my beliefs and relationship with money, finances and wealth? Thanks.*

♦   Write one paragraph honestly summarizing how the issue of money was handled in your family. Particularly emotionally (ease, fear, nervousness, jealousy, appeasement, generosity, arguments, silence...)

_____

_____

_____

_____

_____

_____

_____

• Draw up a list of your family members. Start with parents and guardians; then siblings; then grandparents, aunts and uncles, and cousins.

• Review that list of people who surrounded you as a child and divide them into two lists: one for your paternal side and one for your maternal side. If re-marriage was a factor, give that branch of your family their own list as well.

• Arrange on a pair of facing pages the constellation of personalities you grew up with in a chart something like this, with yourself at the centre:

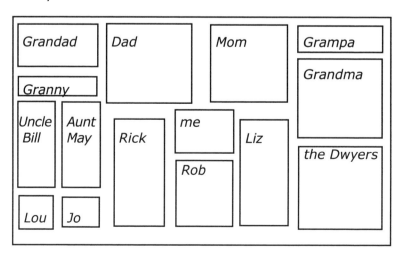

*   Fill in what you know of their financial personalities and priorities. Were they spenders, penny-pinchers, mysteries, well-off, broke, worriers, sneaky, flashy, successes, disasters, labourers, professionals, business owners...? Don't protect them, don't praise them, just be factual.
*   If there's a lot of people, or a lot of history to summarize, feel free to give an entire two-page spread to each side of the family, or groups of siblings, and so on. As long as you can keep them all out and visible where you can scan them all at once for perspective.
*   Include what you know about financial successes, crises, businesses, careers, investments, properties, lifestyles, *etc.*.
*   Also, how do you remember the *tone* of their behaviour with money and possessions, their gift-giving tendencies, their dress, their homes, and so on? Especially their moods about money.
*   Stepping back and looking over the family, do you see patterns? Recurring traits? Opposite reactions? Start circling, highlighting, drawing connecting lines or writing in notes.

Souvenirs, mementos and other clutter
*   Next, sit back with a pen and a couple of fresh pages of your journal and let your mind drift between family events, beginning with these:
    holidays, vacations, birthdays, graduations,
    family visits, meal-time conversations,
    reunions, large get-togethers...
What were they generally like? Do you recall incidents involving money, gifts or possessions that were embarrassing, frustrating or threatening (including "learning a lesson")? Note them, including the people involved.
*   Make special note of your parents' proverbs, quotes and lessons about money, rich people, security, saving, work, *etc.*. Such as "Money doesn't grow on trees." "You have to work hard for your money." "Do I look rich?" "The banks are crooked." "It's just money." "The stock market is for the rich." "Easy come, easy go." "Nobody can afford that." "You can't have everything you want." "It's hard to get ahead." "When it comes to money, women/men are..." And so forth.
*   Did they have pet phrases routinely pronounced about one's own finances? Such as, "I'm no good with money." "I don't have a head for investing." "I can't even balance a cheque book." Write them with the corresponding family member.

+ Did your parents say such things about *each other's* financial skills? Note them too.
+ In some cases, especially where there was deliberate silence about money, you might have to infer what the lessons would have sounded like.
Or perhaps it was conveyed by teasing or jokes – especially cultural traits, such as being Scottish or Dutch. If you can quote directly that's good, but the important thing is what messages you came away with.
Alternatively, you may have witnessed arguments and worse over financial situations - write down the sorts of things you heard, *highlight* either things yelled in a rage, or systematically leaned on with the intent to control someone else.
Write a list of these "lessons".
+ Do other influential individuals come to mind, like teachers, coaches, in-laws, friends' parents, *etc.*?
+ You may find other relevant thoughts bubbling to the surface over the next few days. Don't dismiss them, or think, "I'll remember that later..." Show them some respect and write them down!

Familial beliefs have influenced your thinking and behaviour regarding money and wealth. Including opposite reactions! Do not underestimate the gravity these exert on your financial circumstances. Especially the ones relating to Mom & Dad.[1] Bear in mind, we are not criticizing or judging these people, we are just being realistic about their influence, and especially your resulting conclusions.

Caution: do not justify, excuse and rationalize on their behalf; and do not shrug off what the Holy Spirit has just helped bring to mind. As an adult you might be tempted to dismiss them and say, "It was just his way of coping," or "It was just a bicycle," or "But we were just kids." As a child you were absorbing it all as truth and experience. Maybe you want to be nice about it now, but until you're willing to examine what was really going on, you cannot actually be understanding and compassionate. Just glib.

How can childhood stuff matter so much?
Because your character, core values and behaviour are pretty much decided by age six, and cemented into place by age 12. Not your opinions and knowledge maybe, but your base state and inclinations. I'll give you a personal example. When I was five years old, my parents took my two younger brothers and me to the Detroit

Zoo. Don was probably three, Neil was still in a stroller. It was a hot summer day and Mom asked, "Do you boys want a pop?" Don cheered, "Yeah!" and happily reached up both hands – I think he was an Orange Crush guy. I politely declined.

A little while later, Dad asked if we wanted some ice cream. "Yeah!" said Don, and I said, "No, thank-you."

Of course this got my parents wondering and Dad asked why I didn't want anything. I explained, "I don't want to owe you too much when I grow up."

So Dad just explained, "You don't have to pay me back, just do the same for your little boy when you grow up."

Satisfied, I had ice cream.

Now where does a *five-year old* get a concept like that? And think he has to restrain himself because of it? I don't know where I got such an idea. My parents were, and are, generous and thoughtful, we had an ideal childhood and I'm not aware that debt was ever a problem, much less discussed. I must have overheard something somewhere – an overheard adult conversation, television, radio... who knows? But it stuck in the mind of a little boy and had already shaped my willingness to receive.

And it didn't stop there – my wife will tell you that I still have to be reminded that it's okay just to receive, period.

But I'm much better.

So a non-traumatic, normal and happy childhood can still leave you with clutter to clear out of your root thinking and beliefs.

Clearing that clutter
Now I'll give you a pattern, a template, of how to deal with this sort of accumulated stuff.

We'll start with the beliefs, maxims and proverbs you picked up. Let's say you remember hearing your dad and your favourite uncle agreeing that, "The rich don't care about anyone else." (You can substitute one from your list as you follow along.) Remember, even if it only *seemed* reasonable, or *felt* true, then you agreed and it stuck. Even if you wouldn't agree with them now: in that case, you are the proud owner of mixed messages!

And those misperceptions and myths are like pushpins (or rivets!) that hold bad finances in place. So a distrust of rich people will prompt you to do all kinds of little things to make sure you're *not-*

rich – either undoing any good thing that threatens to make you well-off (like saving and investing) or prompting you to do negative stuff like blowing your budget, procrastinating on retirement savings, splurging on the wrong things, and so on.
If you have a belief, your emotions and subconscious will just keep making suggestions and taking shots until the right moment and circumstance comes along to fulfill it.

Pray with me:
Father, people I know and love have passed on to me all kinds of beliefs and ideas that aren't helpful now. Please help me clear out the stuff that does not serve me well.
Lord, this thing about, "_____." is flawed. So it's false.
Father, I forgive _____ for teaching me this lie, for every way it has shaped my thinking, and for everything it has cost me, especially financially.
Please forgive them too.
I intentionally release them from any guilt or debt because of this – they owe me nothing for it, not even to admit it.
In fact, I bless them to learn a better way from you and prosper themselves.
I also forgive myself for believing this lie, for taking it on, and for every way it has hindered or damaged my finances by _____. (What were the implications? Keep this part about yourself and what you've done.)
Father, I'm sorry for every way this lie interfered with your generous vision for my life. Would you please forgive me for taking it on and acting like it was true?
Thank you.
Now, Holy Spirit, if that was the lie, then what is your truth?
(Listen, and write the first line that comes to mind.)

_____

_____

Thanks, I'll choose to believe that instead.
And I am rich in _____!
(Now cross that belief off your list.)

Well done!
Repeat this process with as many pieces of bad thinking or advice

you identified on your list. *Even if it takes a couple of sittings* – how badly do you want to see change in your finances?

You may see there's a particularly deep wound, or a repeated cluster of related splinter beliefs, but be patient and work it through. If it becomes overwhelming because money was adding fuel to an already dysfunctional situation, such as marital strife, you may need to take the issue to a counselor.

One test for how well you've dealt with any of these myths is to say it out loud and gauge whether it still 'feels' true, rings true or you'd say part of you still believes it. If so, quiet yourself and ask yourself, "Is there a related lie still there?" and listen for it. If you can look at the lie or read it out loud and you sense that it just doesn't 'stick' anymore, it's probably done.

If there's a 'Yeah, but...' attached as a rationalization, perhaps masquerading as compassion, understanding or loyalty, it's still flawed and worth getting rid of. God will give you something better than an excuse or rationalization.

And in every place where truth supplants a lie about money and finances, you can begin to prosper and bear good financial fruit. Like a garden that has been weeded and pruned.

There are deliberate elements and angles covered by this prayer model which are important, so I wouldn't advise skipping parts. I don't want to take a bunch of space explaining all of the aspects, but it's like some weeds that grow back no matter what you do to the leaves, stems and flowers at the surface of the ground – if you don't get at the whole root, it'll be back. So the prayer is intentionally thorough.[2]

I am confident that you will experience a sense of relief as you clear these things up – kind of like when background noise such as an air conditioner switches off and the relief makes you suddenly realize how the constant rumbling or whirring was weighing on you. The relief is all of physical, mental and emotional.

If you feel strong emotions surfacing as you go through this process, that's good. Don't be afraid to acknowledge ownership of what's been there beneath the surface all this time. Actually, the degree to which you acknowledge your feelings of disappointment, anger or pain, and release them along with the forgiveness and blessing you're giving away, the more thorough a job you'll be doing of clearing the clutter.

It's important to acknowledge the emotional costs because they have been a *huge* factor in your financial struggles. If you deny their importance, or even existence, you are despising a legitimate part of your self and this process will be a waste of time. If fact, it will fester with internal resentment. In my experience as both counselor and counselee, honest acknowledgement is a powerful dynamic in freeing up these areas.

The next section is fairly major too, so spend some time with your list for this exercise before you go on to tackle the next.
. . . .

Character resuscitation
Here's a hard thing about Jesus' teaching that reflects how ruthless we need to be with our mental junk.
You don't have to be a professional athlete to be athletic.
You don't have to be a court judge to be judgmental.
You don't have to physically tangle with the wrong person to be adulterous.
You don't have to actually kill someone to be murderous.[3]
That's hard, but not harsh. He was getting at the condition of our hearts and minds, *including the way we categorize and treat our images of people up inside our thoughts and in the backrooms of our memories.*

Neurological science has demonstrated that if you close your eyes and remember vividly, with sights, sounds and sensations, what a past experience was like, the same neural pathways re-fire as if you're actually involved in that activity. Top athletes have done this for years – it's called *mental rehearsal* and it generates the same brain/muscle neural activity as actually running a 100-metre dash, sinking a foul shot or hitting a home run. It's not released to your limbs, but within your brain, and to your mind, it's the same set of neural pathways. Including the attending emotional content. There's just a provisional directive to remain in your chair with your eyes closed. Maybe that sheds light on why Jesus said that thinking something through is morally significant even if you don't tangibly go through with it: it makes you the same kind of person.

This also relates to what I call *The Diesel Jetta Effect*. I bought one of these Volkswagens from a friend, and suddenly they were everywhere! And not just any model of Jetta – particularly the diesels. My brother noticed the same thing when he took care of it for us while we were off traveling for a couple of months: "Sheesh, I didn't realize there were so many of these on the road." Obviously, it was only our perceptions that changed – mathematically there weren't any more diesel Jettas out there, but our experience/awareness of reality was altered.

This same dynamic is in play when you judge others. Suddenly you notice so much of that characteristic in their life. And in others too! But actually *our sensitivity* to that perception is the thing that has changed – that judgment is now a fixture in our own mental grid. Your conscious and subconscious is compiling a dossier to build a case around your judgment. You are personally invested in it and now *you own it*. So Jesus said,
    "As you judge, so you will be judged, *with the same measure*."[4]

All very interesting, now what's the relevance to my finances?
If you have judged your parents in the area of finances, money, work, provision, and so on, then you will find *the same measure*, the same dynamic, operating in your own life. Doesn't matter if you now think you now know better – it's in play.

While this is true with people you judge in general, this is *especially* true concerning your parents. Besides the 'Judge not' clause, consider that the commandment to "Honour your father and mother..." also carries a guaranteed effect "...that it may go well with you in the land."[5] *Ergo*, in the areas where you dishonour them, things will not go well with you in that same area. The judgment dynamic is actually compounded in light of this command+promise.

So, if you judged your father as 'a cheapskate', you'll spend your days handling money in ways that are pushed and pulled by the gravity that judgment exerts on your own behaviour:
  ◆   you'll perceive ways in which your dad kept proving out your expectation,
  ◆   other father-figures, such as mentors, coaches, teachers and employers, will exhibit similar characteristics,
  ◆   if you're a guy, you'll find yourself doing what you so disliked in your dad to your own kids, students, employees, *etc.*,
  ◆   if you're a woman, your husband will be swimming against

that same current you've created and be inclined to do the same things,
* or you'll over-compensate in efforts to do the opposite by force of will, which isn't freedom either.
In my wife's and my counseling experience, we've heard women say, "I feel like I've married my father."
This is that.

Alternatively, judge your mom as 'a hopeless case' when it comes to money and guess what you'll be struggling with. Either in yourself, your spouse or other influential females like your bank loan manager, supervisor or pastor's wife. Ever catch yourself thinking, "Man, she sounds like my mother!"? (Hopefully you've *never* made the mistake of saying, "You're just like your mother!" during an argument.) Given that we all posess a full palette of human characteristics, moods and traits to draw from, guess who's generating The Diesel Jetta Effect and actually drawing that particular behaviour out of them.

Now, there's an important difference between judging someone and recognizing behaviour. It's okay to acknowledge that, "Dad was uptight about money, including when it came to us kids." That's recognizing how he behaved and we need to be honest about the effect that had on you. But you cross over into judgment when you decide, "Dad's a cheapskate." Then you've *labeled* him, his identity and his personhood. And based on that pronouncement, you're set to reap something analogous because you've...
* dishonoured him (per the commandment),
* judged him (per 'Judge not') and
* done him injury in your virtual-reality, good-as-real neural pathways (per 'mental rehearsal' and Matt.5).
Heavy, eh?

There is also an upside to this delving
Thankfully, the good news is that you, and your own finances, can be freed of the ongoing, self-fulfilling, cyclical consequences of those judgments. You made them, and with a little bit of help, you can clear them out. Here's how...
* Ask the Holy Spirit, your counselor extraordinaire, to reveal areas where you crossed the line from recognizing how your father and mother handled things, to judging who they were as people. Look over your entries for your mom and dad on your family chart and note your realizations, *particularly if*

they became labels with negative emotions attached, such as "miser", "reckless", "gambler", "manipulative", "hypocrite", "unreliable", *etc.*
List them here, or on your family chart (if it isn't getting too crowded):

_____

_____

_____

_____

_____

Take the first label on your list and pray with me, out loud, like so:
Lord, I admit that I judged my father as _____.
I admit that this was wrong of me and I'm sorry for carrying this offense in my mind, in my relationship with him, and even with you!
Please forgive me. Thanks.
I now renounce that judgment and I cancel every related 'reason' I've held onto that influenced my thinking, emotions, spirit, body, relationships and finances.
Thanks, Jesus, for bearing the consequences of my judgment, so I don't have to.[6]
Holy Spirit, where I've dishonoured my dad, would you give me something to honour him as? (Quick, first thing that comes to mind, fill it in here: _____.)
Thanks, I choose to focus on that instead.

Repeat with each judgment or label about your dad that God shows you. If there's a lot of them, it's okay to group similar ones, as long as you acknowledge them specifically. Don't worry if this seems formulaic – that in itself doesn't make this glib. The point is how serious you are about changing things at your end of the equation.

That was Dad, this is Mom
Now, let's do the same process regarding your mother. If you need to take a break and do this in another sitting, that's fine, but I suggest you not wait long – a cooling off period can work against

you by tempering your willingness to view imperfections in your upbringing.

Let's do one together now. Take the first label on your list relating to your mother, roll your shoulders, allow yourself a smile and pray with me (aloud):

Lord, I admit that I judged my mother as _____.
I admit that this was wrong of me and I'm sorry for carrying this offense in my mind, in my relationship with her, and even with you!
Please forgive me. Thanks.
I now renounce that judgment and I cancel every related 'reason' I've used to influence my own thinking, emotions, spirit, body, relationships and finances.
Thanks, Jesus, for bearing the consequences of my judgment, so I don't have to.
Holy Spirit, where I've dishonoured my mom, would you give me something to honour her as?
(Fill it in here: _____.)
Thanks, I choose to focus on that instead.

Please understand, examining this stuff closely is not disloyalty or being negative – you are liberating your experience from the dulling gloss of sentiment or denial. Which means you will also have renewed compassion and appreciation for your parents' positive intentions, gestures and actions within the context of imperfect circumstances.

If you're unwilling to acknowledge the struggle,
how can you fully appreciate the effort?
Be assertive with this kindness.

But what if I had great parents?
I relate to that. My folks are great: generous, supportive, patient, hospitable, considerate, encouraging, thoughtful... all those things. But I came to a point where I realized that my experience of God's generosity, patience, kindness, *etc.*, was modeled on my parents. Which is a good way to start, but He is so much more! So I had this huge, happy comfort zone with God based on my parents' virtues – a wonderful way to grow up, but this became the extent, the frontier, the limitation of my experience of God. And I had to press past. And more to the point, my perceptions, reactions and interpretations were still my responsibility to deal with.

The process has begun

We've tapped some of the family culture issues involving money in your personal history and the way in which they embedded themselves in your thinking and deeper beliefs to become self-fulfilling prophecy in your finances. Not only with the Diesel Jetta Effect, in terms of perception, but also subconsciously and emotionally, with the related gravity these things have exerted on your desires, motivations, impulses, decisions and results.

Plus, you can see that there are spiritual principles in play where the decisions in your heart, and the things you've spoken out, have a way of coming back around. The properties built into God's creation conspire to draw our attention to these anomalies, not just as mechanical cause-and-effect (though there is that), but also as God's willful intention to provide you with *the feedback and opportunities you need* to resolve this stuff. So don't be discouraged because you've been carrying this stuff around for decades – everybody's got their own.

Just think of this as a wonderful occasion for change.

Next, we'll take things down to another, even deeper, level.

. . . .

That was now, this is then

You, or your parents, or grandparents may have gone through some times of cultural deprivation. The Great Depression, The Second World War, rationing, prejudice, an evacuation or displacement, a famine, or worse. The amazing thing is how resilient people, families, communities, cultures and entire races can be when circumstances sweep away what is dear to them. Including their means of making money, supporting their family and personal dignity. Those are amazing stories and we need to be aware of them, able to engage with their meaning.

However, the mentalities, coping mechanisms, beliefs and strategies that get people through hard times can become encumbrances if they don't change along with the circumstances that made them useful, even crucial, for survival. Part of our survival mechanism is the ability to make some things automatic:

expect less, share more, complain less, try harder,

be practical, make use of what you already have, and so on.

Much of it commendable. But perhaps no longer the dominant themes you need to flourish in the here and now:

flexibility, imagination, optimism, expressiveness, boldness, risk-taking, mobility, global thinking and so on.

Give careful consideration to your family's cultural background and historical experience and weigh out what is still going to be help-ful and what programming needs to be simply appreciated for its role in the past. Including their working group: farmers, dentists, politicians, cab drivers and police all have their own subcultures and modes of thinking about money and its meaning.

Jokes and humour are often clues – you can still keep a sense of humour about things as part of your appreciation, but ask your-self if you're still operating by those rules. If so, your family chart may reveal those old parameters – let's take them through a simi-lar prayer model as we just used for judgments. Hand over your heart:

Lord, I am thankful that I grew up in a home and family with a _____ culture – I know there are some very positive and helpful, even necessary, aspects that I want to keep. But I can also see some weaknesses, or old strengths that have become hindrances, specifically:

_____

_____

_____

So while I honour my forebears, and will celebrate their strengths and contributions, I now break unhealthy bonds and links to beliefs and mindsets that would now hold me back from living out of your abundance. Father, I believe that in their place you have... (one for each hindering trait you identified)

_____

_____

_____

Thanks Lord, I choose those instead.
I am rich in _____!

Talkin' 'bout your g-g-generations

You're now off to a great start in clearing up intellectual, emotional and cultural interference in your own finances. Let's go deeper still.

You carry within you a tremendous inheritance. That can be in terms of wonderful physical attributes such as eye colour, natural dexterity or childbearing hips. Or regrettably, deficiencies such as congenital health weaknesses like diabetes or developmental problems. This is your physiological inheritance at the genetic level. It's early in the game of deciphering and contemplating the human genome of DNA, but one of the more interesting scientific observations has been how personal experience shapes our cellular, even genetic, make-up. The stuff that happens to you, and by you, actually moulds the configuration of your DNA.

One might think you come into the world with a determined make-up and that's the constant that you work from all your days. What we're discovering is that circumstances also shape us at the cellular level. Not just triggering weaknesses such as high cholesterol, but we are actually imprinted at the cellular level, at the genetic level, by temporal events. Experiences are actually encoded not just in our memories, thinking and subconscious body language, but into our bodies. It's called genomic imprinting. These experiences and circumstances can then be passed on to following generations via the blood line.

Simple negative examples would be pancreatic damage from eating and drinking ridiculous amounts of sugar, inducing diabetes. Or liver problems from alcohol abuse. Or circulatory problems from reckless fat intake. Evidence mounts that habitual emotional responses also induce ailments such as arthritis and skin problems. These can all be cultivated in an otherwise normal body and then passed on to the next generation.[7]

The revelatory thing is that decisions, actions and experiences, even the electrical activity of our thoughts and emotions, also register change in your body's genes.

You are carrying an inheritance at many levels. Starting from the most external, you have inherited cultural and national characteristics (not in a rigid sense, but inclinations, expectations and tendencies). Financially you can also inherit family wealth or debt.

Emotionally, we intuitively know that we inherit some predisposi-
tions – I suspect because of the associated neurochemicals released
by our mother's emotional experiences and into our bloodstreams
while in the womb.

You have obviously inherited your physical characteristics and your
baseline emotional makeup. And from the DNA research we've
just discussed, you have also inherited the impact of generations
of experiences, circumstances, perceptions and interpretations
embedded at your genetic level.

Similarly, at the spiritual level you also bear the imprint of your
ancestors. If traits and circumstances are embedded and passed
on, then surely you have an inheritance of blessing passed to you
as well. This is another glimpse of why Jesus said our spiritual
restitution requires being re-birthed spiritually.[8] And then we get
to work out the implications of that re-birth in our minds, hearts
and bodies – it isn't automatic, but it is worthwhile to choose and
embrace.

Spiritual imprints
When you sketched out your extended family money tree, you may
have noticed trends and patterns. Hopefully some encouraging
ones and perhaps some disturbing ones. Just as there are cultural,
familial, mental and emotional undercurrents to these patterns,
there are also spiritual undercurrents largely stemming from the
promises of God's Path of Blessing and the Path of Alienation that
we discussed back in Chapter 2.

So, can anything be done about what you've inherited spiritually?
Yes. At the physical level, there are limits to what can be done
about your height or male pattern baldness, but things get quite
malleable as we move through the mental/emotional spectrum into
your spiritual makeup. You've been working on the conscious and
subconscious levels, now let's do some work at the spiritual level,
where we can free up the flow of generational blessings in your
bloodline and clear out blockages of generational clutter.

You are what you eat & drink, thank God
The Bible is clear, the Lord releases blessings and benefits into family lines that can run through our genes for a thousand generations.[9]
But also that negative consequences can be borne and passed on
for as many as 10 generations – let alone our tendency to perpetu-

ate and compound them.[10] The good news is that God's creation is designed to provide feedback, self-adjusting opportunities to recognize and resolve those negative influences, including the ones we haven't been aware of. So let's make this an occasion!

We'll apply a similar pattern from our previous prayer models...
  acknowledging,
    forgiving,
      renouncing and
        replacing
... and we'll add the nourishment and joy of bread and wine. By physically ingesting your prayers, we'll apply them to your paternal and maternal bloodlines, right down to your cellular level.

Again, you'll need pen and paper, but also some other elements:
+ Get some red wine – de-alcoholized wine if you abstain, but try to find something nicer than reconstituted grape juice.
+ And some bread – *not* regular leavened bread – Jewish *matzo* if it's available, a Mediterranean flat bread would work.[11]
+ Take your chart of familial financial trends and write two lists of words that characterize what you see on your *father's side* of the family: one list of positives and one of negatives.
  On one side you might have "security", "generosity" and "success". On the other side, negatives such as "unemployment", "victim" and "investment losses".
+ Do another couple of lists for your mom's side.

Let's invite God's input and guidance, and remember that we're anticipating a *good* time:
  Holy Spirit, please help me to hear what you're saying to me, spirit to spirit. Thanks.
  Lord, I know that you love my family and have always had wonderful plans for us. Would you please join me, infuse this bread and wine with your spirit, and help me to free up and restore your best designs for my life which were meant as my inheritance?
  I know it's going to be great!

  Heavenly Father, I appreciate the blessings that have come down to me through my family line. I also admit that as a member of this family, related by blood, I also bear the consequences of their selfish thoughts, harmful words and destructive acts – I bear a share in our collective guilt, even

in my own body.
But I choose to forgive my parents, grandparents and even
my ancestors for the struggle and alienation that I have
inherited from them and experienced myself. And for all that
this has cost me – especially in my money and finances.
And I forgive myself for every way I've played into these prob-
lems through my beliefs, attitudes, speech and actions.
Jesus, you made free payment for me and my family, which
you bore in your own body on the cross, which I now accept,
specifically for these generational patterns of bad finances.
Please heal me, even at my body's cellular level with this
bread representing your own body, broken for me. Thank-
you.
Break off some of the bread and eat it, with gratitude.

Now pour yourself a glass of wine – a glass, not one of those little
thimble things they pass down the church pews.
Take your list of family stuff and the list of negative financial traits
or experiences from your dad's side:
Lord, I admit that these negative financial patterns of (read
them out) _____ *are in my family, especially on*
my father's side – I forgive my dad and his ancestors for
how I've been affected. And I'm sorry for playing into them
myself.
Would you please heal my body, soul and spirit of this inher-
ited, generational, financial dis-ease?
Let this wine act as your blood transfusing mine to purify my
generational bloodstream on my father's side. Thanks.
Take a drink and consider that scripture says, "The life is in the
blood".[12]

Having worked through the paternal patterns, do the same with
the wine for the financial characteristics on your mother's side.
· · · · ·

This is great! Now, I'm going to pray for you:
I'm probably not in geographical proximity to you right now, but
I figure we must be somewhat entangled by now! Put your hand
on your chest, smile and read this *out loud* on my behalf as I pray
for you...
Father, I bless my friend for their honesty and transparency.
I speak release to your inheritance of family blessings that have
been blocked or diverted from you. Father, let those blessings

now flow freely into their circumstances, body, soul and spirit. I'm calling them forward now, all the way back through the generations, on both sides of the bloodline.

I bless the paternal financial provision and prosperity, and I bless the maternal comfort and nurture, to cascade into your finances. Lord, release sources of money, old and new, into my friend's life. Starting NOW! Let it come.

Now, I bless you as a son/daughter in the family to thrive and prosper in every way, especially in your relationship with money.

I bless your family inheritance to return to you and multiply.

I bless the positive, helpful aspects of your culture to flow freely in your finances.

I bless you Lord for your kindness and life.

I bless you, my friend, for all the good that you will do with this new freedom.

Father, release it!

I love praying for people!

For the next little while, repeat as needed
You may find over the next days and weeks that stuff related to these prayer models surfaces seemingly of its own accord – memories, sayings, opinions, names, places, and so on. That's normal – some of it just takes a while to work its way to your recollection. If you don't have this book handy, and you think of something while you're riding the subway or working at something else, write it down in a note to yourself. Please don't postpone because you think you'll remember later, because your rational/skeptical mind may protest and try to bury the issue again. Better to take two minutes to deal with it then and there.

You already know enough of the pattern:

Admit – recognize where you've been wrong.

Ask – being forgiven is humbling, not humiliating.

Renounce – break its influence by renouncing it specifically.

Replace – swap in a constructive belief to be grateful for.[13]

And the process isn't over – you've just learned a couple of very useful tools that you could apply to other areas of your life, such as relationships, food, social interaction, sexuality, self-care, time management, devotional life, work style, and so on. I've no doubt that you'll find relevance in just about every area of your life. The good news is that you can recognize these matters and do something about them.

The even-better news is that it gets better and better. Even if you find yourself in a season of deep and unsettling inner work, the seasons change and you'll be prepared for the next season of growth and freedom. I don't know if it will become what we'd call 'easy', but *it does get better.*

Now that you've started, I don't suggest going at yourself with hammer and tongs – that's not what life is for. You can trust God to use people and circumstances to lift these things to the surface of your attention when the time is right. He's patient to let some things lie if there are other things to take care of first. And he's generous enough to bring it back around again for another try if you miss the opportunity. If you find yourself in an undesirable circumstance, thinking, "Oh, not again!" or something seemingly random leaves you wondering, "Now where did *that* come from?" take that as your cue to do an internal check:
  • If this is the fruit, what's the root in my background or experience?
  • Is there something familiar about this situation?
  • Does this person remind me of someone in my past?
  • Do I have an emotional "zing" relating to this place? Or these people?
  • Is there something in me that attracted this event into my life: fear, selfishness, embarrassment, guilt or need for comfort?
And you'll know what to do.

Whatever you do, be frank with yourself about your own role and responsibility and don't accuse or blame shift – these are your circumstances and you're the only person who can benefit from them. Turn that bruising into a blessing with admission, forgiveness and renewal in your thinking.

Once you've worked with these exercises for a little while, you'll be able to just skim off stuff as it bobs to the surface. Now that you're attuned to some of the dynamics, you'll occasionally notice things linked to people, places, occasions, *etc.*. But you know what to do: now you don't have to be swept along by, or get sucked into, the old patterns that have been discouraging and hurtful for so long. You can see it for what it is, and now choosing a different way of thinking and behaving for yourself will be easier.
And remember, *you are rich in _____!*

Note: If you feel unsure about the validity of hearing God's truth as his thoughts flowing into yours, *versus* wrestling with your own perceptions by yourself, my good friend Mark Virkler has given me permission to include an appendix summarizing his teaching on the subject. You'll find it at the back of the book. It's a quick read and it has helped revolutionize the devotional lives of thousands of people.

1 John & Paula Sandford, the founders of Elijah House Ministries, have brilliant teaching and ministry in this area, and I'm deeply indebted to them. Their ideas have shaped some of my suggestions here.

2 Chester & Betsy Kylstra's prayer ministry templates synthesize several counseling models in a similar way. I recommend them to you, including their book, "Biblical Healing and Deliverance".

3 Matthew 5

4 Matthew 7:2

5 Deuteronomy 4:40. The Sandfords have particularly powerful teaching in this area of judgments and vows.

6 To sum up the cross: the innocent paid so the guilty could go free.

7 "The Biology of Belief", by Bruce Lipton, PhD, explains how molecular physics affect our biology. I think he oversteps by saying surface responses to environment are the seat of intelligence, but the bio-chemistry is interesting.

8 John 3:3. And perhaps also why the ramifications of our selfishness were physically borne in his body.

9 Exodus 20:6

10 I suspect that a lot of the spiritual makeup that we carry from previous generations is what is often misinterpreted as "past lives", reincarnation, ancestral worship and other forms of spiritism.

11 It amuses me the way some churches try to practically apply so much of the Bible, yet when it comes to the intimacy of the Lord's Supper, they opt for bread with leaven and not-wine.

12 Leviticus 17:11-14

13 If your parent was largely absent, even missing, God can still show you things to be thankful for, even fundamental things like your nationality, safety, health, stature, eye colour, or artistic inclinations. Ask, expecting to receive, and you'll hear.

Chapter 7
Clearing the Clutter, part 2
The Weed-whacker of Eden

Let's take stock of how things are going.
How was dinner? Was it a stretching, meaningful experience?
How much money are you carrying around in your wallet?
Are you using your "I Like Money!" declaration and entangled money jar/statement daily? (I keep mine right beside my desk so I don't miss it.)
Are you more comfortable relating to, or talking about, money?
Have you checked off some things on your Top 101 requests?
Are you saying, "Thank-you! Thank-you! THANK-YOU!"?
Did you try complimenting people?
Are you doing better with receiving compliments?
Have you started work on that financial conundrum? (pg.41)
Any further insights after dealing with that family financial clutter?
Are you consistently, insistently reminding yourself, "*I am rich in _____!*" with *every* financial action and transaction?
Thwacked anything lately?

It's fantastic that you've taken time to do significant work on your thoughts, beliefs, emotions, body language and behaviours with money. You should congratulate yourself because too many are either too embarrassed or discouraged to try something new, and too few are willing to embrace change. So they remain stuck in the same scenario from year to year to year. You've probably noticed that no matter how much some people talk about stuff out of their surface thinking, little actually changes. *You are now on a different path.*

The Weed-whacker of Eden
Now we venture into a thorny, tangled garden: your religious finan-cial clutter. And I use the word "religious" deliberately to differ-entiate and separate out the human element of your spiritual life. You see, God is not religious. Never was and never intended us to be. In fact, it's the kind of thing that got us barred from Eden:

religion is where mankind (and it usually is men) will take what God offers and say, 'Very nice, thank-you. We'll take it from here.' And all manner of grief ensues.

Religion is where our selfishness, need for comfort and will to dominate or ensnare kick in and we feel compelled and justified in commandeering the best of what God has generously provided in order to twist it to our own dissatisfaction.
So let's not confuse your spiritual life...
    love for God, His love for others in you,
    and the joy of participating,
with your religious life...
    your favourite opinions/offenses, expectations/limitations,
    concerns/gossip, preferences/control, and so forth.

And you know, some of that stuff wouldn't be half so bad if only it was consistent, but we spend most of our time and energy forcing and maintaining makeshift fixes between those competing ideas, conflicting opinions and partial conclusions that we've accumulated during years, if not decades, of listening to various notions about life with God. No wonder so many lose interest and/ or energy for it.

For now, let's stick to the effects of religious teaching, interpretation and application upon your understanding and experience of money. We've looked into your family's input and what can be done with that, now let's sort through some of the flawed religious teaching and mixed messages you've taken on regarding finances, wealth and money.

Since most religious church sources cite the Bible, we'll start with a selection of religious assumptions and their scriptural allusions – you'll then be better able to sift through other specimens you've picked up. After that, we'll sort through some of the church-culture-based contradictions in your thinking so you'll be equipped to cover off other experiences, opinions and quibbles as they come to mind.

The B-I-B-L-E
I was raised in a church denomination that highly prizes the truth and relevance of the Bible. I'm grateful for that. Throughout my church, para-church and pastoral ministry experiences, I have always found the Bible a dependable source of truth, perspective, comfort

and inspiration. I don't believe that will ever change, but my *understanding* of the Bible changes and grows with time, experience and investigation. And I've seen belief in the Bible go wrong.

In some cases, respect for the Bible can become an unhealthy reverence where this compendium becomes virtually deified as the fourth member of the Trinity. How many times in history has the Bible been quoted in resistance, even defiance and persecution, of the activity of God? Pretty much every time. Usually by proponents of the previous surge of biblical understanding – that was Jesus' own experience, that of the prophets before him, and every reformative movement in the Church ever since.

Fortunately, we can grow in our understanding of scripture. I trust that you don't read, interpret and apply the truths of scripture in exactly the same way that you did five years ago. And five years from now, your faith and understanding will have grown some more. We need to live with and love the scriptures, not get defensive about our current understanding of it.
We don't grow out of it, we grow into it.

So let's examine some aspects of a few widely held viewpoints about what the Bible says. Not to undermine, but to refresh and encourage new growth.

Judgment ≠ Condemnation
Sometimes we need to deliberately jar our comfortable old assumptions about passages of scripture. For instance, we've already talked about how judging sets you up to manifest the very qualities you despise in someone else. And how you will sooner or later reap what you've sown through your thoughts, words and actions. Those are demonstrable dynamics that yield feedback about the condition of your own heart. And you may have been conditioned through sermons, seminars, books and roadside billboards to think of them as being strictly negative. They're bad news, aren't they? They mean trouble. They bode ill of God's displeasure with you.

But are they threats, or are they truth?
What if those same scriptural dynamics hold true in the other direction? When a matter goes before the courts, does a judge's decision always go negatively for the defendant? No. A judgment can be favourable. The court often even awards damages. As I've said a few times so far: If it works, it works. So, what might happen

when we turn the negative on its head to become a positive? What if you 'judged' your dad as 'a hero' for being perceptive, helpful and compassionate? Would you be fated to become what you've judged and become more perceptive, helpful and compassionate yourself? Would you reap more of the perceptiveness, helpfulness and compassion that you've sown? With the same measure?

Why not? At the very least, your appreciation and admiration would surely motivate you to think, speak and act in similar ways. You'd create better circumstances for yourself, thought-by-thought, conversation-by-conversation, decision-by-decision, and action-by-action. And your surroundings would shift accordingly to accommodate your revelation about your dad. People around you would perceive those qualities, respond positively to them and reinforce the change. You'd see things outside your immediate grasp starting to line up with your new, improved perception. I venture that it wouldn't be long before those paternal traits blossomed in your own life. You might even become that same kind of 'hero' to someone else because we become what we judge.

Let's take that up a level now. Would God be pleased with you for labeling your dad that way? Sure. Might you reap some of God's favour or blessing in your life for similarly honouring your Mom? You bet. "What you sow you shall surely reap" doesn't have to be ominous, though it's usually presented in that negative light. What if we looked at it as a promise? An offer? A helpful hint?

In the context of an abundant universe geared for expansion, growth and fruitfulness, this dynamic was meant from the beginning to be a life-giving, encouraging phenomenon to multiply goodness. It's our persistent negativity that has cast the sowing and reaping dynamic in a dour, disapproving, religious tone.

Let's try it
- Go back to the parental stuff you worked on last chapter and choose the biggest judgment you cleared up regarding your Mom.
- Pray with me:
  Lord, I believe that you originally designed the sowing & reaping principle for blessing and abundance.
  I'm so grateful that where there used to be a curse, a blessing is going to spring up!
  Help me to have vision for it in my heart.

‣ Now take that honouring word, which you swapped in to replace your judgment, and write it here: _____.
‣ Close your eyes for a moment and think about that attribute as it relates to your Mom...
Notice how it makes you feel to know that you experienced that through her. Notice any visual memories? Or do you hear her saying something? Is there a physical sensation, like warmth in your chest? Does it make you smile?
‣   In this space, write an instance of when you experienced that attribute with her: *I saw/heard/felt this in Mom when...*

_____

_____

_____

‣   Based on the truth of that precedent, let's imagine four more ways that it could manifest in your life again in the near future – perhaps with her specifically, but open it up to other female figures as well.
For example, if you chose to honour your mom as 'thoughtful', you might recognize that in the past, she...
Never missed doing something special on your birthday.
The next four manifestations of your judging her as 'thoughtful' might be that...
1) She spontaneously offers to take the kids for the weekend.
2) Your manager remembers your extra effort when she reviews your salary.
3) The lady you buy your next house from lowers the price... and then throws in all the appliances.
4) The woman at the airline check-in counter bumps you up to first class. ("Thank-you! Thank-you! THANK-YOU!")

We'll write in either the present or future tense, but don't push it too far out into the distant future. (If you're still struggling to see how judgment could be transformed into something positive, press through! It's your conditioned assumptions that we're taking on here.)

Let's finish your example in this space, and feel free to GO BIG with the possibilities you can reap, as you shrug, smile with heart-felt

appreciation and say...
I recognize and honour my mother as _____.
I see this in the time she...

_____

_____

I expect to reap this honour I sow when she, or another woman...

1 _____

2 _____

3 _____

4 _____

Now let's do the same with a transformed judgment about your dad. Go back to the virtue you swapped in for a judgment and remind yourself of that admirable quality you connected with him. Allow yourself to embrace that characteristic and its significance to you. Do you get a visual? Do you hear anything, like his voice or his favourite music? Do you remember the feel of his whiskers or smell of his aftershave? Does it produce a sensation in your body? When you've really engaged with that quality, fill in these lines:
I recognize and honour my father as _____.
I see this in the time he...

_____

_____

I expect to reap this honour I sow when he, or another man...

1 _____

2 _____

3 _____

4 _____

Now you can expect to reap what you have just sown. You've just set the sowing & reaping dynamic into motion to your benefit. The circumstantial details may vary, so allow for some creativity in how God and his creation answer, but it will come. This is as much about your mindset of expectancy and increased capacity to receive as anything else.

Required assignment: tell somebody
What we attest to, for others to hear, is a powerful tool that shapes our circumstances. Make sure you share with others the qualities that you recognize and are thankful for in your parents. And if you want more of it in your life sow it into lives around you – make sure that's how you treat your spouse, or your mechanic, your students, the boss or the grocery clerk. Do unto others this way and you will find that others co-respondingly do unto you.

Premium assignment: tell them
Find a way to honour your folks within their hearing. Say something publicly at the next birthday. Toast them at Thanksgiving. Write your Mom an ode and read it out for your family this Christmas. Next time you golf with your Dad, remind him of something he did for you and tell him what character quality you see in that.

If your parents are not around, do it in a classified newspaper ad. Or place a plaque through your town's parks department. Use the specific words you identified in this exercise to express what's now in your heart.

Please don't put this off – make plans *now*. These things happen far too infrequently. Or too late.

So, there you go. The religious notion of judgment as something to fear has been opened up to become a life-giving and healing dynamic.

So let me ask, is the origin of the principle of sowing & reaping not God's generosity? His original design in Eden? His assurance that fruitfulness is his primary directive for you? Yet how many times have you heard "What you sow, you shall reap" presented in encouraging, generous words, in an enthusiastic tone of voice or with energetic body language? Even a smile? Think about what you learned instead...

Pray with me, out loud, with *oomph* and a smile:
Lord, I admit that "You reap what you sow" has had a nega-
tive spin for me, and I've incorporated that into my thinking.
(Thwack!)
This was not your intention, and I forgive the preachers, teach-
ers and authority figures who turned your promise into a
threat – please help them see this bias and I bless them learn
a better way too.
For myself, I recognize the flaw, I was wrong to believe it and I
surrender that stronghold in my mind.
Please forgive me and open my heart to embrace hope, vision
and confidence in a fruitful, abundant future.
I choose instead to remind myself that I have also sown a lot of
good *things with my thoughts, words, actions, money, efforts*
and skills.
And now, for every good thing I've sown which has been dor-
mant, (turn up the oomph!)
I declare a new season of reaping good things:
Great ideas, encouraging words, practical help,
immediate cash and high rates of return,
increased energy, health & strength,
distinct and unique abilities,
new techniques, new friendships and fresh opportunities!
Thank-you, Lord, for your generosity to me!
You are making me rich in _____!

Now would be a good time to hug someone, tell them you love them, phone a family member, write a letter (a real one, not an email) or buy someone lunch. Reach out!

Now about those Bible passages...
One of the most dangerous things believers can tell themselves is, "*I know* what that Bible passage means." That's like looking at a roadmap and saying, "I know where Vancouver is." There's a degree of truth to that, but you've only begun to get a glimpse of the city's arterial location, and only in one narrow sense. Not the road conditions. Not the traffic laws. Not the traffic patterns. Not the mountain scenery, riverfront or oceanfront. Not the hills. Not the weather. And nothing about the movie industry, financial district, the shipping patterns... let alone where the best Chinese food is. Obviously, the more you visit there, even live there, the further you can mine the experience of getting to know Vancouver's location.

The same with scripture. Saying 'I know' chokes off your ability to learn, grow and move into a fuller, healthier, wiser understanding. Rather you could say, 'I know this much...' or 'My understanding is...' Otherwise you'll be cemented into your old information and be in very great danger of missing it when new, relevant situations arrive. Even in the case of past problems, you can probably look back at the Bible passages that helped you through, and now time and experience help you see both those occurrences and the relevant scriptures with a different, deeper appreciation.

If you're apprehensive about being open minded about scripture, may I ask you to at least be open-ended? Bible passages are kinda like cats – you can hold them up and turn them any which way to look at them, play with them and pet them before you drop them, but they land right side up. Unless you have ulterior motives to deliberately force them in some unnatural manner. Trust your Bible and your spirit's ability to recognize truth and wisdom to take care of themselves and land you on your feet.

I didn't intend for this book to be yet another set of competing opinions thrown into your own internal clutter of financial advice. Nor a sermon or Bible study. I'm just going to toss into the air a bunch of quotations and clichés relating to scripture and finances and give them a different spin. I'm not saying they're bulletproof doctrine, or that there aren't other relevant, helpful views, I just want to open up and air out your rusty, rote assumptions so the Holy Spirit can get in there and work them out with you. Hopefully in a refreshing light that will serve your desire to view and handle money in a healthy, new way.

So, whatever tangle of conflicting notions your Sunday School teachers, pastors, denominations, books, commentaries and church business meetings have left you with regarding 'what the Bible says' about money and riches, and especially 'stewardship' (brr-rr-rr) let's blast some petrified old paradigms and see what God will do with them.

Wealth in the Old Testament
Adam and Eve – Talk about fresh opportunity and limitless resources! It would take a good sized book to mine all the relevant lessons of both versions of the creation story.[1] But here's the crux for now: God said Adam could "eat from any tree except the tree of the knowledge of good and evil [he was already sur-

rounded with 'good', so the only thing Adam really stood to gain was 'knowledge of evil'] for when you eat of it [personally experience it] you will surely die."

Notice he did not say, "because I'll kill you." But don't we make it sound like God said that? What are your emotional responses to that passage?
    Does it sound like a threat?
        An ominous command?
            A trap?
Or a single caution about consequences amid an abundance of life-giving delights?
Which one looms larger in your thinking? Which spin were you given?

Later, upon being disqualified from the garden, God explains what Adam (now Adam + Eve) will then face. The pain, sweat, thorns and thistles were manifestations of the 'evil' they were about to live out, having gained knowledge of it. Such as one of their sons murdering the other.

As we discussed earlier regarding God's offer through Moses of the two paths set before us (blessing and not-blessing), I submit that for us born outside of Eden, we're looking at a matter of degrees. The extent to which we are straining for a living "by the sweat of your brow" (striving and frustration) illustrates the extent to which we are living out of our knowledge of evil, *i.e.* fear, selfishness, guilt, shame, deception, deprivation and scarcity. In our work experience this shows up as possessiveness and territorialism, spoiled and missed opportunities, bad relationships, bad management, inertia, avoidance, stonewalling and discouragement. Sound familiar?

However, there is also a HUGE upside for us. We can also experience fruitfulness, multiplication, opportunity, cooperation and generosity to the extent that we live and work out of the 'knowledge of good' that God originally intended. The mixed bag we often experience is simply the logical result of the tangled and mingled beliefs and motives we harbour in our hearts and minds.

Noah was wealthy – Think about the scale of that project! With no corporate sponsorships, tourism revenue or product placement deals. Noah *had* to have been a landowner.

Job was rich – Job had it all but he was pretty religious and superstitious in his understanding of God's character. He thought he had to contractually cover off his kids' carousing by buying him off with extra sacrifices. This was typical of pagan religious understanding, *i.e.* contracting with your chosen deity and appeasing him/her/it in exchange for protection and prosperity. (Sound like anyone you know?) Job's losing everything he thought was his, and then his health, was devastating but he bore it. His wife's (understandable) meltdown challenged him, but he stayed onside by not accusing God. But his three buddies' religious theories of clutterization churned him up and goaded him into resentment.

When God saw things had gone too far for his friend, he intervened, made a rare personal appearance and exploded Job's perspective into a wide-open, panoramic, Technicolor, 3-D immersion course in God's wonder and genius – not an angry, domineering and belittling lecture, as we're prejudiced to believe. As a result, Job dealt with his clutter, he prayed for his friends (the kind of stuff we've just done regarding your family clutter) and he was restored above and beyond his previous state, in terms of both children and wealth.[2] Job was temporarily pushed down by disastrous circumstances, but on the other side of it, the Lord's generosity and prosperity sprang back exponentially with Job's new understanding.

Abraham was God's friend, and God made him rich – True, but at the same time, Abraham dampened his own destiny. Abraham's dad, Terah, was a successful pagan idol maker in Ur, and *he* was the one who undertook the spiritual pilgrimage to pursue Abraham's revelation about a land of milk & honey (nurture & inspiration) called Canaan.

Unfortunately, they got stuck halfway in a place called Haran. Terah "settled" for years in this pleasant spot – not coincidentally named after his dead son. Something emotional kicked in for Terah and it blocked him from ever seeing Canaan. By the time Abraham buried his father[3] in Haran and felt free to move on, he was already rich, but he needed to get back on track with his calling.

Centuries later, at the time of his stoning, Stephen pointed out Abraham as an example of Israel's incessant delay and resistance to the blessing and prosperity intended by the Holy Spirit.

Lesson: A classic case of 'the good' (Haran) interfering with 'the best' (Canaan). God's generosity is a constant, so don't fritter away your destiny by trying to keep everything normal, sensible and manageable. GO BIG! And don't assume that because you're prospering materially that you're attaining your destiny.

Abraham tithed – Well, once that we know of. Abraham's famous 1/10th gift to Melchizadek, a proto-non-Jew (if you will)[4] was a one-time gift, not a pattern of regular giving. And it wasn't even his own money. It had been stolen from Sodom by an opposing warlord and Abraham recovered it when he rescued his nephew Lot and family. As the story is told, it looks like Melchizadek laid on a banquet for Abraham's returning war party and Abraham responded with a tenth of the booty. It seems the king of Sodom didn't have such a grateful heart, but he did offer to cut Abraham a deal: keep all of the recovered goods in exchange for the return of the human collateral (who must have been in slavery and/or financial bondage to Sodom). Abraham refused – some money comes too expensive.

What we can draw from this is that Abraham hived off a tenth of the material gain from his campaign to bless God's priest in thanks for his generosity.

Joseph went from rags to riches – True, but first he was the favourite son of a rich man – a precocious kid. When a string of disastrous and arguably undeserved setbacks threatened his life and destiny, he not only endured, he gave his best effort to whoever he found himself subservient to. Even when things got worse. Because he decided to promote the interests of his masters, first as a household slave and then a convict in prison, he flourished. As far as he was thrown down, pushed down and held down, he was eventually launched exponentially higher to a place of national financial responsibility for all Egypt in agricultural and economic planning, and famine relief.

In terms of his own success, it probably didn't hurt socially or financially that after he became prime minister, Pharoah married him off to an Egyptian priest's daughter and Joseph joined the Egyptian priestly class. Reconciliation and healing with family is something that can't be bought with cash, but Joseph's position facilitated the opportunity to work through his heartbreak with his brothers and father.

Was Moses really a penniless fugitive or bedraggled old shepherd? – Aaron's baby brother and a survivor of Egypt's one-child policy, Moses grew up in opulence as a ward of Pharaoh's daughter. When he became a royal fugitive for murder, he probably didn't flee Egypt empty-handed with nothing but the shirt on his back. When he got spooked by his Hebrew bro', he likely went on the lam with a significant bundle of cash. Why? Because the owner of a prosperous livestock operation, Jethro, let Moses, a wanted man in his 40s, marry his young daughter: marriages usually had strategic and financial benefits factored in, which a shrewd manager like Jethro would have considered. (I wonder if Moses had previously married into the Egyptian upper class while he was in the royal court. Likely. So much for divorcées being unfit for ministry.)

God expected, and got, the best – The designs he gave Moses for the Tabernacle in the desert were elaborate, the materials were the finest, and the workmanship was exquisite. And he wasn't embarrassed by it. Why should we? He did, however, keep the design to a very approachable human scale. Shouldn't we?

The Law of Celebration – Through Moses, God was proclaiming an atmosphere of celebration and gratitude in his house, in the capital and out in the communities – a generous, healthy mix of food, drink (including alcohol), music, barbeques, feasts, festivals, family camps, theme parties, friendship and laughter. The law was about relief from guilt, not revenge; to stop offences from spiraling out of control; communal problem-solving, not control and punishment. Even the commandments begin with the exhortation to love, and the others, as Jesus later pointed out, are about how to live out of love for each other.

King David was rich – True, but the dark areas of his heart (for sex and power) were amplified as God, though Moses, had warned would happen with the choice of a human king. David's polygamy and harem (institutionalized promiscuity and adultery) led to tragedy after tragedy in his own household and the nation. And all the worse for the women. (The amazing thing is how the women were even taken into consideration, given the times, such as Bathsheba's restoration and promotion to queen: contrast the fall of Vashti.)

And when it came to war and power struggles, David was typical. His military audit (why would he count his troops if he didn't either plan to use them or worry about needing them?) unleashed a deadly plague. And by the time David was dying, he was tutoring Solomon in political assassination.

Still, David's attitude toward money was one of generosity and devotion, leading him to set up a financial foundation and trust for the first bricks and mortar Jewish temple in Jerusalem. His reward was God's promise to perpetuate his lineage.

Solomon was gloriously rich – True, because he first won God's favour by putting wisdom and justice for his people ahead of selfish indulgence. *Unprecedented* riches were God's reward. And he handled it well for a while. But again, his genetic kingly desires for sex and power corrupted him and his wealth amplified his degeneration. He became spiritually dissolute by appeasing his foreign wives' demands for recognition of their occult religions. He also became a political tyrant, hence his son's macho metaphor of "whipping your backs with whips". Solomon's finance & trade strategies introduced 666, signifying spiritual corruption fueled by gold – was Solomon the first multi-national corporation?

The Other Judges and Kings – Prosperity and national security were the barometers of Israel's spiritual state. When spiritual corruption settled in, they suffered. And this wasn't about some Levite's kid putting up black-light posters and yin/yang medallions in his room. We're talking full-on, devilish occult, including girls and boys born into a lifetime of temple prostitution, ritual human sacrifice and freak-out demonic frenzy. By the time God dissolved first Israel and then Judah, the kings were steeped in it. And yet, God's patience was consistent, and to the degree that the nations repented they immediately returned to safety and prosperity.

The Prophets – God had his messengers do some crazy things in his attempts to get people's attention. Like walking around nude for a year, stuffing underwear into walls, being fed by ravens, calling down fire from the sky, and marrying an out-of-control tramp. But money was a secondary issue. In fact, the prophets were generally well off financially. Most were landowners and community leaders. Some were high ranking government officials. As an example, Jeremiah was a man of prominence whom God instructed to pay full price, in cash, for some land just as invading conquerors were closing in. Given that Jeremiah died as a refugee thereafter, this had to be one of the worst real estate speculations on record, but he was making a prophetic point about God's plans for the future of the land. So Jeremiah was well off, but he made his wealth, health and freedom completely available for the Lord to 'spend' as he wished.

That Malachi text[5] – A perennially abused passage. The context of this book is a rebuke to the Levites and priests, *i.e.* the clergy, not the congregation. Compromise, complacency and resentment had crept into the ministry and God was confronting the temple leadership on all points. Not the farmers, herders, craftsmen, homemakers, merchants, labourers, *etc.*. When it came to the matter of tithes and offerings, he was dressing down the management, not the givers.

If we can just shut off the mental tape loop that insists this is about God *p-l-e-a-d-i-n-g* with the congregation to give more to the church, we can see that something was awry with how the temple's finances were being handled. Apparently somebody was trying something a little too creative instead of bringing the whole tithe into the house so the temple staff could all be provided for. God is busting the leadership for financial mismanagement, corruption and scandal. God's normal, generous flow of blessing was aching to be released, but not until the leadership repented.

And yet how many times have you heard this passage quoted at offering time, with no context, to chide congregations into digging deeper? Mega-*thwack!*

The lessons so far
+ There is undeniable linkage between material wealth and spiritual health, but one is not a direct guarantee of the other. Many of the key figures in scripture were wealthy – they owned land and livestock, had large amounts of gold and silver, were usually financially responsible for large groups of people such as extended family, and servants and their families. Some degenerate people were rich, but their corruption was rooted in spiritual and/or sexual issues, or lording military and/or political power over others. But in the main, financial prosperity tended to be a benefit of living right.
+ We see examples of how money amplified the weaknesses in men's character – it wasn't the money, it was what the money revealed about them and put within their grasp. The lessons regarding integrity are most vivid when ample money affords ample opportunity to move toward either prosperity

or depravity.
* The misperception that carried over into the New Testament era was that financial affluence was a badge of God's favour. Money is just money, and it didn't prevent people who loved and served God from living that way.
* But neither do we see financial struggle treated as a spiritual virtue. Periods of deprivation sometimes served to refine character in the form of feedback (as in, wakeup call). Particularly when it was arguably undeserved. When one's character is under pressure in a refining process, there is a corresponding exponential reward, including financial prosperity, on the other side of the test. It's still about the heart, not the financials.

Wealth and the New Testament

"Jesus was born poor" – Humble yes, poor no. His Bethlehem crib time in a manger was a function of family crowding (everybody and their uncle was home for the census registration) not inability to afford a commercial inn.

Also, at some point in the first two years of Jesus' life, a group of highly educated and devout astrologers (we don't know how many) bearing gifts of gold, frankincense and myrrh traveled to honour Jesus the newborn king. Those were *expensive* gifts. In our cash-flush and Christmas-crazy culture the magnitude is hard to appreciate.

Let's indulge in some conjecture, starting with the gold. Under Rome, a single gold coin represented 25 days' wages[6] – about a month's income if you assume a 6-day week. Let's take a nice biblical number like 40 and suppose that the magi brought 40 gold coins – that's over three years' income, or conservatively about $125,000 to us.[7]

Personally, I think that's low given that...
* the magi's stature warranted a royal audience with King Herod;
* these notable men's gifts were for (they thought) an earthly king, and a celestially favoured king at that – their gifts would have to be of royal calibre;
* they traveled for days, perhaps a week or two, atop animals, from a foreign country, which must have involved armed guards – not a shoestring operation.

I venture that we're talking about more than a purse with 40 coins.

And then there were the other gifts, the frankincense and myrrh, which were also widely traded commercial commodities. So assuming that the other gifts were comparable in value to the gold, we could double or triple the value of the first gift. Taken together, this was more money than most people of that era would see in a lifetime. Shortly thereafter, Jesus' family fled as refugees to Egypt to elude Herod's death squads. Maybe this was the money they lived with during the family's exile.

Jesus' birth and infancy were humble, socially awkward, even perilous, but finances were not a worry. They were starting out rich.

"Foxes had their holes, but Jesus had no home" – But he had a treasurer! (Judas Iscariot, unfortunately.[8]) And his ministry was partially financed by women who must have been affluent enough to not be deterred by controversy or controlling husbands. So was Jesus complaining about his ministry trip accommodations? Hotel rates? Real estate prices? Or was he expressing the price of alienation and the *emotional cost* of his mission? Things that money wouldn't alleviate anyway.

"Jesus sent Peter to catch a fish with a coin in its mouth in order to afford the temple tax" – Wait, wait, wait. Was the ministry *that* broke? Was cash flow the problem? Or was he modeling for Peter something about how God's abundant creation generously provides for our needs? For oneself *and* for others? Through surprising sources?

Money was one of Jesus' favourite metaphors – In fact, the number of New Testament verses that address money, financial matters and possessions abound. Some literal, some allegorical. Money was neither spiritually irrelevant nor inherently anti-spiritual to Jesus and the apostles.

Jesus said your finances foreshadow your spiritual progress – Context helps here, but specifically he said, "So if you have not been trustworthy in handling worldly wealth, who will trust you with true riches?" He was rhetorically asking how anyone can expect to be trusted with spiritual power and authority if they don't have the focus and integrity to handle money well (illustrating one's quirks

& clutter). Remember, Jesus wasn't angling for offerings, he was addressing what money revealed about people's hearts.

For example, he blasted Pharisees who could tithe fanatically and yet hardheartedly withhold financial support from their own aging parents and justify it religiously by invoking The Corban Clause: assets tied up because they're dedicated to God's service, *i.e.* "Gee, I wish I could help Dad, but my hands are tied – our assets are willed to the Temple Beautification Program." Shame! But we clumsily conclude this passage as meaning, "Wealth is bad." Actually, "Religion is bad." The energy of money reveals it as such.

So demonstrating integrity in working with TIME+ENERGY in the form of money is actually an indicator that you'd be able to handle higher spiritual forms of TIME+ENERGY. This harmonizes with...

The Little/Much Principle[9] – Jesus said that if you're faithful with little (that is, consistent, honest and dependable) then you can be trusted with much greater things. The corollary: Don't expect the "much" until you're good with the "little".

This certainly holds true when it comes to money. We like to think, "It'll be different when I have more to work with." Sorry. How you're handling your current income, spending, debt and investments is the blue print for exactly how you'd do with more money. And also, as Jesus indicates, how you'd handle spiritual matters, which will affect a lot more people more profoundly. Until you clear your clutter, you'll just produce more of what you've already got. More money will simply yield the same proportion:
    assets minus debt,
        income minus spending,
            fulfillment minus stress.
We'll get into this again later, but Jesus is saying the same thing as contemporary self-help spokesmen are saying, "How you do anything is how you do everything."[10] This is why we're working on your internal wiring rather than promoting a clever budget or fool-proof investment strategy.

This is a bit of an aside, but it does relate: Who's further ahead?
  * The person who fantasizes about supporting all kinds of missionaries and hosting a bed & breakfast for burned-out pastors and creating a centre for the arts... but hasn't a clue what to do about the money for any of it?

- Or a successful businesswoman who hasn't got an altruistic bone in her body but employs people, supports the local community, and grows her business honestly?

Which one is reaping what they're sowing?

Both.

Think about it.

What did Jesus do with his money? God never asks us to do anything he wouldn't do himself. In fact, he prefers to go first. Which is why he stopped Abraham short of sacrificing his only begotten son, Isaac. So, could it be that Jesus first learned to handle worldly wealth himself before moving on to spiritual power and authority in public ministry? Perhaps he himself made such a dramatic lifestyle change as a precedent for what he might expect of...

The rich young ruler – This section of the gospels[11] often gets broken up, but it runs before and after this specific anecdote for a larger picture. The context for this exchange between the RYR and Jesus was he was taking on religious people "who were confident of their own righteousness and looked down on everyone else."[12] In that context, this successful, wealthy, young Pharisee and synagogue leader claimed to have kept the Law to the letter and wanted confirmation that he'd earned himself eternal life – I surmise that he thought himself a rare example compared with the people Jesus was hanging out with.

Jesus didn't go on the attack or curse the guy's wealth. He said that the Law's provision to make him perfectly righteous was to sell off what he possessed, give to the poor (the very people he was looking down on) and follow him – as in, "do likewise", indicating that this had already been Jesus' own experience.[13] The RYR could neither cross that social divide nor muster the faith to do that kind of sowing.

The cliché interpretation is that Jesus is defying wealthy people in general to liquidate all they own and divest themselves before they can follow him. But one of Jesus' key criticisms of the Pharisees was how they made experiencing God's kingdom onerous and exclusive. Why would he do the same?

Bearing in mind Jesus' encouraging, generous heart, I think he was actually making the RYR a kind offer of something better: to move from obeisance, striving and self-righteousness under religious expectations, and into Jesus' lifestyle of excitement, trust and miracles. Grace. He was explaining the Law's end-game and offering the young man a way out of the box of saving himself via the Law. And it seems Jesus was disappointed that the man did not stick around long enough to learn this scripture episode's REALLY... BIG... POINT...

**"It's harder for a rich man to enter the kingdom
than for a camel to pass through the eye of a needle"**

Some like to debate whether or not this was a humorous one-liner, like swallowing a camel or having a baseball bat hanging out of your eye (think, 'Monty Python'); or if the city walls actually had a night security entrance called The Needle's Eye that a man could barely squeeze through. Either way, the camel stays outside. Jesus is not saying the rich are essentially doomed. Jesus meant that it's hard for *anyone*, even the rich, if you're going to try to make it via religious striving and performance.

People were under the widespread impression that being rich meant you were God's version of the teacher's pet. Jesus was deliberately shaking up that assumption. So naturally Peter's nervous follow-up question was, "Well if it's impossible for these prosperous, tithing, Bible-memorizing, clean living, missionary-sending, churchgoing, conference-attending guys... then who *can* be saved?" Jesus' wry answer: Anyone, when it's God doing the saving.

Remember, the issue kicking off this whole episode was not wealth – it was superiority. And Jesus was getting heat for hanging out with socially un-superior people including not only the poor but also rich people, such as...

Zaccheus the taxman – Unlike the rich young ruler, this successful tax collector got assurance of his spiritual restitution because Jesus saw a change of heart and his commitment to make financial res-titution where/if called for. Jesus doesn't ask him to quit his lucra-tive career (or sell all he had and give it to the poor), Zak was just elated to be accepted by Jesus and pledged to operate honestly. Which reminds me of this parable...

"The unjust steward" – *sigh...* we need to ditch some of these misleading subtitles.[14] This allegory perplexes people because they simplistically conclude Jesus is commending fraud. But the fired manager is not asking the debtors to falsify records, he's running around getting the account holders to pay down their balances. The owner wasn't being ripped off, he was seeing large influxes of cash that had been tied up in arrears for too long (hence the tense situation). And the manager, whose livelihood was at stake, was making a favourable impression on prospective future employers as a real go-getter – why else would they "welcome" him into their own employ? Not if they knew he would falsify receipts. And in the end he's commended (rewarded, restored, given recognition) by his original employer. This is not financial advice: it's a *me-ta-phor.* An illustration. This one's about evangelism. And Jesus did advise to use wealth this way.[15]

The widow in the temple – People mistakenly use this to paint poverty as a virtue. It's a cliché afforded by people already living in rich countries. When Jesus said that the two coins she gave were more than the attention-seeking Pharisees, he had just finished blasting the Pharisees for devouring widows' houses, and not-so-coincidentally, in walks the widow. He was obviously talking about her trusting heart toward God. No question. But in church circles we bend that around to mean, "So it's more godly to be poor like the widow than to be rich like the Pharisees." No, that misses the point: it's better to have that much humility and trust in God, not in one's self and/or money.

"Right, so if you're poor like the widow you're in more of a posi-tion of faith." No! Granted, wealth can make it easier to lapse into complacency (the broke lapse into worry, anger, resentment and depression) but the rich will get their opportunity to take faith-filled risks that will similarly test their limits and their hearts, because "to whom much is given, much is required."[16]

The way Paul explained it was "For if the willingness is there, the gift is acceptable according to what one has, not according to what he does not have."[17] Think about that, and hold it up against the examples of the widow and those Pharisees.

Personal cost is a given – In this world, one's spiritual life should not be servant to material ambition. That's backward. But if you have the heart to sow temporal possessions, like houses, invest-ments and community ties, for the sake of serving others, Jesus assured that you will reap...
    the same
        many times over

in both this life and the next.
(And along with it, your share of discomforts, misunderstandings and even persecutions.)
And we see the believers in Acts taking this to heart.[18]

Unfortunately, it's trendier than ever to make small-s spirituality a lifestyle component, like installing a reverse osmosis water filter, buying a minivan or retirement planning. When you have money you have more options and more opportunities to share. At least in the sense that the availability of money is not such an obstacle. But you can't buy genuine spiritual motivation or influence – Simon the sorcerer found that out when he tried to buy spiritual power from the disciples.[19]

"The poor will always be with you" – This actually sounds callous and dismissive until you understand that Jesus was quoting a familiar Old Testament directive to make sure we care for the poor: "There will always be poor people in the land. Therefore I command you to be openhanded toward your brothers and toward the poor and needy in your land." Deuteronomy 15:11

Other classic parables
The talents – A business illustration about what we do with our potential. Jesus was comfortable using money as his metaphor. The main point: you get exactly what you believe for. Clear your clutter! (More on this one later.)

Jesus is "the pearl of great price" – No, *you* are. Jesus was describing his own mission to metaphorically divest himself of everything to redeem you. That it was a field he purchased indicates that he expects to do some cultivating, giving the land a good working over.

Lazarus and the rich man – This is a biggy. The immediate message is to warn the wealthy not to overlook the poor. But many take this to be about the rich going to Hell while the poor get a hug from Abraham.[20] Wealth is again a metaphor. If we can snap out of this mental tunnel vision of turning everything Jesus said into condemnation of wealth, or that his embracing the poor meant he had to reject the wealthy, we'll realize he was trying to shed light on the bigger, spiritual situation.

First, this Lazarus wasn't an actual person – the name can be taken to mean "helpless", a nice literary flourish on Jesus' part.[21] As for the rich man, the contention was that neither being racially Jewish (descended from Father Abraham) nor religious (having the law and prophets) will save. Jesus' deliberate, in-your-Pharisee-face provocation was that the spiritually starved and diseased Gentile less-than-dogs would be received into Abraham's promise even if the religiously privileged Judah (Abraham's son with five brothers) habitually passed them over at their (temple) gates and hoarded their spiritual wealth. The dead rich man is in anguish of soul because he's been separated from Abraham and left out in the valley called Gehenna, which was a defiled dump outside the city and famous for murders and the stench of garbage fires – not a religious torture chamber (*me-ta-phor* – like the gate, crumbs, sores and dogs).

This is about Abraham's blessing and promise extended to the Gentiles, not revenge on the wealthy. Jesus didn't have to tell people he loved the poor, but he continually provoked the spiritually complacent. The larger issue is that this parable needs to be read in the context of the conversation kicking off this and other parables in this series: the sower, the lost coin, lost sheep and lost son. All about Jesus' embracing people who have lost their way.

Lost sheep, lost coin, lost son – Not about us: about him! Who needs a lecture about just how pathetically lost people can get? People need to know how God values us, misses us and celebrates when he has us back. Why did he use these fables? Jesus was celebrating this phenomenon in real life and he was getting flak for it. This series of financial illustrations culminates in expensive, lavish gifts for the alienated-but-restored son (think, 'sinners & Gentiles') vs. the hardworking-but-resentful first-born son (think, 'religious Pharisees') who begrudged the father's generosity and was oblivious to his own wealth. Again, there's no enmity here between wealth, money and spiritual life.

The vineyard workers – Men hired over the course of the day receive equal pay. Is this an allegory for flat-rate pay in ministry? Or the egalitarian nature of the after-life? Nope. He was foreshadowing his own intention to include the latecomer Gentiles, which he could already see was resented by the Pharisees who had toiled for ages under the hot sun of the Law. I'm sure he understood that even his own followers would struggle with the idea. And they did.

The fool who dies dreaming of surplus – After a bumper crop, this farm owner's only thoughts were of how to contain his good fortune. The point is that his heart was geared to *self*-reliance. Jesus was tweaking the nose of materialistic tunnel vision, the wastefulness of fretting and a heart to hoard food in a time when hunger was an ever-present threat. Priorities. This lines up with Jesus' advice to use temporary worldly wealth to generate spiritual treasure that endures.[22]

The Apostles, their Activities and their Advice
+ The rich shared, they didn't have to feel guilty about having something to share – they gave parcels of land as gifts because they were in a position to do so, not because they felt they had to jettison wealth. One couple got smoked because they faked it.
+ There are consistent reminders to share with the poor. They were encouraged to follow through on pledges of financial support for struggling believers in other provinces of the empire.
+ Wealthy church members were sharply told it was their responsibility not to make the financially strapped feel inferior – even if it meant eating at home before gathering for a communion meal.
+ Paul had deep relationships with slaves and owners, men and women, Jews and Gentiles – money and status did not interfere.
+ Paul learned to be content and engaged with both little & much. He could afford to sponsor Timothy's pilgrimage to Jerusalem.
+ Paul believed he was worthy of financial support in ministry, but in one case he chose to set up a tent making business (as in profitable and money-making) to avoid the taint left by prior religious leeches.
+ Paul also wanted Christians to prosper so they'd be in a position to respond to the needs of others.[23]
+ James had a few things to say about money. He's sharply critical of quarreling fueled by greed and self-interest... anything that isn't done from humility, generosity and kindness. Including faith as a hollow theological opinion that doesn't manifest as action.
+ In his letter, he also stated that business plans need to incorporate humility and spiritual sensitivity. And he delivers a blistering Christ/Dylan-like tirade against people who use

wealth to take advantage of others.
* And he says being double-minded will nullify your requests in prayer. (Ask yourself now where you're at with your "I Like Money" declaration, your money-magnet jar and your 101 requests. Ask yourself if they're too much bother, or if you're really that interested in change.)

Laodiceans, look out – John delivers a message from God to the believers in a wealthy city renowned for high-quality gold, fine wool garments, expensive eye salve and a tepid thermal spring that produced undrinkable water. The city was so affluent and fiercely independent that they declined disaster relief funds when an earthquake flattened the place in A.D. 60. God's point wasn't that their wealth was bad, but that it had enabled them to become complacent and uninterested. Again, money was merely highlighting the condition of their hearts – the commercial activities were relevant illustrations to riff on.

Okay, enough for now
There are too many citations of money, wealth and riches to cover them all here, but I hope you're seeing patterns:
* Jesus welcomed both the poor and the rich, but he attacked injustice and attitudes of superiority and privilege.
* Financial illustrations worked really well for what he was saying.
* Personal wealth is secondary, not contrary, to spiritual riches – but you *don't* want to get them reversed.
* Being anxious about money and lifestyle is counterproductive – scarcity is not a virtue if you then worry about it. Neither is affluence if it interferes with our willingness to respond to God's leading.
* Being consumed and distracted by finances is worse – whether you're rich or poor.
* Jesus was surgically separating the Siamese twins of wealth and righteousness because the Pharisees could no longer see the difference, and everyone else had bought into that mindset.

In our Christian cultural mindset, we're accustomed to either being spoon-fed our conclusions, or grazing until we find what we'd prefer and indulging that. This is why I am not advocating any particular financial lifestyle: whether you decide to excel at generating large amounts of money to work with and share, or take the route of self-denial in order to sync up with and serve a group of people more effectively, or something in between... in any case you need to be healthy about money to do things well, in a state of peace and grace.

Your understanding of what the Bible says about money (or rather, the internal contradictions and conflicts you are juggling, balancing and holding in tension within your mindset and emotions) are what have you immobilized, idling or running just to stand still. That's what holds you between tensions such as desire/distrust, blessing/suffering, work/rest, abundance/scarcity, losing/receiving, and so on.

The big point: "Be not anxious"
Jesus said not to be anxious, fretful and distracted with money, clothing and food. "Running after" these things speaks of anxiety. Unfortunately people usually *are* anxious about their finances at some level and to some degree. When we don't have much-money, we naturally tend to fret about it. Yet we cling to anti-wealth clichés which only keep us living with marginal finances and financial stress. *So stop buying into the silly myth that having not-too-much-money means you're somehow free.*

Perhaps you will be called to dramatic giving, self-denial or self-sacrifice. And it may be in a particular instance, or for a defined season or as an ongoing lifestyle. But how free and available will you be to respond to that call if your credit cards are maxed, your savings account is empty, you're stressed about paying rent and caught in a dependent cycle of living from pay cheque to pay cheque? There are no prizes being handed out for wishful thinking. You need to intentionally change your anxiety-producing circumstances, starting with your beliefs and emotions surrounding money.

I'm not saying that being wealthy makes one immune to financial stress. But I would say that having a healthy income and accounts makes it easier to be honestly at peace with money.

Here's another manifestation of being anxious.

The deception of benign scarcity: 'Not too much' & 'Just enough'
There is this misleading, pervasive mentality of 'benign scarcity' in and around the church. So many people, out of the fear of

becoming presumptuous or flamboyant, deliberately downgrade their material expectations, dampen their motivation to generate more money, deflect blessings and pass up opportunities because of vague assumptions that flourishing financially will somehow 'change' them and distance themselves from friends and family. As if! They kid themselves into thinking that if they have not-too-much money then they'll be free from its corrupting influence, that they probably aren't hurting anyone, that no one will be critical or offended, and they'll be less *un*happy.

Because money could disrupt their lives, their relationships and priorities.

Just getting by is success enough.

Thinking small is a sign of humility.

A last-minute bailout by God is an experience of grace.

Financial brinkmanship is the way of faith.

Rubbish! That is inverted selfishness papered over with half-baked piety. If we look outside of ourselves for a different perspective, *i.e.* the sake of others, then having 'just enough' means...

+ you don't have much to share,
+ passivity prevents you from helping where it's needed most,
+ not having to commit to taking risks (I mean, other than "faith" that God or some other sympathetic soul will help the money "come in" just in time),
+ you can avoid the added work and responsibility that success and prosperity will generate (aka, the fear of success),
+ you have a narrow comfort zone that kills through neglect and passivity, leaves the suffering without options and smothers hope,
+ and it's actually a backhanded way of saying, "I'm mostly interested in keeping my own butt barely covered, and not very motivated to mobilize money and people in order to help others."

The religious comfort zone *kills*
The 'just enough... not too much' thing is a cop out. It's a cover for preferring not to get involved. Actually, you *need* surplus money before you'll be in a position to contribute to the needs and encouragement of others. If Jesus' assurance is that the Father already knows you have need of the necessities, then where is the virtue, faith or growth in aspiring to survival budgeting? What employment will you generate by having 'enough' to retire on? How will your inertia encourage a struggling local business? Should some-

one congratulate you for contributing so little to the local tax base? What gratification or congratulation do you suppose you'll garner for knowing exactly where your talent is buried?

What we're talking about here is actually a personal emotional complacency, because in order to be wealthy you'd have to change. In order to see better financial results, you must behave differently; in order to behave differently you have to change your thinking; in order to think differently you have to believe new things and abandon old ways; in order to believe new things you'll have to 'feel' right and energize, not dampen, your emotional and motivational state.

Sometimes the religious will despise the feel-good factor as being either self-gratifying or frivolous. And then they wonder why people aren't flocking to their sides. Mediocrity is not the same as the fellowship of suffering with Christ that the scripture forearms us with – that kind of suffering for his sake (for the sake of his compassion, his purity, his passion for people) is what James said we could count as "all joy". Not stressing over car repair bills. James' all-joy suffering is backed by an underlying confidence and pleasure in the greater good that is being accomplished for the sake of others. That's different from the kind of suffering that Jesus continually confronted and reversed: physical suffering (healing), emotional suffering (love & peace) and spiritual suffering (deliverance). Including financial anxiety. This is true at both the individual and organizational levels.

Aspiring to have 'just enough' money ('barely enough' more like) as some sign of humility is the problem, not the solution. And it is endemic among church folk. What people are really saying points to a root emotional issue and belief, *i.e.* I should not have to change because...
   a) my finances should just cooperate and do the changing for me;
   b) God should make money appear on my terms;
   c) I don't want the responsibility of wealth;
   d) I don't want to give up my 'free time' to generate more money;[24]
   e) all of the above.

The fear of money
Okay, if you really want change in your experience with money, not just talk about how you wish things were different (and that's a

massive shift) then *you* are the one who has to change. Not money – it will not change for you. Or for anyone else. *You* have to do the changing. And in order to change, you're going to have to admit that you're wrong about something.

Easy to say, easy to nod, hard to do.

I still laugh at how difficult I made this for myself, but it comes down to this:

I didn't have more money because I was *wrong*.

And I'll say the same to you:

You don't have more money because you… are… *wrong*.

Money doesn't care what you think. Neither does oxygen – it's just there. All around you. Ready and available. And if you decide it's more noble to use less oxygen and breathe shallow, or even hold your breath, oxygen will not become alarmed and suddenly funnel its way up your nostrils and into your lungs. But it's there for you when you're ready.

Most people who have little money to spare or work with say, "Wouldn't it be great if…" kidding themselves, thinking they now 'have vision'. They say they want something different, but they really don't – they are just soothing themselves. They just want the discomfort to stop and refuse to face the fact that the pain is actually their friend, their messenger, their signal to try something else. Something unfamiliar, something unsettling, something that will stretch and even hurt for a little while. Their comfortable prejudices still reign and the Lord is willing to let them keep reaping it until they've had sufficient to surrender, lose the comfort blanket and embrace some discomfort.

For your experience with money to change, it has to feel unfamiliar, strange and uncomfortable. Like when your joints are bending further than they should, like your skin is stretched too tight, like your tendons might tear, like your muscles are burning.

Most Christians just want to sit and receive "deeper revelation" or supernatural blessing that will prove out their mediocre opinions so they don't have to give up their crummy preferences. They'd rather be wise in their own eyes. What they need is to be confronted, and even offended. Fine, let them have their meager results and keep blaming the rest of the universe, especially the devil, for their own lack of money. We create, and receive, what we really want, and what most people want is to not have to bother changing.

It's time to ditch the small-minded religious fear of wealth
So many believers have this and as a result "rich" continues to be a tarnished word. You don't have to fear riches – fear of anything is not a solution.[25] If you have faith, the opposite of fear, then you can look past the issues that money tends to magnify and stir yourself out of dormancy, and really deal with the root problems. Yes, it entails greater responsibility, greater amounts of time and work, and a greater need for personal accountability, but here's the choice:
Help save lives or stay in your comfort zone.

A good friend of mine has come to realize that money is simply a tool. When he did carpentry and home renovations for a living, he bought a bigger, high-quality wood router and a larger, more expensive, compound mitre box saw. And they made his work easier, faster, less wasteful and more enjoyable. He didn't go to work just so he could use the tools, but they made it more of a pleasure to work. And serve his clients well. Same with money – more money can enable you to work, serve and enjoy what you do. Money makes it easier, faster and less wasteful. And fun. Similarly, when I bought a better-quality guitar, there was a tangible difference in the quality of my experience with it and I can take even more delight in playing, leading congregational worship... even practicing! In both scenarios, money helps. A lot.

There is this kinked logic that equates financial success, even wealth, with selfishness, insensitivity and waste. As if our only options are either meagerness or luxury. And if we opt for meager then that makes us morally superior. Do I hear a *thwack!* out there?

Unfortunately there are some high profile examples of gross and tasteless opulence tarted up as 'blessing'. I don't even need to specify them – you know what I mean. They give prosperity a bad name – I don't even like using the word 'prosperity' because people have become so defensive/protective about the term. Even superstitious. But again, money is simply amplifying the state of somebody's heart and they're compensating for something. (I'm talking about 'them', not you, right?) Taking the charitable view, excesses are just another opportunity for mercy to be needed, sought and found. So let's not take it so personally.

I mean, think about it. What kind of desperation is being comforted there? What need for coddling and pampering? What gaping yaw of need can you fill by hurling gold-gilt pianos and stretch limos into it? Compassion is what's in order, because they won't stop until they come to the realization that it doesn't 'work'. God's already applying his loving pressure on their hearts and you can trust him to be at least as persistent and kind with them as he's being with you, *i.e.* helping them get to the point where, like the parable of the Lost Son, they will come to themselves. That moment will be both terrible and sweet.

Hand on heart, and smile with amusement at yourself...

Lord, I admit that I've judged and despised the opulence displayed by some Christian ministries, denominations and churches, both historical and contemporary – that's just my opinion, not my right, not my place, and I've been wrong to do so.

So, I renounce my judgments against them – please forgive me for holding it in my heart, agreeing with others and even mocking them. Thank-you.

I now choose to bless them to prosper in grace, healing and finances,

and I ask for my own release from any reaping I've been doing in my own finances as a result of my judgments. Thanks.

In the meantime, don't let distaste for how others have handled things put you in a reactionary posture of despising good uses of ample amounts of money. You just get on with it.

So back to you...

The opportunity you have is to handle money differently and by example lead the way out of deprivation and frustration with grace – for yourself, your family, your employees, your congregation, your co-workers, your community and especially for poor strangers who are living in overwhelming circumstances. That would be the poor, the working-poor, the single parents, the homeless, the addicted, the abused, the incarcerated, the persecuted. Motivation enough? Yes, or yes?

If yes, then let's do something to rev up your internal financial generator.

Paul encouraged the relatively well off Christians in Corinth to follow through on their good intentions to give financial assistance (money) to their brothers and sisters in Macedonia, who had themselves responded to "the most severe trial" with "overflowing joy and their extreme poverty welled up in rich generosity."[26] An amazing display of character. So Paul reminded the Corinthians that Jesus himself, "though he was rich, yet for your sakes he became poor, so that you through his poverty might become rich." I know there's profound truth in that on the spiritual/moral/cosmic level, but don't disqualify literal monetary wealth, which is after all the context of his counsel here. The subject on Paul's mind is generosity with money.

On the same topic, Paul also assures his beloved friends that while he wants to see them "excel in everything – in faith, in speech, in knowledge, in complete earnestness and in our love for you ... *see that you also **excel** in this grace of giving.*"

"Excel in the grace of giving." That takes money.
   Lots of money.
More money than 'enough to get by on.' Surplus money.
   Excess money.

"Excel." How does one excel in anything?
   By taking it seriously.   Aiming high.
   Thinking big.   Going for results.
   Focusing.   Devoting energy to it.
   Taking courses about it.   Studying it.
   Being well above average.   Strategizing.
   Making a plan.   Looking for opportunities.
   Taking a risk.   Modeling after successful examples.
   Deciding that you can do it too.   Committing to it.

Unfortunately, money/career/business/investment is a pursuit which very few churches openly encourage, let alone facilitate, people's potential to excel. Well, maybe when it comes to asking for offerings – more on that later too.

Furthermore...
In the same context, Paul assures the Corinthians that "God will make you *rich in every way* so that you can be *generous on every occasion*,"[27] and as a result people will experience gratitude and joy in God. Remember, the situation is financial, so it is a disservice to the scripture to deliberately exclude wealth. Of course "every way" means a lot of other things too, but not to the self-conscious, prejudicial exclusion of money, which is the warped and discour-

aging assumption we foist on ourselves and each other.

Notice who gets to go first:

"God will make you rich ...*pause...* so you can be generous."
He's not asking for blood from living stones. For something you
don't have.
And like Bono said, "My God isn't short of cash, mister." God isn't
anxious about money – he could solve the world's financial crises
with little more than a sneeze.
**God's goal is not to make you rich,
it's for you to become generous.**

You don't have to be rich to be generous – Paul lauds the Macedo-
nians for being generous despite their own poverty. And I believe
they reaped generosity when they needed it for the generosity
they sowed.
But this passage *is* saying that you need money for every occasion
in order to be generous on every occasion.
And to be *really* generous you might *really* need money.

Why? Because bigger gifts are better? No, because of the scale of
the need, the scale of the faith required to bring justice to bear on
those needs, and the enormous scale of God's compassion.
Does that work for you?

Hand on heart:

Lord, I accept! You can work on me!
Make me rich...
*   And give me an occasion...*
*   So I can be generous!*
And may the credit, thanks and satisfaction come back
around to you!

Exercise: God's idea of 'seed capital'

[*Note:* Remember that one of our chief aims right now is to break
out of your mental norms that are perpetuating your financial
frustration. Be open to something different for a while. So for our
purposes, by 'occasion' I'm not talking about your usual church,
favourite charity, current building campaign, ongoing personal
project or someone you're particularly concerned about.
If the finances of one of these concerns looms large in your thoughts
these days, let's mentally park that off to the side so you're free
to come back to it later.

Put your hand on your head, and pray this:
   I understand that _____ is important,
   but I need to learn something different just now.
   So Lord, I'm leaving _____ in your care
   and I will come back to that when this is done.
Your subconscious should be content to wait on the issue and not crowd your thoughts with it, given that you've acknowledged its importance and committed to re-visit it later.
Just make sure you *do* come back to it later.[28]]

Get into a relaxed position, roll your shoulders, remember a time when you relaxed in a sunny spot, such as a porch swing or a dock on the water. How was the view? Did you hear wind or water? How did your body feel?[29]
When you feel strongly engaged with that sense of peace and content-ment, smile, use your key and remind yourself, *"I am rich in _____!"*

Now pray with me and just notice where your thoughts go:
   Father, I want to exercise gratitude for how you've already been
   generous to me. Teach me how to be generous your way.
   Your scripture says that you will make me rich, for the sake of
   an occasion, so I can be generous.
   You also said that you will supply seed for the sower [30], so I'll
   take you at your word.
   I trust you to supply both the occasion and what you want me
   to give.
   Lord, what's the occasion this time? Who will it be for?
   . . . . .

What did you get? A person, a group, a situation, a location?
If you have to go back and try it again, just reset, get back to that peaceful posture, ask, listen and accept what comes to mind. You don't have to mentally scamper around looking for an answer – let it come to you.[31]

Write it here, with today's date:

_____ - __/__/__.
Do not write any amount, even if you think you got that too.

Choose a timeframe for God to work with: a week from now, 10 days or two weeks. Whatever feels right.
Note that date here: __ /__ /__.

And in your own words, tell the Lord you are committed to setting aside whatever 'seed' he supplies between now and then. Tell him now.

There we go. Now, it's up to God to supply that seed, NOT you. Watch what extra money comes to you over the next while, *over and above your expected income*. Your pay cheque does not count. Nor do overtime, outstanding invoices or scheduled interest income. Only what comes spontaneously. This is not about regular giving from what you normally earn. This is about God supplying seed for you to sow into whatever just came to your mind from him.

* If you get an unexpected refund or rebate, put that aside.
* If someone gives you a cash gift, put it aside.
* If somebody pays for something that you'd already allotted money for, such as a meal out, so that suddenly frees up some money, separate it out. (Including what you would have used your bank debit card for in lieu of cash – something that would have gone on credit does not qualify.)
* If a cashier gives you too much change... give it back!
* If you find a coin, that counts. There's no such thing as a small amount in this case.

After the 7, 10 or 14 days are up
When that date arrives, come back to this space and record the amount that he supplied, however large or small, here: _____ .
And use your key to thank him that *"I am rich in _____!"*

Follow through and sow that money where he suggested, confident that ultimately the credit and satisfaction are his. If it's a small amount, that's all you give. If it's a large amount, God bless you with the faith and excitement to give that too.[32]

Record observations, thoughts and feelings that come to you here:

_____

_____

_____

I want to underscore the importance of writing this stuff down. Don't just get ideas and figure you'll remember later. Just reading these things could very well inoculate yourself against them. While we're still working on your ability to hear God's thoughts coming alongside your own, writing it down is a tangible, legible sign to your own self, and to him, of your sincerity.

Financial healing in the Church
The fruit of financial, emotional healing can definitely show up in your congregation's finances. To illustrate, you might be familiar with the passage that describes the fruit of the Holy Spirit's work in one's life being "love, joy, peace, patience, kindness, goodness, gentleness and self-control."[33] That's a lot of fruit and a lot of emotional content. Feelings. In fact, you can't have any of those qualities without embracing the associated emotions.
And guess what: they all feel good!

Now, what if you could...
Express love with gifts of money or stable financial support;
    En-*joy* money and celebrate with it;
    Be at *peace* with money;
    Have the *patience* (resilience with clarity) to see your finances thrive;
    Demonstrate *kindness* and mercy with money;
    Promote *goodness* by financing worthy causes;
    Be *gentle* with money, rather than manipulative, garish or grasping;
    Exercise *self-control* over your financial behaviour?
Would that be a healthy spiritual scenario? Of course.

And what are primary obstacles to feeling good about money and finances?
    Bad experiences.
    Harmful circumstances.
    The lingering pain and apprehension from financial wounds and failures.
And of course that big pile of information, observations, perceptions, opinions, theories, conclusions, lessons, beliefs and habits that accumulate and coagulate around those events.

Family is family
Pastors, if your ministry's finances aren't healthy and thriving, don't blame the congregation. Look to your own familial financial programming. If a platoon of millionaires suddenly joined your congregation and dumped baskets of money into your church's coffers, you'd soon find yourself in the exact same place finan-

cially – whether that's sinking, stuck or stumbling. You'd just have more of the same – a bigger budget to fall short of, bigger plans that have been stymied, or more stressful ups and downs. Like a lottery winner. Remember, your church's money is simply highlighting what's really going on. Finances are the symptom, not the problem. It may be that you're simply reaping in and through your ministry what you've personally sown in judgment from your own upbringing.

Or you're in a not-habit of not-reaping what you have been not-sowing into your church's people.

The Creation, of which your church is a living expression, is giving you financial feedback about what's in your own heart. It is incumbent upon you to look for parallels between the finances of your ministry (church family) and your own upbringing (natural family). So...

How does your ministry's financial state make you feel?
Not what you *think* about what's happening or not happening – stop and reflect on where things are at and consider how that leaves you *feeling.*
    Stuck? Nervous? Resigned? Timid? Resentful? Contentious?
Stop and write it in here:

_____

What words describe the mood among your members and leadership team about finances in general, and especially about money itself? Are you sure you know? Are you sure they can really tell you? Write what your impression is here:

_____

_____

Then consider the humbling prospect of getting honest feedback, understanding that it will be difficult and awkward for whoever you ask. Even if you don't think it should be.

Do your church's finances parallel your family's while you were growing up? Do you see the analogies? The limitations? The crises?
On the left, write five current aspects; on the right fill in parallels from your family life:

My ministry's money mood	My family's money culture
1)	
2)	
3)	
4)	
5)	

Are your spiritual brothers and sisters behaving in a way that reminds you of your natural siblings? Both good and bad?

Is a spiritual father figure, or perhaps the elders (church-fathers) in your congregation, displaying a characteristic you struggled with in your dad?

Is something that angered, frustrated or hurt you as a child now being echoed by 'Mother Church'?

Step back from the problem and look for the pattern
There are so many possibilities and variations that we couldn't conceivably cover them all in this book, but if you're still not connecting with the emotions involved in your money & your ministry & your ministry's money, try one of these to kick start your thinking:

 • How do you honestly feel about the gilded-lily media ministries?
 • "No pastor should make more than the average income in his congregation." Where's the blessing in "average or less"?
 • "We can underpay ministry staff because they can live by faith."

* "It is, after all, a sacrifice to serve the Lord."
* "God wants you to live in affluence because your nation is favoured by God – wealth is your right as a believer."
* Stewardship = doing things on the cheap.
  'Free' is worth the hassle.
* The church encourages excellence, except in business and making money.

Where any of those rankle, and peace is not the arbiter in your heart, you've got issues and they will manifest in your ministry's finances. Consider this seriously:

If you've got the fruit, you've got the root.

And in his unfathomable patience and mercy, the Lord is *presenting* you (as in a present or gift) with another opportunity to remove that hardened, brittle, stony bit of your heart and allow him to replace it with resilient, flexible, soft flesh. Remember this is not about blame, it's about responsibility.

If you recognize the parallels, I suggest flipping back to *Chapter 6: Pruning Your Family Money Tree* to do the work of unhooking those family dynamics from your ministry's future. If you resolve those issues within your own heart, you'll see the spiritual freedom reflected in your personal finances and your ministry's finances too.

The egg and the chicken

Here's another dynamic. As the pastor's finances go, so go the church's. And *vice versa*. It's simple enough to understand that if a church is struggling financially that can lead to the rationalization that it's okay for the pastor's family struggle financially as well. Wrong, but understandable. So the pastor gets underpaid. But that energy current actually runs in both directions.

I've seen this is especially true where the senior pastor operates from a key man position, in a top-down, paternal fashion like an owner, sole proprietor or chief executive officer. The pastor's financial programming exerts influence at every level – materially and spiritually – based on his sense of conviction (what feels right) about the ministry's finances, his staff's pay levels, his personal income, and even the finances of the congregation's families. He will continually be broadcasting his own perspectives, beliefs and expectations about money at different levels (remember: body language / tone of voice / content) and he *will* shape the members' own expectations and experience.

Alternatively, if you're in a church that's essentially driven by a board structure that cycles pastors in and out, and you're on the committee or board that helps to govern salary levels, vacation time, benefits, health care, bonuses, and so forth, consider this very carefully: the way you treat your staff is the way your congregation will treat your church. Treat your staff well and you will see resulting health in your church's money moods.

In either case, the same holds true:
Sow generously, reap generously;
    or, sow sparingly, reap sparingly.
Share the ministry's success monetarily, and the resources for
    further success will multiply;
    or stifle them and you'll find yourself stymied.
Be openhanded with them and watch the church's finances
    open up;
    or squeeze them and you'll feel the pinch.
Honour your people financially and the Lord will honour your
    other spending plans;
    or renege, and you'll find God's promises somehow
    not-materializing.

If your strategy is to see how much bang for the buck you get from your staff, don't be surprised if the members are more interested in what they get out of church than how they can contribute. As Paul said, we should be competing with each other only in the sense of trying to outdo each other in love, encouragement and kindness. Otherwise, you may find yourself caught in the... um, tension between platform exhortations for generosity, and the in-house, behind-the-scenes realities.

And no, the irony will not be lost on people. They will respond. Either to your encouragement or to your chagrin.

If you're in a leadership capacity and you want to see your ministry's financial health flourish, consider how you're treating those within the spiritual household. If you want to see generosity flowing, guess who gets to take the lead.

Check the car-o-meter
On a lighter note, think about this one. If you want an idea of how healthy a church's finances are, look at the staff's cars.[34] They are very likely revealing metaphors for the tone of the ministry

in general.
+ What shape is "the body" in?
+ Is the interior cluttered or tidy?
+ Is it a mechanic's poster child or a credit to the congregation?
+ 'High maintenance'? Running on borrowed time?
+ Does it make a success statement, when in fact it's financed to the hilt?
+ Is it built to last or will it be turned over every few years?
+ Does it have style and presence or is it plain, unremarkable and unnoticed?
+ Cheering or boring? Homely or garish?
+ Is riding in it a fun or worrisome experience?
+ Is it a rolling embarrassment with a couple of ineffectual religious sentiments slapped on the bumper?
+ In general, is it a vehicle for ministry, or a liability?

I am still perplexed by the number of (verified) stories of pastors selling off Mercedes Benzes or BMWs because others objected (or might object) to the optics. Even when it was given to them, and despite the fact that they tend to be more reliable in the short term and more economical in the long run. So they trade for some bland, unreliable, money-sucking econo-model that deteriorates and depreciates rapidly. Sad.

Think about the different churches you've attended. The different pastors you've known. I think you'll I see that when it comes to finances, the scripture, "As a man thinketh, so is he." applies at the congregational / corporate / organizational level too.

I like what Martin Luther had to say on this:
I have held many things in my hands,
* and I have lost them all;*
But whatever I have placed in God's hands,
* that I still possess.*
If we surrender and deal with our stuff,
  we'll be amazed at what we're left with.

So, are you ready for more freedom?
  To shed the burdens of the past?
    To transform old obstacles into new portals to fulfillment?
    Let's go...

1 Genesis 1:1, 2:4

2 The matter of Job's daughters, their intrinsic worth, their inheritance and status is huge, given the cultural context.

3 Remember how Jesus got impatient with someone who wanted to wait until he'd buried his folks before following his calling?

4 A Christ-figure: prophet, priest and king, ministering in Jerusalem to God and Gentiles (pre-Jewishness and outside Abraham's line).

5 Malachi 3:10

6 A gold aurelius equaled 25 silver denarii; 1 denarius was standard wage for a day's labour.

7 40 gold coins = 40 month's salary @ $3,125/month (half the average Canadian household income) = $125,000.

8 Would Jesus have not realized Judas was embezzling? Perhaps there was more to Jesus' thinking than protecting the cash reserve…

9 John Arnott.

10 T. Harv Ecker.

11 Luke 18:18

12 Luke 18:9

13 Remember, Jesus came to fulfill/complete/satisfy the Law. He was blameless under the Law, so it's reasonable to think he'd already done what he proposed to the RYR. We're no longer obliged except to live by the spirit of the Law – its loving intentions. Besides, under the Law, giving to the poor is like lending to God, who will repay because he's no man's debtor, so the RYR stood to come out well if he could manage the faith and get past his class-consciousness.

14 Luke 16

15 Luke 16:9

16 Luke 12:48

17 II Corinthians 8

18 The atmosphere wherein people were laying gifts at the apostles' feet to serve the needy, including the proceeds of real estate sales, did not buy them immunity from persecution. It wasn't long before Stephen's murder and a wave of persecution that scattered many of the local believers.

19 Acts 8:18-24

20 Luke 16:19

21 It gets better: Lazarus ("helpless") is a variant of Eliezer ("God helps") which was the name of Abraham's servant – his Gentile heir prior to Isaac's arrival.

22 Luke 12:16-21

23 II Corinthians 9.

24 In this case, free time is a misnomer because it's costing you a lot – directly and indirectly.

25 Fear of God is a different thing – we could probably use more words for 'fear', like the Greeks had for 'love' and the Inuit have for 'snow'.

26 II Corinthians 8

27 II Corinthians 9

28 This dynamic also really helps in other contexts, such as when you're studying or working on something while other concerns weigh on your mind.

29 Don't deliberately paste Jesus into this scene, but you may sense his presence with you.

30 II Corinthians 9

31 If what came to mind is a personal project or pursuit that leads to a bigger dream or purpose, that counts!

32 If nothing comes in, don't worry about it, God's probably preparing you in some other way for now. No guilt! Come back to this exercise later, perhaps after you've finished the rest of the book, and see what happens then.

33 Galatians 5:22

34 Years ago, an evangelical satirical magazine (yup) called *The Wittenburg Door* [sic] ran a photo contest in search of the worst pastor's vehicle. Funny, in a sad way.

Chapter 8

Clearing the Clutter, part 3

Let's Make This Personal

Well, seeing that I haven't offended or shocked you enough to put you off completely with that last chapter, thank-you for sticking with me. Because this chapter is kind of a long one, but it comes to an exciting conclusion, so stay with me, tackle what's ahead. It's fine if you break it up into a few different sittings because we're going deep and long.

Oh, and remember to track whatever extra 'seed' God provides for you as a sower and follow through on sowing into that circumstance you identified. Through this, your heart is learning to be Spirit-led when occasions present themselves rather than...
    seeing a situation
        thinking about whether you should give or not
            deciding what you can give
                based on what you suppose you can afford.
This is a great way of taking the striving out of giving and allowing the Lord to direct, rather than our interpretations and opinions about tithing and so forth. I would love to hear about how the Lord responds in your case – please visit my website at www.healingyourfinancialsoul.com and tell us your story!

And I bless you for your willingness to embrace change. This kind of change is not easy because it involves coming to grips with what you'd rather wasn't true:
    things about ourselves and people we love,
        the decisions we used to be convinced of,
            all the time, energy and resources (including money)
                already invested in thinking, believing, talking
                and acting as if they were true.
It's hard to let go of your right to think you were right all this time and accept that the outcome is proving you wrong.

Don't take that as a personal criticism. In a very real sense, it's pretty amazing that we're all still here and sane. Our minds are so complex, agile and adept that they will not balk at the assignment of carrying contradictory, conflicting, self-fulfilling and self-defeating expectations, no matter how frustrating and painful the external circumstances become as a result. That's how skillful, imaginative and accommodating your mind is. You're actually more brilliant than anyone has ever given you credit for!

Brilliant, but burdened

Right now, your brain is processing massive amounts of information – to stay sane, your mind is consciously aware of a fraction of it all. That leaves a huge amount of processing to go on below your stream of thoughts, observations and noticed sensations. So there's lots of capacity maintaining a lot of autonomic, automatic input and feedback, including outdated or negative thought patterns and belief programs, especially if emotional content fuels them with a sense of urgency, pain, need or gratification.

The upside is that this is also the subsurface cauldron where innovations, inspirations, thoughtfulness, motivation and nobility can spring from.

The downside is that this is also how people get so embroiled in toxic, co-dependent relationships, and even go on to rationalize, accommodate and fulfill their own worst conscious fears – such as the son of alcoholic parents who despite all he's seen, heard and felt, goes on to cultivate his own alcoholic dysfunction. Or a woman who accepts and enables an abusive relationship. Despite what one might 'know', the mind makes this kind of paradox possible. Because it's been asked and because it can.

The subconscious is very agreeable and willingly takes on an assignment even if it's self-defeating because the conscious mind, the figurehead, is preoccupied with just coping with the moment via momentary options and preferences chosen in order to navigate safely through the 'now'. Survival.

The assignment gets downloaded to our mix of emotions, subconscious, and even physical body language, without necessarily canceling the mouldy-oldy mandates that are now no longer relevant, or even counterproductive. Even if the new input is desperate and objectively not true (such as, "This will help" or "If this flops, then I'll get to relax" or "I don't want to be noticed") the mind quickly and cleverly finds ways to accommodate both the latest directive and preserve the old ones. Or will implode on itself trying.

It takes tremendous energy to maintain the tension and effort of juggling both your true, healthy motivations and beliefs, and all the accumulated momentary expediencies – that gap, and the energy maintaining it, is what we call 'stress'. It's the difference between what you really want and what you're still trying to make work.

So if your job causes you stress,
 if your relationships cause you stress,
  if your commitments cause you stress,
   if your finances cause you stress,
...it's because you are not functioning in harmony with your true desires. Your surface thinking, speech and actions are out of sync with your deeper values.

Some of that is because you need to adjust your thinking, habits and circumstances; some of it is because you've got sub-surface in-fighting going on between old directives. If you're into computers, you might think of this as conflicts between pieces of legacy software.

All we're doing here is stopping long enough to acknowledge, interrupt and cancel the manky, skanky old routines and programs, and reintroducing the element of free will – choice.
 Then you're at liberty to review, edit, unburden, clarify, simplify, and streamline your belief system.
 Then all the energy and subconscious effort that has gone into maintaining outdated contradictions can be devoted instead to the results you really want:
  focus, purpose, accomplishment, fulfillment.
Whatever those look like for you – peace at home, opportunity for your kids, encouragement for others, help for the needy, a better job, a profitable business, an extra goat in the backyard, whatever.

So although the delving we've been doing can be unsettling, a bit embarrassing, even painful, it's controversy with a purpose – to unseat outdated beliefs and perspectives that may have made sense at the time, even worked temporarily, but are now undermining and sabotaging your capacity to attract, generate, retain and handle money.
This disruption is worth it.

Creeping accommodation
Of course it gets awkward. It confronts strong loyalties. When Jesus

upended the money tables in the temple, cleared out the livestock and generally wailed on the businessmen, it was more than awkward and disruptive. But it was similar to what you're doing now. Jesus probably looked like a Jew assaulting his own temple and tradition – but he knew to discern and divide between God-inspired intention and 'creeping accommodation'. Out of his love for the true purpose of the temple (to be a house of prayer for all nations), he saw a situation that had devolved into exclusive, self-contradicting behaviour. And he knew it had to be reset, put back in order, and boldly confronted with the temple's original, intended purpose. As upsetting, even confusing and chaotic, as that was.

But let's think for a minute about what the back-story may have been for things to have reached that point. The commercial activity he attacked was in all likelihood the result of a long series of bits of feedback, discomfort, complaints, committee reports, recommendations, motions and decisions by well-intentioned people to solve logistical problems and make the temple operation more convenient for the visitors, to improve security, to accommodate the volume of traffic (human and animal). At each point, each change made sense, solved a little problem, smoothed things out and brought in more income. And they eventually created a mess at odds with the temple's own purpose.

Hence, Jesus cleaning house in a dramatic, provocative and disruptive manner. Controversy.

This is the nature of rules 'n' regs: a series of glitches, anomalies, odd exceptions and problems builds up a thick layer of preventative measures to fortify against imaginable recurrences. And rather than accept the temporary inconvenience, over-splash and trickle of exceptions, and occasional mop-up duties, we wind up with this onerous codex of preventative measures and protective 'policy' that smothers the very source of inspiration.

There came a gradual turn, a shift by degrees where the well-intentioned motivation to serve the experience of the
     customer / member / visitor / user / public / congregation
became a barricade of requirements and policy to serve and blanket the
     host / organization / company / department / ministry.

It's human nature. It's the way of human institutions. It's the way of government, bureaucracy and culture. The cooperative created to provide benefits becomes a blockade of controls. It's why institutions, both public and private, become so frustrating, discouraging and even antagonistic to their own constituents.

The point, please
This is exactly what we do to ourselves. Internally. It's why we find ourselves financially stuck, bound up and entangled.
   A one-off reaction becomes, "I'll never help *them* again."
   An acceptable margin of error becomes, "It's such a hassle."
   A temporary setback becomes, "It doesn't work for me."
   Someone else's progress becomes, "I don't have what it takes."
   An in-flight adjustment becomes, "Steer way-ay-ay clear."
As an individual, your own Internal Department of Rules 'n' Regs has understandably cultivated a complicated tangle of self-perpetuating policy that stands between you and financial abundance, responsive action and profitable ventures into new areas of attitude, speech and action.

So these chapters are about deliberate controversy. You and Jesus stepping in and upending the tables of good intentions, felt needs, accommodations and accumulated policies that have evolved to a point where they're self-serving in spite of you. And against your original purpose to grow, be fruitful, multiply, prosper, thrive, celebrate and live in a constant state of gratitude.

This is why we're cleaning house:
   You were created to be a thanks-giving generator!
      You're designed to be a blessing transmitter!
         You're meant to be an opportunity & reward magnet!

And although external circumstances have provided you with the resistances and complications you've accepted as 'part of the game', you still have time to undo the tangle and get back to your God-intended purpose.

So push past feelings of being awkward or disloyal or exposed. Welcome this internal controversy, because without a period of controversy and disruption, you (like the temple in Jerusalem) probably can't get back to that original purpose to prosper and thrive.

And this is not to disrespect everything that has brought us thus far. We should respect and honour the tangible efforts, willing

hearts and determined minds of people who have gone before, and often paid dearly for their willingness to embrace what was needed for their time. For example, if you've moved on from one church tradition to another, speak fondly of your heritage. Humour helps, mockery doesn't. The same goes for previous employers, bosses, employees, partners, *et al.*
Including the bad ones, and you'll soon see why...

Now let's get personal
Remember way back we talked about the differences between blame and responsibility in your financial circumstances? Well, we're about to dramatically re-shape your internal landscape regarding money by re-solving lingering personal financial dilemmas, crises and disasters by sorting between blame and responsibility at levels deeper than opinion, reason and rationalization.

Why? Because no matter how long ago they occurred, the disappointments, frustrations and stresses that you've incurred run deeper than your surface attempts to shrug them off and move on. Even if you've "changed your mind" about them and acknowledged the emotional upset, the impact is likely still rooted into your beliefs, subconscious and even your physical body.

The impact of financial trouble resonates deeply. Otherwise, when those negative situations arose, you wouldn't have found them such a physical drain on your energy, your face wouldn't have gained a wrinkle or two from the stress, and I can guarantee that your body language and posture were registering how you were feeling too. (Lord knows, mine did.) Those experiences reverberated deeply, and set into motion entire mechanisms of emotional responses, physical expression, reflexive decisions and compensating behaviour – all the internal counterbalances and rationalizations that you're still using mental and emotional energy to maintain.

My visual analogy is the kind of vaudeville act I used to see on The Ed Sullivan Show. A balance artist would place a plate on the end of an upright stick and spin it. The plate's centripetal energy kept it balanced there and he'd start up a whole row of sticks & plates. Soon he'd be dashing back and forth behind the row of plates & sticks, adding spin when they lost momentum and started to wobble. His objective was to keep as many plates spinning as possible before any toppled to the stage floor. A lot of people feel like that in their day-to-day lives. Right now it's happening inside you and your soul is deftly keeping as many plates spinning as it can.

And just because you consciously want something different doesn't mean that all of your background emotional platespinners, subconscious functions and body-language management teams 'got the memo'. Or feel that they've been properly heard out. They are, in all likelihood, still bearing the effects of discouraging circumstances, shabby treatment and bad news – the stuff that made you suck in your breath, your stomach sink, your chest feel heavy, your head spin, your shoulders slump, your voice drop, your eyes lower, your conscious attention zone out, your energy evaporate... You're physically remembering those moments and sensations right now, aren't you? It's because they still reside in your body language, your autonomic nervous system, your emotions, beliefs and subconscious thoughts.

If it was possible to be completely detached and objective, we'd be physically, emotionally and subconsciously resilient in the face of...
 * a bad management decision
 * a dive in share prices
 * a bully you no longer work for.
Objectively you might try to tell yourself it doesn't matter. After all,
 * you didn't decide to close the department
 * you stayed the course when the market dumped your stock
 * the bully didn't make you go to work.
But the related stress took its toll. Especially if you thought and felt like you had no choice in how you were being affected.

Your finances probably continue to tell the same tale. Just because your conscious focus has found other matters to glom onto, don't assume that your entire being made that corner. Your conscious mind finds it (all too) easy to flit from idea to idea, to reverse decisions, rationalize and choose to look the other way. So you can change jobs, switch careers, close the business, lay someone off, find a new broker, cut up your credit cards, write up a new budget, try a new diet... whatever, because these tactics promise help.

But beneath the surface, it's like those Japanese soldiers lost out in the jungle for decades after World War II ended – they continue to operate in survival mode because they never got the order to stop. Your faulty old "truths" are like that. They're underground, deftly avoiding detection, preserving themselves, ready to lash out if confronted and running something of a guerilla war against any activity that doesn't conform with their old information and convictions.

And don't think that just pouring more money over these issues will solve them. The wealthy are not exempt.

'Stuck' is still 'stuck'

A dear friend was describing what a frustrating, turbulent experience it can be to buy clothes. "I'll go into a store I like and tell myself it's okay to be good to myself and buy something I like, that fits well and feels good. But then I get home and feel guilty for spending the money – I feel terrible.

"So the next time I need something I'll buy something cheap instead, but I can tell the colour is wrong, the cut isn't right, the fabric doesn't hang properly and I'm not going to be comfortable and confident. So it stays in the closet, and that's a *complete* waste of money. I know it doesn't make sense and I can reason and argue and talk to myself all I want, but I just get tied up in knots inside."

Sound familiar? Everyone has those internal second-guessing sessions about spending money.[1] The thing is, this humble soul I'm quoting is worth millions. A couple hundred dollars one way or the other won't make any difference whatsoever to their bank account. But what a difference it would make to their enjoyment and performance both at work and at home. These things loom large for everyone and we will continue to be driven back and forth with emotional reactions until we change our beliefs and emotional state regarding money. Having a lot of money doesn't solve it because the money just highlights the old emotional patterns from one's upbringing, programming and past experiences.

I know of a man from a wealthy background – it's all inheritance money running generations deep. He flies everywhere first class, he'll never have to work or worry, the money is there in perpetuity. Problem is, every time he attempts to start something of his own – businesses, real estate deals, personal projects – they always fizzle. He doesn't get wiped out, but he gets nowhere. Success eludes him. So he's actually stuck at the level he was born into and is conditioned to accept as 'normal'. At least he's stuck being rich, but what does this pattern of frustration do to one's personal motivation and sense of self-worth among his peers?

Clearly money is illuminating a self-fulfilling, internal pattern of beliefs and expectations.

So, you can be rich and have these issues, or you can be broke and have these issues. Personally, I prefer the wealthy scenario. But just as both rich and poor share the issues, both can also be free of them. When these things get sorted, the poor are more likely to succeed at solving the poverty of their families and their communities, and the successes of the rich will generate economic effects of increased employment, more money circulation and more participation in their community's growth and prosperity.

Cumulative carry-overs

When something like a traumatic financial event (such as being cheated) or persistent pressure (like a toxic work environment) impacts us emotionally, it leverages our inner balances and counterbalances to compensate. Kind of like playing 'Crack the Whip' when you were a kid on a skating rink: the leader (one's surface logic) changes direction with just one or two deliberate steps, but by the time the last kid on the line gets the change, they're hanging on for dear life. Or they break loose and go hurtling down the ice – that would be analogous to stress-induced physical illness. A pep talk and a bit of rationalization won't suffice to countermand the chain reaction that has been set into motion in our emotions, beliefs, bodies, actions and results. They do their very best to hang on.

Simple example: One of my university roommates used to hold his right hand curled at an odd angle against his chest as he dawdled around the apartment. Especially when he'd just woken up. I asked him about it one day and he explained that a year earlier he'd cut his hand badly at work and his hand was bandaged for a couple of months. He developed the habit of holding his hand in this defensive posture because bumping it was sharply painful. Although the physical healing had been done and it no longer pained him to bump his hand, he retained the subconscious, comforting, physical habit of holding his hand like that, particularly when his thoughts were elsewhere and he was going about on autopilot.

We have the same subconscious programs running from past emotionally-charged financial experiences too. Take the old chestnut: "Once bitten, twice shy." Look at the emotional metamorphosis

implied there: from trust and willingness to wariness and pessimism. We carry things over from instance to instance.
    Time does not heal.
        At best it buries.
        And this stuff doesn't keep well.

Everyone's got these incidents in their log book of experience. The good news, actually the great news, is we can turn those lumps of lead into gold. It might not wind up looking like what you'd expect, but it will revolutionize your finances and your future.

Breakthroughs come by breaking *through*
There's something that I've seen clearly and repeatedly during my 15 years' experience in counseling and prayer ministry, both as a layman and as a pastor and spiritual director. I have needed ministry into disappointing, hurtful, even shocking financial experiences myself. And I've learned and observed that a person's willingness to acknowledge, face, tackle and plunge through to the other side of a past experience, rather than expend energy and time trying to ignore, accommodate or compensate for it, determines whether they are ever truly free of its effects.

And not just relieved of the direct negative effects, but able to turn that piece of their personal history into a source of strength, opportunity and generosity.
    ♦ *Strength* because you take away its residual interference in your life, or 'charge' as a friend calls it, and that freed up energy makes you more resilient
    ♦ *Opportunity* because the lessons and level of appreciation (wisdom) you gain cannot be owned any other way
    ♦ *Generosity* because you can multiply the acquired wisdom in the lives of others by being an observable example, by intentionally sharing, and by helping others get through similar challenges.

I guarantee this: If what you've experienced financially
    is a pattern of frustration, deprivation or avoidance,
        it will re-visit you as many times,
            in as many different guises,
                as it takes until you deal with those mechanisms
                    of emotions / beliefs / attitudes / expectations
                        thoroughly.

Why? Because God loves you the way you are,
  and he loves you too much to leave you the way you are.
    Not because he's squeamish,
      but because of how much vision he has for you.[2]

Do we really need to go back over all that stuff?

Usually. In fact, it's to your benefit – they're a source of untapped strength and unrecognized opportunity.

  The points of contention, the areas of resistance, the times,
  places and people in your worst experiences and struggles
  can either be left as bad history and place markers of pain
  and unfairness,
  or they will become your entry points to healing, resilience and
  enlightenment.

Remember, after his resurrection Jesus still had nail marks in his hands and a wound in his side. And they became Thomas' point of revelation and healing.

The good news is that you get to choose which way it's going to be

  The not-so-good news is that God's creation will keep offering you 'opportunities' to solve and re-solve the matter until
  it's done.
  You will keep bumping that sore thumb and wincing in pain
  until you deal with that splinter you picked up.
  It's out of his mercy that God doesn't just shrug off these
  things.

We cannot change history, but if you're willing, you can take away its lingering, frustrating power over you.

  You can neutralize the gravity it still exerts on your core beliefs,
  moods, thinking, hopes & expectations, choices & results.
  And after, you'll witness God's way of leveraging those things
  to great advantage.
  Redemption isn't just salvaging what's left – it goes beyond
  restoration to transformation.

Including in your relationships, if you're willing to push through to the other side. Offenses, wrangling and challenges, once you've come out the other side together, actually become part of your shared history, and reasons for enduring friendship. Even humour.

Calling it what it was

We can be honest: anxiety and ambition bring out terrible things in people's behaviour, and money and finances amplify matters:
*   The abusive employers, the crooked investment dealers, the stingy parents, the controlling spouses, the manipulative friendships,
*   the negligent policies, the domineering teaching, the fine print, the politics, the advantage taken,
*   the failed businesses, the bad loans, the bounced cheques, the missed opportunities, the negative performance reviews,
*   the broken word, the confiscations, the foreclosures, the torpedoed deals, the plugs pulled, the questions left unasked and unanswered,
*   the cheating, the reneging, the stonewalling, the stealing, the sidestepping, the dropping, the insecurity, the egos, the jealousies,
*   the crashes, the lies, the betrayals, the surprises, the rip-offs, the shortchanging, the cheap tricks... anything I haven't covered? ...
... any and all of it can be transformed. All of it.

And not just patched, canceled or dropped. I mean redeemed and blessed to become a healthier, richer experience leading to great fruitfulness.
Out of mistakes and deprivations, misuses and abuses, regrets and remorse can come empowering lessons, causes to embrace, encouragement for others. Even prosperity.
And that's what we're aiming for.

Given that no one is entitled to a disappointment-free life, the only constructive option is to bring these things to God and see what he can do with them. Jesus said that unless a seed goes dormant and falls into the ground it cannot bear fruit. He was a personal example. So was Joseph. And Moses. And Job. And look at what they went on to do with their lives.

A dear friend pointed out that we are like grapevines that are pruned where we have not been fruitful... *and where we have been fruitful*. And in both cases, the pruning leads to greater fruitfulness. So if you feel like you've been deliberately cut back or pinched off, or experienced some seasonal winter-kill, then you have the option of choosing to believe for a coming season of fruitfulness in those very same areas.

Your choice. And it won't happen until you choose it.

One thing I know that *never* helps is allowing these experiences to mould us into the role and identity of 'the victim'. Yes, I know from personal experience that sometimes we are victimized, and realistically at that juncture we are in the position of being the victim. No merit in denial. But we have a choice as to whether that will be temporary or *if it will become our identity*. At some point we should be able to say, "I *was* the victim of such'n'such. But *now* I'm a such'n'such specialist. And I work with people who have such'n'such in their lives."

Surprisingly often, the very area in which one is wronged can become a calling and destiny – including financially. Which means more money for you. That's where we're going.

A victim reformed
For certain, a victim mentality will keep you bound to that financial trauma or frustration, and will sabotage any hopes or attempts to prosper financially.

What does it feel like to be a victim? A victim mentality is resignation to weakness and powerlessness, and it becomes one's *modus operandi*. It preemptively disqualifies us and dictates what we will or won't do:
> We don't attempt something because...
> We stay home because...
> We don't start that business because...
> We stick with a discouraging job because...
> We don't learn to play that instrument because...
> We buy dull clothes because...
> We don't save or invest because...
> We avoid risk because...
> We don't get back in shape because...
> We don't buy a house because...
> We let our appearance go because...
> We don't finish school because...
> We stay quiet because...
> We don't take that trip because...
> We get 'seconds' because...
> We don't go into missions because...

It looks like weakness, when actually it is a *powerful* mechanism that blocks, deprives and binds. It steals strength.

That pattern of negative fortunetelling is woven with self-defeating assumptions and stitched together with lies about one's self. The truth is that we all possess
  every positive characteristic
    to some degree.

Because we are all made in God's image...
We are all creative. We all have memories. We can all love. We can all imagine. We can all be brave. We can all communicate thoughts. We can all express our emotions. We all have some measure of confidence. We can all exercise self control. We can all think abstractly. We can all use language. We can all be a friend. We can all plan ahead. We all have bodies that heal. We all have some sense of rhythm. We can all appreciate some form of art. We can all do math in our head.

So I'll repeat:
  We can all do > at least a little > of all things.[4]

This is not pretending or wishful thinking. Given that we're all running on a small fraction of our mental capacity, it's only logical that whatever we need more of can be located, dialed up, intended, cultivated, commissioned and encouraged to excel. Because God placed that deposit in us: his image. Including whatever you needed when that financial crisis came, waylaid you and left you feeling like a victim. You just weren't in touch with it at that time.

The image of God, Christ in you, the mind of Christ, whatever term you want to use, the Lord has gifted you with the antidote you need. If you believe what Paul said, that God will not allow us to be tested (proven) beyond what we are able[5], then the finest form of gratitude you can express is to lay hold of that situation, leverage it, apply it and redeem its place in your personal history and internal belief system. Then you'll be equipped to work out the positive possibilities in your finances.

First, let's take care of you
Let's intercept a circuit in your victim mentality – the self-fulfilling belief/feeling that came out of a financial situation in which you were victimized, and cancel it by tapping into your God-given resources.

Get a pen and sit somewhere you won't be disturbed for a few minutes – make it something upright, not gooshy like a deep couch or recliner. (This exercise works well with a partner to walk you through the steps, but it also works solo.) Let's pray:

Holy Spirit, please be my counselor – which of my experiences do you want to heal and redeem today?

♦ Think of one situation in which you were financially victimized – short-changed, forced out, trapped in, passed over, ripped off, cheated, manipulated by family, mowed down by the market, betrayed at church... Just one. Give it a title and write it here:

♦ How old were you? What stage of life were you in: child, teen, apprentice, employee, spouse, parent, investor, manager, owner? Did you tend to dress a certain way? What kind of physical shape were you in? Your status? Can you remember how life generally felt to you?

♦ Take a deep breath, shrug and picture in front of you a large movie screen showing a favourite place to sit on your own and reflect, like a beach, dock, balcony or fireside, about a stone's throw away. Sitting there is a person who looks remarkably like you at that time in your life – actually, that situation just happened. Notice their clothing and hair; how they're sitting, their posture and body language.

♦ Do you see it in black & white or colour? Note if the colours are strong or muted. Adjust the colour setting to be richer, the focus sharper.

♦ Do you hear anything? Turn up the volume to hear more of the ambient sound around you.

♦ Is the outside frame of what you're seeing distinct or does it roll off? Adjust the size of the frame to take up 3/4 of your field of vision.

♦ Can you sympathize with what that person sitting there is feeling? What they're going through? The sensations in their chest, stomach, joints, shoulders or head? How's their breathing? What thoughts, words or names are cycling through their mind?

♦ Ask yourself, "What do they really need right now?" What characteristic, what personal quality does that person need to come through this in good shape? Listen for the first word that surfaces. Hold that word in your mind.

Write it here: _____

(It might be peace, hope, boldness, vision, energy, tenacity...

whatever comes quickly.)
* Now up and to your left, picture another smaller video monitor, and on that screen an image of Jesus, when his life exhibited that same needed quality. Why do you associate that quality with him?
* Picture that clearly, notice how that taps into and stirs your own God-given capacity for that quality – deliberately lay hold of it with your mind, let it fill your heart and choose faith for it... breathe it in until your cup is brimming and is about to run over.
Thank-you Jesus, that by your wounds, my wounds are healed.
* Then ask the Lord: *Jesus, when my soul was wounded, open and vulnerable, did the enemy of my soul sow the seed of a lie that I've believed because under those circumstances it felt true?*
Write the very first statement that comes to you:

Okay Lord, if that's the lie, then what's your truth? What do you say about that?
Write the first thing that comes:

Thank-you Lord!
[Note: that lie probably sounded like a plausible, realistic perspective – that made it believable. But it's actually a convincing distortion that circumstances sold you, which has been hobbling your progress. Be aggressive about clearing it out!]
* Now let's check on your friend seated over there. Has the scene changed? The mood? How do you feel now when you 'look' at them? Do they look any different? Can you tell if they now feel at peace about that financial situation? Write any impressions here:

+ If they aren't entirely peaceful and at ease, what other quality or internal resource do they need?
Write it here: _____

+ Repeat as needed.
The litmus test is the peace they/you feel about that situation. If your view of yourself in light of that situation is not yet
peaceful, hopeful and confident, look intently and ask yourself again what quality that person needs. Go back to the Lord
as your example and let his Spirit impart it to you as a gift.
Check for any distorted beliefs that seemed 'true enough' at
the time, ask for *his* perspective on it, and you should find
the view of yourself more and more restored.
+ And finish with "Know what? *I am rich in* _____*!*"

Feel good? You've just accomplished several things:
+ Faced a painful piece of your own financial history
+ Sought the Lord about it
+ Let him reveal a self-perpetuating, debilitating belief you
picked up from that incident[6]
+ Let his truth supplant that lie – his truth breaks the yoke
of victimization.

Let the peace of Christ be the arbiter
If, when you check, that impression of yourself sitting out there
still seems to be suffering in some way, then you can repeat the
process as many times as you need. Perhaps from a different
angle, such as the relationships involved, or the physical toll. It
may be that circumstances left you with other false impressions
and beliefs. So,
+ identify the needed quality
+ seek it in him
+ ask him to shed light on what the distorted 'facts' were
+ and ask him for his true perspective instead.

You'll find that his truth flushes away the lies and the debilitating
feelings that help hold them in place – you'll be left with his transforming truth and probably some gem of wisdom.

This process might expand your understanding of Paul's encouragement to "not be *con*formed to (shaped by) this world, but be
*trans*formed by the renewing of your mind. Then you'll be able to
prove and affirm God's good, pleasing and perfect will."[7]

Your homework

You can now apply this model of reflection and meditation to any financial setback you've experienced. So let's be proactive about it and go through as many as still carry any twinge of regret. The earlier the incident the better – your stolen baseball glove, the embarrassing clothes you had to wear, being left behind for lack of registration money. Don't dismiss them as 'normal' or 'childish' or 'growing pains'. They've all helped shape your beliefs about

what you deserve,

what you're worth,

what's likely to happen to you,

whether you'll ever get ahead.

They're all shards of self-fulfilling prophecy that need to be neutralized or they will continue to exert gravity on your decisions (or indecision) with money. In all likelihood, you will continue to exhibit victim behaviour until the experience is resolved

as in, re-solved

at the levels of emotion and body-language.

They're like old landmines lying in wait until you come upon another similar circumstances or opportunities affecting your finances, relationships and personal goals. We cannot change the past, but we can defuse it and take away its power over you in the present and future.

Take a couple of minutes and use this space to list your negative financial experiences such as family disputes, social status & self-worth, living conditions, employment issues, investment disasters, and so on:

_____

_____

_____

_____

_____

Take a bit of time

Will you commit to applying Jesus' model life and the Holy Spirit's truth directly to the emotional and mental wounds that have shaped your perspective, expectations, decisions and relationship with money?

If your answer is yes, then block out time over the next few days (like early morning, lunch hours, a morning on the weekend) to work through that list using this process you've just learned. You'll experience internal shifts and changes as you shed layers of the victim mindset like multiple layers of old wallpaper, canceling self-defeating scripts and programs, and reclaiming your rightful calling to thrive in every way – financial, emotional, vocational, relational, whatever-al. Remember, the proof is peace.

. . . . .

Once stricken, twice wise
So you can unhook old familial myths and messages,
   erase the victim tapes,
      clear the rubble and confusion from old experiences,
         now we move past the events and into higher callings.

In the past, you probably acknowledged that financial wounding but decided you needed to move on – that can help.
Perhaps you acknowledged that you're supposed to forgive and mentally chose that, even said it out loud – that's good.
Even better, you've been able to forgive to the extent that you can be comfortable around that person again or be in a similar context.

But *the best* is when the financial blow you sustained leads past the point of forgiveness to a place where exciting opportunities and pursuits open up for you *as a result of that experience.*
   Mistakes can lead to wisdom.
   Being fired can lead to a better job.
   Business failure can lead to better, more marketable ideas.
   A broken heart can become a softer heart.
   Problems lead to answers.
   Frustration inspires change.
   Deprivation necessitates prosperity.
As long as you're still alive, it'll depend entirely on what you do with it, how you respond to it, where you take it.

You can probably think of people who have prospered in the very area in which they were once stricken.
   ♦ Specialized ministries and charities are often created by peo-

ple who were touched by very negative circumstances, such as a serious disease or social dysfunction, a type of crime or personal brokenness, and so on.

+ A good friend who grew up in an orphanage run by nuns now ministers powerfully in the area of the father-heart of God. Likewise other full-time ministers who had difficult fathers. But God pulled them through that and into a profound understanding and experience of their Heavenly Father, and that became their call to minister to others.

+ The business world is full of successful women and men whose childhood poverty compelled them to build a life of success and wealth.

+ Self-help, self-esteem gurus all have stories of how they used to be weak, rejected, insecure people. That became their expertise.

+ As Joseph explained to the brothers who plotted his murder and instead sold him into a life of slavery, however bad (even evil) people's intentions are, God's intention for good can trump those plans.[8] Not just to make the pain stop, but to turn them into a *cause célèbre*.[9]

+ Although he failed in his rash attempt to help his people, Moses was later used to deliver the entire nation of Hebrews.

+ King David, who was rejected by his own parents, not even considered a son[10], was promised his own everlasting lineage, culminating in Jesus. Where he'd been relegated to minding sheep, David was promoted to shepherding a nation.

Your area of affliction can become your territory in which to prosper.[11]

Think of your financial affliction as a wall, a barricade – well, somewhere along that barrier is a doorway to financial destiny. That door is love. And the key to open that door is forgiveness. I mean the kind of forgiveness that doesn't stop with accepting and excusing what happened. That's a start, and you've probably heard enough about forgiveness to know that we're supposed to make an effort to do so. But it cannot end there if it's to become something that actually empowers you. Jesus differentiates when he says, "unless you forgive *with all your heart...*"[12] This is the kind of forgiveness that unfolds into grace, resilience, new life and even gratitude – as it did in his own case.

And when the weight of regret

and the tension of wariness
    come off your finances,
        you'll see them spring back
        and flourish as never before.

Love is the door, forgiveness is the key
Pray with me:
Lord, I'm willing to learn how to forgive with all my heart,
particularly in this area of financial disasters.
Please teach my heart how.

Whoever your favourite villains are,
    this boss, that partner, those thieves,
        which company, what country, whose bureaucrats,
            her family, his people, their profession...
you've probably had sufficient time to generate profiles of what
they did or didn't do, and what kind of people that makes them.

If your objections and criticisms linger, you will find yourself
dogged by the same profiles of attitudes, outlooks and circum-
stances on a recurring basis, with different faces. Guaranteed.
And you can stop blaming others because you're actually sowing/
reaping and crap-magnetizing your own situation. Problems are
following you and your bread-crumb trail of complaint.

What's worse, whoever was behind that financial disaster is, in a
sense, still winning. Because they've moved on and you haven't.
They're probably not even thinking about what happened. And
if they did they'd still say they were quite entitled, they did what
they had to do, and they've found other people and things to think
about. So if you're waiting for them to come to some crashing realization, have an epiphany or Damascus Road experience... well,
that's not really getting any closer to happening, is it?

More to the point, do you really want to wait for them any longer?
If you're holding out for that, then you're leaving the authority and
control over your life outside their door. You're giving it away.

In fact, if you're still in relationship with this person and contact
hasn't been, or cannot be, broken then you're probably drawing
more of the same out of them. You are fueling that pattern to fulfill your own expectations.

Have you every noticed how some people are so full of rejection that you can hardly help but push them away? Nervous people who make you start feeling apprehensive? Cynical people who draw sarcastic humour out of you? Funny people who prompt you to make jokes? They're fulfilling their own expectations through you.

If that person is an 8-out-of-10 on the Bitterness Scale, but you're only a 2, they'll still find the source of that 2 and tap into it – we always look for what we have in common, like attracts like. You do the same with others, including in the financial realm. Neutralize those negative elements in *your* thinking, beliefs, feelings and body language and you'll see a corresponding shift in how others treat you. Including money itself.

So you're the one who needs to change. And that won't happen until you truly forgive. Not just excuse. Not just tolerate. But forgive, cancel the debt, find compassion for that person, even desire good for them.

And when you genuinely feel compassion for them *and want better for them than the circumstances that motivated them to do you wrong*, you may find yourself inspired to prosper in that very area:
+ to financially support, participate in, or create a business, association or ministry into that same problem area
+ invest in, vote on, campaign for, or advise on solutions to that issue
+ set up or promote a business venture that "finally gets it right"
+ write a book about, create an internet forum for, or counsel others in similar circumstances.

And in all of these, you can prosper financially, emotionally, in wisdom and reputation.

The magnitude of the emotional energy tied to that financial disaster can be turned to propel your passion and compassion for making a corresponding difference in your life and the lives of others. Remember, historically millionaires go broke three times before they make their fortune.

In the end, that failure or trauma can open your path to success, inspiration and passion for that (or a corresponding) cause. In fact, you'll be able to look back on the situation and embrace it as part of the course of events that led to a place of gratitude. Not specifically for what happened, but that this piece of your personal history led you to create something better.

For example, chronic debilitating back pain from a car accident led a good friend of mine to try chiropractic care in desperation for an alternative to back surgery. Not only did the treatments allow his body to heal and let go of the pain, they allowed his back to strengthen to where he's now better-than-new. He already had a university degree, but this accident & healing experience inspired him to go back to school – right back to high school science and math, then a couple of years of university science courses, and then chiropractic college – to become a Doctor of Chiropractic. Now he sees dramatic healing in his patients, his practice is prospering, he has written a book applying principles of healing to other areas of life, and he's taking public speaking engagements on the subject. *That's* flourishing and prospering, and it's in the very area in which he was traumatized. Seeming tragedy became his path to success and fulfillment.

You can have the same in your finances.[13]

Pick someone
Think of someone you consider instrumental in one of the financial disasters you worked through earlier.
Without getting worked up about it, describe in one sentence, as objectively as you can, what that person did to you, or didn't do for you. Write it here:

_____

_____

Pray with me:
  Lord, I need your perspective on this person – would you help me with this?
  Lord, I admit that I have judged _____ for what happened. But I'm ready to move past this, so I renounce my insistence on having the right to judge them for it.
  Despite everything that situation cost me financially, emotionally, physically and mentally at that time and since, I am sorry for carrying this offense in my thinking, my beliefs,

my body language, my finances, my other relationships, and even with you!
Please forgive me for living in reaction to it. Thanks.
I now cancel every "reason" I've held onto to harbour resentment and hold regret in my thinking, my emotions, my body, my relationships and my finances: [14] *specifically that...*

_____

_____

_____

I choose to completely forgive them, as you've forgiven me.
I cancel the debt I thought they owe me: including expecting any realizations, admissions, apologies or repayment from their end.
They owe me nothing now – I will trust you, God, to restore.
I set them completely free, and bless them to live well and prosper in their own finances.

Now Lord, let's exchange my thoughts for your thoughts:
I thought they were (name it) _____.
But you saw they were (first thing that comes to mind)

_____

Thank-you, Lord.
*I now choose to agree with you and see them, **and speak of them**, that way too.*
After all, I am rich in _____!

You probably heard a reason to feel compassion for them. Which is a huge thing in itself. But that's what God is like: compassionate. The good news is that you can use your intention to get on the Lord's wavelength and forgive at an entirely deeper level.

When you do, it unhooks the self-fulfilling mechanisms that you have been either straining against or unwittingly complying with – both have been happening, but true forgiveness strips them of the seeming logic & 'rights' that hold them in place in your thinking and beliefs, and the emotional energy that fuels them.

It's good to write these things down, because you likely won't remember all of it and there are a couple of things we're going to do shortly with what you've been uncovering.

But before we apply this model to other financially frustrating scenarios, there's another facet we need to address.

Now we're ready for you

In many instances, it's easy enough to identify active culprits or passive obstructers and the roles they played in your financial difficulties. But what about the times when it was *you*? This gets back to the issues of responsibility we covered back in Chapter 2: who picked the losing investment, who dropped out, who racked up the expenses, who ignored the warning signs, and so on. As much as you'd like to see forgiveness flow between people, *sometimes the hardest form of forgiveness and compassion to muster is for yourself.*

You can be our own worst critic – you have more dirt on yourself than on anyone else, and a self-perpetuating loop of blame & shame can be hard to break.

Conversely, if you don't think there's anything you need to forgive yourself for in this scenario, it's because you feel entitled to think it wasn't your fault. Which is a dangerous posture too. The problem is, you *did* play a role, even if it was unwitting: a role that cost you.

And part of you knows it. Thinking it was all someone else's fault is not only unrealistic, your heart *knows* better and has been left in conflict with your own surface thoughts. Behind the thin curtain of denial and blame, another part of your intuitive, creative, analytical genius has already compiled a dossier on...
    what you could've done,
    what you should've done and
    what you would've done if you only knew what was coming.
And if your inner critic doesn't get his day in court, he'll become belligerent and take matters into his own hands –
    maybe a whisper campaign of doubt
      a booby-trap of explosive emotion
        or a sit-in of depression and inertia
– until he's been acknowledged and the matter is settled.

The *should'a-could'a-would'a* circuit is like an 'I told you so' – another stubborn little self-fulfilling, self-perpetuating loop. It must be identified, interrupted and satisfied, or it will linger and continue to shape your financial behaviour and results.

To keep the interior dialogue civil, let's establish some ground rules and distinguish between *negative wishes* and *actual choices*, whether taken or avoided.

* "I would've..." or "I would never have..." is negative fortune-telling and impossible to prove or disprove. Eliminate 'would' – it's not fair to you.
* Edit out accusative vagaries like, "I should've known" or "I did nothing" or "I should've said something." Those are too indistinct and unfair.
* In fact, let's eliminate 'should' completely – in hindsight you mostly know the 'shoulds' already, so let's get down to whether there actually was a tangible, doable 'could' possibility.
* 'Could' only counts if it's specific, like, "I could have called" or "I could have refused."
* Phrase it concretely, rather than a 'not' statement. For instance, "I skipped over..." is more tangible and palpable than "I did not admit..."; "I ignored..." is less nebulous than "I did not take seriously..."[15]

Me *vs.* Myself *vs.* I

So, let's go further with that financial debacle we were last working on. You'll need a pen, and probably a journal or writing paper.

Relax, shrug, breathe and...
> *Lord, thank-you for my analytical abilities – I choose to entrust them to your wisdom and compassion.*
> *Father, I can't change the past but I want to resolve my role.*
> *I give myself permission to recognize my own responsibility when _____ happened.*

Take your pen and paper and, sticking to the facts, start writing with:
> *Looking back on it, I can see that I...*

Stop writing when you sense that line of thinking has run its course...

> *Now that I've brought all this into the open,*
> *Lord, despite what it has cost me, cost my loved ones, and cost others, would you please forgive me? Would you remove my*

shortcomings from me and relieve me of this burden? (Another shrug and deep breath.) *Thank-you.*
Lord, I acknowledge that if you can forgive me, I can forgive me. (Next, slap your thigh for emphasis as you declare, with oomph...) *Therefore I choose to drop this case against myself* **NOW.**
Instead, I direct my heart, my subconscious, my emotions and my belief system, to **cancel all those old directives** *and wait for new constructive projects to work on that are encouraging, wise, fun and rewarding.*
So be it!

While you're in this mode, take a moment to ask the Holy Spirit to let you see, hear or feel something encouraging. Maybe a flow of thoughts, a mental picture, a word or phrase, a sensation... just write here:
Lord, where I thought it was my fault, you saw that...

_____

_____

And as we both know, I am rich in _____!

I suggest you now destroy the "Looking back on it" page you just wrote. With glee. But keep the closing encouragement.

Now you're 'armed and marvelous'
How does that feel? Some people find it a vivid experience, for others it's subtle – both are legitimate. Both are true. Both are effective.

And now you know what to do with the other financial difficulties you listed earlier. Please, *please*, PLEASE be determined about this and apply this model to the whole list. Don't settle for less. It only costs a bit of time, and the rewards will be freedom.

If your inner skeptic objects to bothering to go back and work through the rest, take charge, press through and be thorough for your own sake to resolve your internal conflicts. Don't rationalize and let things linger. And if you suspect there's something deeper unresolved that's disabling your peace, take a few minutes to revisit it for resolution. Let me illustrate:

+ You borrow my company car without my permission and explain later that you were stuck and needed it for a work-related errand. Simple enough, I let it go.
+ Then on your way home you remember that you forgot to fill the tank and returned my car almost empty. Not deliberately, but now you've got something on your mind between then and the next morning. When we chat about it, we both get acknowledgement of how awkward this was and I get the choice of extending the next degree of grace. And we move on.
+ But then it's my turn: I find a cracked taillight. The grace I've extended so far was sincere but didn't cover this as well. I don't know it was you, but rightly or wrongly our working relationship will be affected by some tension until the next level of resolution comes.

It's the same for you internally – forgiveness can only be effective if it's proportionate to the degree of honesty and magnitude of the infraction. Including for yourself. There is great freedom on the other side of acknowledgement, so it's healthy to be completely honest with yourself. Not to re-hash and rehearse and beat yourself up, but to be thorough. And sometimes it takes a follow-up visit to get to the bottom of it.

Do yourself the same favour. It's a bit of work, but it's a rewarding, effective use of time – certainly more than devising financial strategies that you'll wind up subconsciously undoing. Again and again.

When you've gone through your list of financial struggles, keep the positive encouragements you received and just a shorthand list of the events. We're about to use those to reveal potential opportunities to move into your financial destiny.

Forming a future
The financially stressful times of your life, the jobs, the relationships, the investments, the businesses, the disasters, the living conditions, the school years, the home life... *they can all serve you, even though they felt negative at the time.*

Now that they've been defused with forgiveness, we're going to do a bit of forensics and sift through them for clues about your financial calling and destiny. We're looking for trends, themes, patterns and pathways for your relationship with money.

Consider the first financially negative situation you've worked through, and let's break it out according its various components by filling in some blanks.

Take a two-page spread in your journal, or on a full sheet of paper and create a grid with spaces for these columns. Start with these blanks if you like:

What: The general mode of what happened: Was it theft, debt, firing, spending, investment loss, under-employment... ?

Who: The role you played: leader, follower, customer, client, investor, student, member, employer, employee, volunteer...

Who else: On either side: family, peers, gender, culture, age, regulators, career or industry, religion...

Where: The context: local/international, urban/rural, single group, widespread association, industry, culture...

When: Timing: your stage of life, education or career, or activities (while commuting, vacationing, working, graduating, grieving, wedding planning)...

Why: Factors like the background, conditions, history, trends, news, mindsets, culture, gender, motivation...

How much: amounts, relative importance, the purpose of the money (living, saving, playing)...

Lay out your answers along the top blank line of the following grid so it looks something like the example on the following page:

214 Healing Your Financial Soul

What	Who	Who else	Where	When	Why	How much
unemployed, erratic farm income, basics only	mother, 2 kids, volunteer	Mennonites, rural, farmers	Hoytquit County	university, kids 1-6yrs.	stuck, long commute, no child care	2nd income or business, $25k/yr.
inheritance						
bank hassles						
bad timing						
re-po						
fire						

Now do the same with the other money struggles we've been working through. It'd be great to have five or six to populate the grid. Don't forget to include childhood experiences – adult experiences are often a re-telling of what happened when you were 12 or younger.

When you have the chart filled in, pray with me:
Lord, would you give me eyes to see?
What's really going on here?
Please help me recognize strategies, deficiencies, themes, needs,
    trends, and tendencies.
Start circling, underlining and drawing arrows on the chart where you see parallels, common elements or perhaps opposite extremes (reactions).

You might notice, for example, that there's an issue with salespeople, the idea of selling and self-promotion. Or lack of long-term planning. Or procrastination. Or quitting. Or interference. Or illness. Or poorly chosen relationships.

Summarize your observations here:

_____

_____

_____

_____

Bounce this off someone you trust
From here, you need a strategy. If you have a mentor, life coach, small group leader or pastor, or accountability partners that you interact with regularly, consider taking these observations to them for some feedback and perspective. The Bible says we can receive confirmation that what we received truly came from the Lord, by bouncing it off two or three spiritual advisors: "For in the mouth of two or three witnesses every fact is confirmed." So always bounce your insights from the Lord off people who are ahead of you and in a position to give you honest feedback. (Showing them the actual journaling is generally more powerful than just describing it as our paraphrase is never as potent as God's original.)

When it comes to the personal implications of what you're discovering, you may recognize an area of weakness in your life. Perhaps a need for self-discipline and consistency. Or a more optimistic attitude. Or that you need a more independent work situation. These sorts of needs or shortcomings can only be remedied once they're identified, so get some objective perspective.

If you see a pattern of a particular kind of person, or kind of behaviour, or repeated incidents that have a theme (theft, vandalism, conflict, *etc.*), does it sound like an earlier personal experience? I suggest carrying it back to resolve the financial issue from that angle – it may be that money has, once again, been highlighting a lingering self-fulfilling belief or expectation.

It's bigger than you
Looking beyond yourself, you may see that there's an opportunity to solve the same problems for other people. As I alluded before, these could lead to
  • full- or part-time business or career
  • public sector work
  • ministry or consulting
  • volunteerism
  • academics or your own research
  • forming a support or advocacy association
  • fodder for a book on the subject, and so on.

Perhaps there's a niche that would serve a widespread but unconnected group of people. Or a narrow, overlooked group of people. Or an underserved location. From your chart you might see
       issues at college for students from home-school backgrounds,
           training needs for women in farm communities,
               financial issues facing single fathers.
               If it affected you, it probably affects others.
If it happened in your life, it has happened in the lives of others. And it could well be a new line of passion, compassion and purpose for you and your finances.

Unlocking your future pursuits
So, let's get your Innate Creative Brilliance Department working on some constructive action that will redeem and leverage those negative situations into rewarding new ventures. Among your observations there is probably a good handful of aspects that can be turned around to good, or opportunities to solve similar experi-

ences for yourself and other people.

For this activation, you'll need to go get your journal or three sheets of paper, plus your keys... as in car & house keys.

+ Choose the three most significant, traumatic, confusing or entrenched money-related patterns that surfaced on your grid. You can take them from the "What" column of the chart, or from the summary of observations you derived.

+ Give each one an illustrative title, like the working title for a college course or magazine article. Make them positive and proactive, *ex.*, "Graduate Rich: Who says students should be broke?" or "The Finish Line: How I quit being a quitter".

+ Take a couple of pages in your journal and set them up like this, with the list of titles on the left of the page, then add the Strategy and Tactics columns, leaving ample space for notes:

What	Title	Strategy	Tactics
1	" "	a)	
		b)	
		c)	
2	" "	a)	
		b)	
		c)	
3	" "	a)	
		b)	
		c)	

+ For the next column, take a minute to consider your first title and propose a general solution for that scenario: Sit back and think, if your cousin came to you asking for advice about the same situation, what would you suggest?

Digging for new research,   fresh training,
more recreation,   private counseling,
better equipment,   consulting an expert,
hiring some help,   a change in surroundings?

Think of three suggestions for each title. Keep them in terms of a general direction (not specific actions such as a person to call or place to go). List these three under "Strategy".

+ Do the same for the other two "What" titles.

You'll need some uninterrupted time for the next step

We're going to use those titles to employ a bit of drama as a way of subconscious brainstorming for creative, specific, tangible tactics to implement those strategies – and it'll be one of the easiest things you've ever done!

As we've pointed out before, your agreeable, tireless, observant, creative and loving subconscious is ever at the ready to accept assignments – so instead of occupying it with remorseful replays of past events, negative second-guessing and fearful fortunetelling, we'll launch some optimistic, constructive clusters of creativity and strategic planning. You often hear people refer to "my creative side", "the practical part of me" or "the romantic in me"; or maybe "something in the back of my mind" or "rolling around in my imagination". In all likelihood, you have said such things too. This is normal. So let's set into motion some positive, helpful and creative projects and programs that will generate a whole roster of fantastic, fresh, innovative and wise courses of action.

+ Okay, with your keys in the hand that you'd normally hold them in, get comfortable, sit-shrug-breathe, and invite the Lord to this creative session:
  Holy Spirit, you're the best counselor there is.
  Please join me as I consider new possibilities that open
      fantastic new opportunities to see your kingdom come.
+ Put your hand on your head and affirm that...
  I am blessed with a profound, active and creative mind.
  And hand on heart...
  My heart is for the Lord, his people and me.
+ Have you noticed where your best ideas and insights occur to you? Is it in the shower, in the car, in bed before dawn, while jogging, thinking out loud, talking with a friend, while writing or playing your instrument?

Pick a good scenario and fix it in your mind: Where are you? How's the view? What objects surround you? Any people? Is there a preferred time of day?
Identify the sounds you might make, the ambient background sounds, a song or phrase running through your head.
What does your body experience? Heat? Breeze? Motion? How's your breathing? Are you gripping something? Standing or sitting? Remind yourself how and where it feels in your body.
Allow yourself a moment to re-enjoy that setting, smile and wordlessly let your gratitude flow because *"I am rich in _____!"*

+ Holding that scene in your thoughts, let's state your premise out loud:

I'm calling a meeting with the creative, imaginative, visionary problemsolving sectors of my mind. If you want to have some fun and excitement, sign in.

You may 'see', 'hear' or just 'sense' your mental resources rallying like volunteers. Probably several. (If you're unsure about this, read this footnote.[16] Otherwise, stay in the flow of the moment...)

+ Hold either your car, house or office key as if you were about to use it, smile and table your first project:

This is going to be great! I'm looking for great ideas, tactics and practical steps to implement strategies for these three creative projects. First one:

Read the first title from your grid and its three strategies out loud.
Then continue...

If tackling that project appeals, I want a creative team to work with the Holy Spirit to generate dozens, even hundreds, of fantastic ideas on how to do this.

Give me something new and awesome – be bold, be daring, make it fresh, go crazy.

And over the next few days and weeks, every time I use this key (squeeze it), *that's a cue for feedback. I want to hear all of it. And I will take it seriously.*

Go now, start right away and have fun!

Right, next project...

and repeat to assign the other two strategies.

As you proceed, allow hope to rise in your heart, let the excitement bubble up, the anticipation build.
And close the meeting with *"I am rich in _____!"*

Be prepared

It's now underway. Thoughts and ideas are going to bob to the surface of your thinking, **especially when you're holding that key and about to start your car or unlock a door.** When they come to you, say, "Thank-you!" and either repeat the idea out loud or jot it down immediately.

Use your *"I am rich in _____!"* proclamation freely, with gratitude and enthusiasm.

As they occur to you, write those action steps into the chart under "Tactics". Add them to your current to-do list and act!

You'll think of someone to call,
    remember a course you once considered,
        think of a place to go for a drive,
            get a business idea.

Whatever comes, follow up on those promptings. Show them some respect and you'll find the flow will respond with increasingly creative and inspired possibilities.

External shifts and occurrences

Not only will you find ideas floating into your stream of consciousness, external circumstances will start speaking to you.

You'll also notice books and magazines catching your eye,
    bits of overheard conversation reaching you,
        scriptures jumping off the page,
            song lyrics taking on new meaning...

It's a variation of The Diesel Jetta Effect we talked about.

Your subconscious is doing two things for you:

1. Scanning for material, networking concepts and connecting the dots within the constant tide of information, ideas and resources all around you to formulate something new.

2. Using sign language, like a game of Charades, to speak to your conscious attention so you can choose a course of action.

Remember, creativity is rarely *ex nihilo*, it's usually an imaginative re-combining of what's already around.

And it's bigger than that. The Holy Spirit is leading, God is creatively re-arranging the world to encourage, support and supply you with what you need to grow and forge

a dream into a destiny,
    good intentions into great experiences,

and pleasant notions into forward motion.
He is opening the way for you to walk into a new way of living, doing things, meeting and working with people, applying yourself and making a difference for yourself and others. All of this basically comes down to you actively participating in his vision for your life.

Don't worry about whether or not you're getting carried away with your own ideas – if they're good ideas, they're way more likely to be God's ideas than if you don't look for ideas at all.

And if you're open to God steering as you make progress, you'll get there. But he can't steer a stationary object. Make a move! It surely won't happen if you park on your talent and passively wait for his return.

Remember, Jesus did this with his own disciples. They weren't furiously taking notes during his ministry. Jesus said that the Holy Spirit would remind them of what they needed to be conscious of from all they'd seen, heard and done. In fact, just by telling them that, he was seeding their subconscious minds with the directive to be prepared to retrieve stuff when circumstances demanded. In fact, it was years and decades before the components of the New Testament were written down. He understood the human material he was working with, and we are of the same.

Well, that's enough to work on for now. Be alert and anticipate good things!
In the next chapter, we'll talk about some practical matters as you pursue your plans.

Together with me... *"I am rich in _____!"*

---

1 Back in my young, corporate, yuppy-wannabe days, I under-spent on a electric blue suit that only ever made one public appearance.

2 I'm not saying that everything that happens to you was intended and sent by God. He is not an abusive father. But in a fallen world, circumstances will provide plenty of occasions that we experience and perceive as random – the human race generates problems that visit people as probabilities. For instance, your community probably won't deal with the social problem of drunk driving until there have been enough seemingly random and senseless deaths. Then they'll step back and say, "Wait a minute, there's actually a pattern here and we need to do something about it." So that's actually circumstance offering

222   Healing Your Financial Soul

feedback on the scale of an entire community toward positive change – the dead passenger's grieving family experiences it as random and pointless at their level. But then, they can choose to transform even that tragedy into an expansive, missional opportunity to heal that very social ill, e.g. MADD, or Mothers Against Drunk Driving.

3 Usually, I'm the one who needs to say it. If you don't, or won't, you're handicapped.

4 Barring some forms of clinical or developmental disability. This is not "human potential" as we fret about in the New Age movement – their mistake is embracing self-sufficiency as an option to refuse the source of sufficiency we find in God through Jesus. But let's not throw out our God-given potential in fear or spite.

5 I Corinthians 10:13

6 Matthew 13:24

7 Romans 12

8 Genesis 50:20

9 I suspect this an aspect of God's sense of humour. Or at least irony.

10 He was probably illegitimate, the result of an extra-marital affair. I Samuel 16:10-11, Psalm 27:10, I Samuel 17:28,29

11 Genesis 41:52

12 Not as in, "I really, really, really want to mean it." As in, from the very core of your being.

13 In fact, a negative experience is often a negative indicator of a potential calling and destiny – if you turn to face it, you can choose to leverage it into fulfillment.

14 This is probably what they should have or could have done instead.

15 The brain finds the words no, not, none, never and so on, a slippery concept. If I say you, "There is no such thing as walrus ice cream," no matter how awful that sounds, your mind still goes there and immediately formulates what a cold, fishy, chewy experience that would be. It's more effective to re-phrase in a concrete form to grapple with.

16 Don't worry, this is not about mental fractures, multiple personalities or opening yourself up to deception. It's just a visual tool, a one-man or one-woman mini-drama to kickstart your capacity to generate creative ideas, not much different from spreading ink squiggles on paper (writing or doodling) as a vehicle to activate your thinking. Remember the scripture, if you ask your father for bread (sustenance) he won't give you a stone (a harsh rebuke); if you ask for an egg (a new possibility), he will not give you a scorpion (a nasty intruder), Luke 11

Chapter 9
Income and Outgo

Do you still use your *"I am rich in _____!"* declaration? I mean besides when you're reading and working through this book. Use it *every time* you find, receive, pay, give, plan or even daydream about money. It reinforces your thinking in a positive, encouraging direction and shapes your ideas and decisions to line up with that statement. Circumstances represent a swirl of possibilities and potential – you must be proactive about mastering your thoughts, the statements that come out of your mouth and the things you do with your money. When you do, you'll find yourself less and less likely to make counterproductive, resigned or compromising decisions that fulfill self-defeating impulses. Your mind needs a different place to go.

When you remind yourself this way of your heart's true desires for your finances, you'll be more secure and more confident to turn away from the temptation to opt for momentary self-comfort (and the self-condemnation that follows). You'll create shifts in...
  * what you read, think about, seek out, sign up for, attempt and accomplish;
  * where you'll go, what you'll spend money on (or not);
  * who you'll spend time with, who you'll seek out, who you'll go deeper with, who you'll hold at arm's length;
  * what kinds of ideas will surface in your thinking, what you'll dwell on, how you'll view challenges, what solutions you'll try, what new things are needed, what risks to take, how 'good' is 'good enough'.

It's not magic, it's being deliberate and intentional about cultivating a creative, consistent and constructive mindset about money. It's part of taking charge.

"Thank-you, *thank-you,* THANK-YOU!" should become your reflexive response when something, anything, good comes your way. Go big, be vocal, put your body language behind it.

Have you been acknowledging and compiling your 'key' tactics from your Innate Creative Brilliance Department? Even if you don't immediately recall them, I'd bet that if you went back to that Title / Strategies / Tactics grid right now, they'd start coming right back and you could immediately fill some in. If it's been a few days, go back now and see what comes back to you as you contemplate the chart. Remember, little ideas, like little seeds, count – don't shrug them off. We're going to talk about putting those into action shortly.

About that money jar

Now that you've had some time to work with it, have you built up a stash in your entangled money jar? If so, you've repeatedly heard the sound of money deposited every day and kept your goal of financial abundance fresh. Speaking out your intentions daily helps you steer and shift your own thinking and circumstances. I know of a man who has set up his internet business' online sales so that his computer makes a cash register's *cha-ching* sound every time someone buys something from him. It's a very happy sound, and an encouraging one – it continually reminds him that

+ his ideas and efforts are interesting to people,
+ he is doing something valuable and helpful for others,
+ he is continually reaping financially for it.

Take the money and walk

Okay, count up the money from the jar and go open a long-term savings plan with it. *Not* a savings account. Make it a no-minimum, no-load, no-setup-fee mutual fund – you'll probably find them available at your bank. Choose one that's invested in equities (stocks, not bonds or "balanced" portfolios of stocks and bonds) that are listed on the general stock market of your country. Don't go for an aggressive, cyclical or industry-specific sector of the market (by the time the activity there has you convinced, their up-cycle is probably over). Watch out for set-up fees and penalties, there's no reason to pay them. Make sure the plan reinvests its returns in additional units of the fund so your money will start working for you and generating growth momentum of its own.

Every three months, empty your jar and deposit its contents into this account – that's long enough to accumulate a respectable amount, and probably enough to register how it is accumulating, without being unsettled by ups and downs in the market from day to day or week to week. This fund is for years and decades, and it starts now.

And short of an emergency, don't *ever* cash it, or shift it to another kind of investment idea or expenditure. This is not for spending.

Never, not ever. Its purpose is to seed forward motion into your financial mindset, growth in your net worth and a positive momentum in your thinking about money – not to be yanked back into day-to-day distractions and notions. If you are faithful with this 'little', then God and his creation will start sending 'much' for you to be faithful with.

The gross amount of money from the jar is secondary – its purpose is powerfully symbolic and encouraging. And symbols are powerful, like a flag, coat of arms or anthem – they provoke deep responses, even for the cynical. Never dismiss the jar or this investment account as window-dressing or frivolous.

And your 'Seed for the Sower'?

What have you observed from your 'Seed for the Sower' exercise? What money came into your life to be generous with? Have you followed through and given that money for that cause or occasion you identified? Don't hang onto it, it'll go skanky like day-old manna.

If it didn't go so great, or not at all, don't dismiss it and move on. Or try to make up for it by just giving something anyway – the Lord is looking for hearts that are willing to learn to be responsive, not so much hearts that are willing to make up for things.
      He doesn't live in regret,
      so don't try to cultivate regret with him.
If the money came and you have it, give it. If not, just acknowledge that and re-start the 7-, 10- or 14-day time frame. Or just try it for today and tomorrow – start small and build a history with generosity. *Nobody starts by giving away millions*, so there's nothing lame about beginning with just a few coins or bills.

Why not take five minutes, right now, before reading on, turn back to 'Seed for the Sower' in Chapter 7 and give it a fresh start? It's okay to be in the process of learning this stuff – if it was automatic … well, it just isn't. Learning from your mistakes is still progress as long as you're willing to try again.

Take a fresh look

Your income is your opportunity to do something wonderful. To create a new direction. Even if you're only earning a small income right now. It comes back to the Little/Much Principle:
      He who is faithful with little will be faithful with much.

Notice that there's an implicit promise that being a good manager with a smaller amount leads to having larger amounts to work with. In fact, barring a Cinderella-style inheritance, starting small is the ONLY way to arrive at your desired state.

And this is born out in Jesus' parable of the three managers who were given one, two and five talents to manage.[1] ("The Parable of the Talents" is another fable begging to be re-named. It should be something like, "The Story of the Three Money Managers". Or just "The Investors' Parable". And how many times have you heard it presented as a parable about 'talents', as in 'skills', to avoid the awkwardness of talking about money? *Bruh-ther.*)

Now, we could spend the next few days just riffing on the two versions of this parable in Matthew and Luke, but I'm only going to make some quick observations and suggestions from it.

First notice that the master was rich. Really rich. Jesus was fine with that.

Also, he allots *money*. Not sheep or seed or fishing nets. MONEY. And quite a bit of it – in Matthew's version about $15,000, $30,000 and $75,000 respectively if they were talents of silver.[2] Given that the managers were endowed with different amounts to work with, the owner must have given it thought and had different expectations of them. The boss doesn't give them orders as to how to use the money, they were left to work it out, make decisions and take initiative.

Next, the two good managers doubled what they were dealt. One was rewarded with new responsibilities for managing five cities, the other two cities. If one was peevish, one might say that they were treated unequally and there was even more disparity after the rewards were handed out. (That would be a poverty mindset raising its annoying little head.) But the point is that they both got huge promotions, and they were both given increased responsibilities as a result – they didn't go into semi-retirement.

(**Important tangential point:** If you wish you had more money because then you could take it easy and wouldn't have to work so hard, then the sentimental comforts of those daydreams are probably all the reward you'll see. Wealth requires increased creativity and effectiveness and leads to increased responsibility, opportunity and work[3] – not necessarily working harder, as in strain and stress, but smarter. It'll also be work that's a lot more effective, rewarding and fun. Unless you're talking about indolent inheritors of wealth, you'll find that the wealthy are creative, productive people... *thwack!*)

Back to the parable

The delinquent manager is criticized for not at least thinking to put the money out for loan interest. But it's not about the lack of initiative and performance. Matthew touches on this issue, Luke's version spells it out: Jesus defines the lousy manager's real problem: not his results but *his beliefs*.

And he exhibits pretty much everything we've been covering in these pages. Specifically, the lies and misconceptions in the manager's heart about his employer's character:
"It's because you're a harsh man with unreasonable expectations." (Have you heard a version of this at work?)
He uses blame as an excuse to avoid responsibility. Back to the blame/responsibility thing.
And he brings on himself exactly what was already set up in his own thinking. Negative fortunetelling.
His opinion/complaint/judgment of the owner – "I knew that you are a harsh man" – whether based on fear or resentment, becomes self-fulfilling prophecy.
And we've talked about how dangerous "I know" is.

All he had to do was deposit the money somewhere people who care about money would do something with it. That's all. Maybe the master wouldn't have been thrilled, but perhaps a corollary of "To whom much is given, much is required" is "To whom little is given, only a little is required."

Yet the single-talent manager was still getting an opportunity to do well. Or at least better. Earning just one talent could have set him up in a nice position. You probably know someone like this: the guy who says,
"If they'd only give me that promotion,
they'd see what I can really do."
Nuh-uh. You're already showing them what to expect.

Tangent

There's a very common expression of the poverty mentality that says, "If you pay me more, then I'll start being more valuable." It doesn't work that way. That's like saying you'll start doing a few sit-ups once you're in better shape. *If you want to be promoted or get that raise, you need to be over-delivering first. Sow!*

You *will* reap – and if you don't reap in that place, the blessing due you will skip your employers or customers and come around to you some other way. (Maybe even in a non-taxable form!) Your employers and customers are in a favourable position to partici-pate in your abundance, but if they choke then they'll simply miss the opportunity. Your part is to sow and keep your heart open and expectant. I know, it's a bit of a double-standard, but the good thing about a double-standard is that you can go for the higher standard.

To the degree that your company does not opt into being a source of abundance and reward productivity (perhaps because of its own poverty mentality or adversarial mindset), they will begin to lose ground. They might get away with skimming someone else's cream for a while, but in time they will reap a decline somewhere,
    perhaps in the quality of their personnel
        shrinking interest among customers
            or even their own personal doldrums.
Their own access to the Creation's abundance will recede and they'll return to striving and lean times to reflect their own sow-ing pattern.

In either case, keep sowing but keep an eye out – you might reap a different 'much' opportunity for your time and energy.
Then they can keep their 'little'.
The key for you is how well you do at avoiding bitterness.

Back to the parable
When the bitter, single-talent manager's reckoning comes, the master explains that he is judging the non-achiever by his own words – the underperformer reaps *exactly what he sowed with his expectations and not-actions.* His beliefs and emotional makeup dictated his 'reasons', decisions and outcome – emotionally and motivationally abdicating and burying the money.

Fortunately, that's not you anymore. You've wisely chosen to work through a bunch of your own negative expectations, judgments and old beliefs. You can look forward to better results based on better beliefs. So in your case, this should not be a negative, ominous parable.

But isn't it funny how we emotionally position this parable as dire warning? Even a threat? Don't the sermons and Bible study guides make this a perform-or-else tale? Actually, the promise of good things outweighs negative consequences many times over.

There is implicit assurance here that **God is more interested in rewarding than condemning**. The condemnation (rightfully) shrinks to insignificance compared with the commendations awarded. To push the point even further, Luke's version also has the single talent confiscated and handed over to the now-11-talent manager, which provokes the other servants to wonder aloud whether or not this is even fair anymore. Actually, it is more than fair – it's generous. The guy's fired, not flogged.[4] And the talent wasn't his anyways! You thought he should get to keep it? It went to the one most likely to do something really great with it.

Jesus is emphasizing this principle:
 Whichever direction you're choosing,
  you're going to get even more of it!

This is serious. But not grim. We don't call this "The Parable of the Doomed Slacker" – two out of three did really well, were celebrated by the master and handsomely rewarded with promotions to bigger and better things. They flourished. And so will you, *if* you embrace the mandate to take whatever you have been entrusted with now and leverage it – with excitement, optimism and anticipation of those bigger and better things. Including your income.

Get your eyes off of the bitter, resentful one-talent grumbler who got his "I told you so." I am confident that you are *at least* a two-talent>two-city manager, and likely a five-talent>five-city achiever based on the motivation and willingness you've displayed by getting this far in this book.

To conclude:
The poor manager (proverbially) sowed and reaped
 what was already in his heart.
  So did the good managers.
   So did the master…
I'll let you think about that one.

And back to the original subject
In your case, whether the income you are entrusted with now is large-ish or small-ish, what actually determines your results is not the amount but the expectations in your heart. So if you manage well what you have now – not hoarding it, not capping it, not spilling it, not burying it – then The Master and his Creation will respond by providing you with more to work with and greater responsibility to undertake. A positive track record starts with your inner beliefs, and it's already within your grasp.

Let me come at that last point again from a different angle. You cannot wait until you have a bunch of money before you begin managing it well. To recycle the simile used earlier, that'd be like saying you'll start studying once you've got your degree. Any small amount is still an opportunity to start things happening for you.

So by all means start small – it may take a little while, but start! This is why the Entangled Magnetic Money Jar matters – it's not the coins or bills you're putting in, it's your consistency with the 'little' that will attract the 'much'.

Charmaine, as a Life Coach, will sometimes help a client get started with this rhetorical question & answer:
You know how old you'll be by the time you learn
to play piano really well?
The same age as if you don't.
Just start.

As you sow, and how you sow...
No one succeeds by going into a situation saying or thinking,
"Oh, I hope this will be okay..."
"I really wish this would turn out..."
"I really, really need for this to work..."
All the while bracing themselves, being tentative, ready to recoil. All that's really being reinforced is their "hope", their "wish" and their "need" – not their desired results.

So when the disappointment arrives, it's because that's exactly what they emotionally prepared for. Whatever their head might have been saying in false optimism, their heart was busy attracting, manoeuvring and creating based on their beliefs about what could (actually, "should") happen. So it manifests in...
   • self-defeating decisions and muted efforts,

+ hesitations and lurches in their sense of timing,
+ subliminally putting off people who could have contributed and supported the goal,
+ dismissing intuition and missing serendipitous cues,
+ and subconsciously crashing the whole undertaking to prove the insightfulness of their negative prediction.

In other words, the heart's "I knew it" and "I told you so."

If you create a detailed scenario in your mind of what it will be like if it all goes bad, you might like to think that you're being wise and prepared, but that will actually carry more energy and influence than some vague notion of success being a relief.

Specific & detailed   trumps   *Vague & fuzzy*.
Always.

Yes, be wise about a defensive strategy. But you need to sow proportionately more thought, energy and imagination into a clear, desirable, focused, *emotionally-engaging* picture of how great it's going to be and what you're your achievements will

look like,   feel like,   who it'll involve,
how much you'll invest,   the quantities it'll produce,
how much you'll make,   and so on.

Especially the emotional sensations of
satisfaction,   pleasure,   excitement,   fun,
anticipation,   winning,   gratification,
and especially celebration & gratitude.

Get the that *feeling*! It clears your thinking, heightens awareness, invites intuition and spontaneous God-thoughts, and it will rally the generous elements of creation to fulfill your expectations. This is not hype, it's aligning your whole being with the positive ends of your choosing.

If you brace yourself for reasons to fail, you'll get what you expect – it's a prophecy just begging to be fulfilled.

And it's counterproductive to invest proportionately more in disaster avoidance than fulfillment. Remember, most of our mental processing finds words like "never" "no" and "not" very slippery, if not impossible, to register[5] – your subconscious will simply hear and process "lose" "money" "help" and do what it can to "help lose money". Can't help it.

Yes, a fall-back plan will help if it allows you to be bolder about grasping your main idea, but your goals and winning strategy need to be more clear, more detailed and more engaging by far. Here are a couple of things I've noticed about successful people:

*   They are rarely surprised by their success (though sometimes pleased by the degree of their success).
*   Not everyone who succeeds is brilliant. It doesn't hurt, but usually they succeed because they *believed* success was theirs to have and *acted* that way, in their finances, their social decisions, their use of time, their thought life... they aligned more and more aspects of themselves with their goals, invested in them and real-ized them – made them real.

If you're more cognizant of the downside, if there's more nervous emotional energy attached to what failure would mean, that's what you'll produce. In the early pages of this book, we ventured that you will project and attain what you're most clear about. It'll be in your...

*   body language (hands in pockets, lowered chin, eyes down & left)
*   tone of voice (lowered, tentative, questioning)
*   facial expressions and physical responses (cocked head, winces, feet shuffling, eyes dodging)
*   choice of words ("perhaps", "maybe", "could", "I think", "if")

And because everyone has done this, everyone knows the code and will be reading between the lines and understanding what you're really saying despite the verbiage. How else should people around you respond when it comes to their own hard-earned money? Will they buy in? Only out of obligation or pity. Will they help you fail? People instinctively recognize tentativeness and fear and take their cue to back away. And with them they'll take their contributions of time, interest, money and effort.

The tentative person is simultaneously investing in both suc-ceeding and not-succeeding. That mix will be reflected in their results – both investments will pay in kind, and they'll cancel each other out proportionately.

Will God bless and encourage something that you're emotionally and intellectually hedging on?
Which part is he supposed to respond to and bless to multiply:

The faith or the fear?
The vision or the apprehension?
The reasons to succeed or the reasons for holding back?

This is a serious issue because up until now you've been getting both:
To the degree that you are sowing into faith.
To the degree that you are sowing into doubt.

The wild thing about this is that God just might bless your reservations to produce their rightful, correspondingly crummy results. Why? Because if that's what it will take for you to come to the end of your self, *i.e.* get fed up with your self-consciousness, self-doubt, self-indulgence, *etc.*, then he'll let you have your fill.

Because then maybe you'll really get it and choose to believe and live differently. If that's what it takes to get you through the other side of it, he just might help you through that.
Then when you're sick of the fear,
sick of the selfishness,
sick of the lost opportunities,
sick of the lost time and money,
sick of the meager results,
sick of the weakness...
you'll step up and step out into the greater possibilities that he's recruiting for. What a relief that'll be!

He's patient that way, and he knows he's not limited in his ability to turn things around after.

God makes this invitation: "Draw close to me and I will draw close to you."[6] And since God's creation reflects his character, its natural tendency is to behave the same way.
So if you are *partially drawing* toward success, then all the things that comprise success (the people, the money, the facilities, the notice, the opportunities, the buzz) are *partially drawing* close to you.
Conversely, to the degree that you are *not-drawing* close to these things, they are *not-drawing* close to you. So it behooves you to resolve those apprehensions so you're fully convinced and engaged.
Then **your decisions will be single-minded and not so ambivalent.**
Resolve your beliefs, *then* your methods.

I'm not advocating hype or wishful thinking, I'm saying we can make choices beginning with our own perspective and beliefs, and that means taking action with the 'little' knowing that the 'much' will result.

God responds to faith, not wishes
We also know that God is pleased with faith.[7]
And we know that faith and fear are antithetical.
Faith and wishing are not the same thing.
Faith is not defined as "wishing really, really hard."
Wishing is a mixture of wanting something, but diluting it
   with expected shortfalls.
Faith is assurance of the good thing despite the resistance.
Faith is the substance of things not seen, because those things
   don't have to be seen (yet) in order to be real – they don't have
   to be seen in order to be on their way or taking form.
Wishing is resignation to weakness and passivity, faith is expe-
   rience of the strength of God's generous intentions.

Is this manipulation?
Trying to manipulate God is like trying to shovel the ocean: you might make a splash and send out a few ripples, but the only real negative effect you'll have is wearing yourself out on the wrong thing. The only one you'd be manipulating is yourself. (Or possibly manipulating others to participate in your folly and blaming God.)

No, *faith is participation* – God is more interested in *why & how* you engage with him than *what* you're working on. God's love and kind intentions for you are vast. They're actually beyond your compre-hension. So your task is to get yourself out into a different zone, beyond what is now within comprehension – something that lies beyond what you could think or imagine for yourself.

Another important thing about sowing
Where are you sowing?
  • Are you sowing into your dreams and vision?
  • Or are you mostly chipping in toward the visions and goals of others?
  • When was the last time you sowed into your own life by investing in
      a course,   a few books,   a teaching series on CD,
      an on-line seminar,   a paid podcast subscription,
         instructional DVDs,   even a magazine subscription?

+ Or sending yourself to a conference or seminar dealing with finances, money, business, career skills, and such?
+ Have you sown into your own progress by hiring a Life Coach? Or a Business Coach?
+ Are you actively promoting your product, service or abilities to your customers or employers without embarrassment?
+ Have you paid a professional to help you with branding your business?
+ Have you hired an employee to take over and do efficiently what you know you're not so good at – so you can invest in what you do best instead?

If you aren't demonstrating faith in your own potential for financial progress, who are you hoping will barge in and make you?

I venture that if you look at the available income you sow into various areas, you'll see correlating growth.

+ Investing time, money and energy into attending a conference on prayer will yield depth in your prayer life.
+ Spending a week or two of your vacation, plus airfare and expenses, on a short-term missions trip will reward you with an expanded worldview.
+ If you sow into a marriage retreat or seminar, you'll reap dividends in your family life.
+ Invest in a guided fitness program and you'll see benefits in your physique.
+ Sow time and money into counseling and personal prayer ministry and you'll enjoy a freer mind, healthier heart and unburdened spirit.

So, what have you been sowing into your *own* finances?
(I mean, of course, besides this book and the money mindset activations we've done.) Get on the internet and find a financial education course. Once you've sorted through all these background issues relating to money, THEN those budgets and investment plans can actually work. Sow ENERGY+TIME (in the form of money) and your own time and effort into your financial net worth and you will reap in kind.

Sow money, reap money.

Rattle your keys
Now, about that Title / Strategies / Tactics table you filled in during the "Unlocking Future Pursuits" exercise a few pages back – the one using your house keys or car keys. Flip back and look over

your list of Tactics and tell me which ones are the most appealing, as in generating enthusiasm and hope.
Why not start there?

Start by taking one of those tactics and break it down into smaller, more manageable chunks, like...
    getting a catalog,   buying a piece of equipment,
    calling someone,   reading up on the subject,
      ordering something online.

Whatever it is,
  read some reviews,
    get a bit of advice
      and do it!

You've heard the old proverb that a long march begins with a single step. Well, the rest of the march happens pretty much the same way. If you take a simple step, you'll find more simple steps waiting for you. There's nothing wrong with breaking large tasks down into manageable chunks – that's what every successful person does. (Then they hire staff to handle the chunks.)

Get in the game
If there's a skill you love using (mechanical, mathematical, physical, intellectual, artistic, etc.) find the organization that promotes it and start talking to them.
    Read about it. Sow money into a membership.
  Sow your time and attention. Seek out people already doing it.
    Visit them, buy them coffee, buy them lunch.
  Pay to see it done.
    Invest time, interest and money to learn it for yourself.
  And you will start to reap in kind.

If you love to do it, why not do what you love?
Your enthusiasm for it will motivate you to do it well, and there will always be people willing to pay for you to do that. (Just make sure it's something that people want but need help with, or want to know more about for themselves.) The only barrier is sowing the needed money and time into cultivating that passion *and* networking with other interested people until you come across those people who are also ready and willing to sow their TIME + ENERGY into the same thing, *i.e.* pay you. And they are out there.

This also means cutting out time-wasters. Like pointless TV sit-coms, empty online chat, routine social ruts, repetitive games, fruitless committees. Everybody needs a diversion, even a bit of mental bubblegum for a break, but it's just as easy to spend time and energy with people who are motivated and building something financially rewarding, as people who casually play euchre and aren't going anywhere with it. Or want to sit around on couches and talk about yet another 'inspirational' book. Drop out of those groups and take a night course. Invest in a financially rewarding skill and cultivate relationship with others doing the same. Cast your bread upon *those* waters and just watch what floats back as a result.

And be prepared for the fact that these are not one-time investments. You'll need to keep fuelling the fire to go higher, deeper and further. *Commit to becoming an expert and your expertise will find its market.*

Another indicator
What do you naturally find yourself sowing your energy and conversation into? What draws your interest? What's the common element among people you're drawn to? What do you encourage in others? What do you invite others to? What conversations leave you thinking and mulling over ideas?

My wife, Charmaine, is an excellent Life Coach because she's doing what comes naturally: getting into conversations with people about what's really in their hearts to do with their lives. She can't help but get into those conversations and people respond because they sense she's genuinely interested. For years we would leave dinners, parties and activities and she'd be energized by where she naturally found herself going with people in one-to-one conversation. Then one day, she discovered that there was a title for such a person: Life Coach. She promptly spent time researching on the internet and then sowed 17 weeks and a couple thousand dollars into a training program to qualify herself as a life coaching practitioner. Then she invested in a web site or two.[8] She sowed into business cards. She sowed again by coaching a couple of people for free. And she sees wonderful progress in people's lives in Canada, the US and UK. Week after week. Fittingly, her clients too are reaping to the degree that they sow their own time and effort (between appointments) into the insights, suggestions and encouragements they uncover during the coaching process. And their ENERGY+TIME (fees).

So if you've only heard about sowing and reaping "time, talent and treasure" in the context of church life, don't be surprised if an increase in church life is pretty much what you're reaping.

The problem here is that three different things get muddled together:
+ honouring the Lord in gratitude and celebration of his goodness in your life (one aspect being your income)
+ sowing back into your own pursuits to ensure future harvests worth celebrating (your self, your work, your life)
+ participating in the life of your spiritual family.
Not the same. Not interchangeable. Not to be confused.

Yes, I believe that when we are grateful for our material blessings then we should acknowledge and honour God in kind.
And as grown-up sons and daughters in our father's house, it's a commendable thing to support and contribute to the vision, direction and upkeep of the spiritual family's household.

And your financial commitment should reflect your personal values and convictions, *i.e.* if you're committed to ministry to the poor, support a congregation that's actively doing that; if you value a particular style of worship service, participate there, including financially.

But let's drop the three-fer-one pulpit ploy of mucking together celebratory giving with financial support and calling it 'sowing'.

You sow *outside* the church
And when you reap outside the church, then you have something to cheer about and bring to share with the rest of the family. Unless your goal is make the church your vocation: then sow into church work so you'll reap there. (This is why career pastors mistakenly represent offerings as sowing – *they* should sow into their ministry, but it gets fuzzy when they project that on the congregation's members.)

Speaking of which, what about the tithing bugaboo?
I've put this topic at the back of the book for a few reasons:
+ Because when your relationship with money is healed and stabilized, you'll be motivated to live out of a healthy financial mindset, including generosity. I believe you can be trusted.
+ There's too much teaching already in circulation that says

if you fund a ministry, then they can leave it up to God to dump abundance back into your lap. Benefit without responsibility.

♦ Until your own finances are mending, your money mindset clutter sorted, and your emotions, beliefs and thought life regarding money taken care of, there's a strong likelihood that your giving will be motivated by fear, guilt, desperation, duty, manipulation or shame. And I don't want to guide you (back) into that situation. Your relationship with money has to be renewed first.

I hope you're not looking to me for the final, definitive answer to the age-old debate over tithing. There are too many opinions, theories, motives and interpretations out there – some of them well-articulated, some of them badly handled, some of them groundless, some of them helpful. Usually, people just want their own current preferences affirmed.
And you know that's not my style.

And because those lines have already been drawn in a lot of people's minds, there's not much point in arguing. So I'm only going to volunteer some thoughts along the lines of this book:
    prying loose some old assumptions
        clarifying your sowing & reaping
            getting your beliefs, emotions and body language in sync.

Should you tithe because sections of the Old Testament require it?
No, unless you're also committed to abstaining from pork and shellfish, refusing to buy clothing made with fabric blends, stop shaving and grow out your beard and sideburns (for the guys), hiding away for a few days a month (ladies) and prepared to have sex with your brother- or sister-in-law if one of you is widowed and childless. No, I thought not. To be sure, there are wise suggestions and healthy perspectives in the OT law, but we need to make intelligent decisions about how they apply in a circumstantially very different era.

Does the New Testament require Christians to tithe?
Not specifically... maybe, if you want it to. As we've said before, Paul addressed giving and follow-through, but when did he get on anyone's case about tithing? Some argue that it's implicit or assumed within that culture – maybe for the Jewish believers. The apostles and the Holy Spirit came to the conclusion that the only

mandatory expectations for Gentile believers were...
+ avoid sexual immorality (it's confusing and damaging)
+ give to the poor (whether you think they deserve it or not)
+ avoid food sacrificed to occult idols (and Paul softened on this one because interpreting the extent of the boycott was stressing out the folks in Corinth).
They didn't mention tithing.[9]

On the other hand, they had their hands full with miracles, explosive growth and radical giving: such as selling off real estate assets and trusting the apostles to distribute the money well, meals-on-wheels for widows, and devoting themselves to prayer and studying scripture (reasonable to think they were financially supported to be free to do this). Nagging and complaining about tithes didn't initially seem necessary. In fact, giving became so trendy it cost one couple their lives when they faked it.[10] Alternatively, tithing kind of pales in significance in the face of persecution, imprisonment and the impending destruction of Jerusalem, doesn't it?

Could it be that if you're bugged about tithing, either for or against, it's because either your spiritual life or the direction of your fellowship is failing to inspire generosity in you?
   Or that you haven't found an expression of the Church that inspires you?
   Or you need to cultivate your own niche for expression and contribution to the life of your fellowship?
Giving will not solve those – you need to find or create your rightful place, and buy in. The giving issue will become a non-issue if you're passionate. If you're not passionate, find your place of passion.

Am I "under a curse" if I don't tithe?
That scripture in Malachi was primarily addressed to clergy who seem to have been somehow diverting the incoming tithes. God was explaining whatever it was they were reaping as a consequence. Notice God said "you are under a curse" because that's where they'd put themselves through deception – not "I'm going to curse you," as a threat of punishment. And not blaming the congregation. There would have been some ripple effects felt by the rest of the country, but "the whole nation of you", as with the rest of that book, was aimed at the nation of priests.

So is tithing a bad idea?
Not necessarily, unless you're using it to paper over the underly-

ing issues of what you actually believe about God, yourself and your place in the world. Tithing is a bondage if you don't feel good about it. If it's an encouraging exercise in giving, then that's a good reason to be organized in your generosity.

Then is tithing legitimate?

Can be. God loves to see people express love and gratitude in the form of generosity. Like he does. I doubt he's so impressed with people who tithe because they're fulfilling their end of a contract with him. That's a temple tax. He honours people who step out to give because they want to learn faith and experience more of God's generous nature. Will he be so moved by people who tithe because "It works"?

If I give, should it be 10%, and is that before or after tax?

There, see? If you have to ask then you aren't convinced, and you aren't convinced because you haven't yet found your wellspring of inspiration. Interestingly, the financial self-help books I've seen in the general market all advocate giving, charity and philanthropy – some even referring to it as 'tithing' and suggest 10% as a guideline. So, what have they, and some legalistic sects, stumbled upon? That it's healthy and incumbent to simply give for the sake of building up someone else who's struggling, and it's unhealthy to hoard wealth. Generosity attracts more generosity.

That's another thing about the rich (the happy ones, anyway). They have their favoured charities to which they give their money, time and personal connections. And they decide where to give because they're convinced of the value, worthiness and competence of an organization. Rich people are generally generous people. (*Thwack!* if you must.)

If you're concerned about the tithing calculation, then you're still in 'tax' and 'dues' mode. Instead, you should be in a posture of 'growth' and 'prosperity' for your giving – not whether someone's going to be satisfied with their rate of getting.

Personally, I wouldn't go to a church if it wasn't home enough, engaging enough and life-giving enough to mobilize my family's contribution of time, energy, emotions, skills, learning, relationships and money. I don't want to be a consumer who consumes, I want to be a contributor who contributes. If your organization isn't actively cultivating and making room for your non-monetary contribution, then you need to be somewhere else and let them do whatever it is that they're actually passionate about. Or if you aren't taking them up on what they're currently making available, then you need to either create a compatible opportunity that complements their vision, or look elsewhere for a better fit.

So, instead of working out whether a 10% tithe is adequate and then complying, let's look at it from the other side. If you aren't excited about the opportunity to give, then the problem isn't the giving or the amount or the percentage. *The energy of money is highlighting your need for motivation.* Ask yourself what it would take for you to be that moved. Deal with the motivation issue and re-align your giving to be integrated and consistent with that. If your heart isn't engaged, be honest and don't do it.[11]

If you're not doing *any* giving at this point, just start with *something.* "Draw close to me and I will draw close to you." Decide on an amount or proportion of your after-tax income, make it a bit of a stretch so there's a zone of faith for the Lord to cultivate in you, and just see what happens. As God demonstrates his generosity to you, you'll be motivated to respond, grow and prosper in your own sense of generosity. Then the fun and satisfaction of contributing, giving and celebrating your passions will fuel your thoughts and vision for a lifestyle that is oblivious to minimums, scales and requirements. There are people out there with vision to give 90% of their income and only needing 10% to live on. Let's leave calculating 10[ths] of pre-tax mint and cumin to the Pharisees.[12]

But what about faithfulness?
Sure! If faithfulness and consistency is what you're motivated to learn, then that's a commendable thing to do. Not because God needs or expects the money, but because you're cultivating a deeper understanding of life in him that is not subject to surface moods or immediate circumstances. But if you don't find that you're learning, growing and attaining that goal within a reasonable amount of time, a timeframe or season in which to acquire that quality, then review your strategy. You don't want to live there long-term.

I have observed that churches which make tithing an expectation in their congregational culture (sometimes without realizing they're doing it) slip into devoting increasing energy and air-time to enforcement. If they were on the right track, their problem would be either asking people to ease up on the giving or having to scramble to distribute the money fast enough.[13] If a church is not actively, specifically cultivating and celebrating their people's own prosperity in their family finances, careers, businesses, skills, education and investments, then where do they get off complaining about people's lackluster contributions to the program's budget? It helps nothing to blame the rain gauge for the drought.

Unfortunately, there's a lot of teaching out there that says, in so many words, "Giving is your duty and naturally you'll want to give it to us." But if a church is not cultivating and investing time, space, energy and even its own money into the fruitfulness of their own people, then the phrase, "you reap where you have not sown" finds a salient relevance.

This may not be a divine *fiat* to explain God's definitive position, but look at it this way: Do you like receiving obligatory gifts? You know, the ones that blatantly say, "I hope this is adequate because I know you're expecting something." Or, "It's that time of year again, so here you go." You can pretty much tell, can't you? Who is thinking God is any more delighted and touched by that? But his heart *is* warmed by seeing someone who has found pleasure, joy and even celebration in giving. Or at least venturing to *learn* generosity and gratitude. And he's inclined to bless (enable, favour, support, encourage) that intention and action.

I keep hearing about 'stewardship'.
I know, I can't stand it. I grew up with that term, and it's typically misused in several ways regarding a church's corporate finances. First, some committee member's solemn warnings that equate stewardship with passing the offering plate and guilting people about chipping in more so they can (barely) make the church's annual budget. How grim.
Or it's time to ask for additional money for a large project.
Or when it comes to spending it's used as a short form for, "We're doing this on the cheap." Or, "Stinginess is next to godliness."

In scripture, stewardship is not about fundraising or pleading for the survival of the church, or making do with inferior products and services, or deliberately undersupporting their own staff. Stewardship is an individual taking responsibility for their assets, taking initiative, generating and embracing opportunity and producing results worth celebrating (think, *11-talent Manager*). Stewardship isn't about passing the plate for the church, it's about you succeeding with your abilities, creativity and boldness – doing what you do in life well.

So what about 'honour the Lord with your first fruits'?
Yes, that's back to celebration & gratitude. How would you express gratitude to your parents? Perhaps by living in a way that would please them (either being more like them or more like your individual self), or openly crediting their role, influence and significance. You might support their passions with your own TIME+ENERGY. So how would that be reflected in your personal relationship with God?
Blessing the poor, the widows and the foreigners?
Blessing his household?
Feeding the hungry, clothing the naked, visiting the prisoners?
Encouraging other members of the spiritual family?
Giving away the good news?
What motivates you?

'First fruits' doesn't mean a percentage commission off the top – it's about taking delight in God-given provision and productivity, and and giving the best because gratitude is a top priority. Not an afterthought or payroll deduction. Sync up your financial giving with your beliefs, emotions and stated purposes – celebrate it with your money and see where God will take it.

Great, so what am I supposed to do now?
Sow where you want to reap. Where do you want a more fruitful life? Where's your passion? Sow your money where you'd sow your ENERGY + TIME. And sow generously, not as an obligation or expense item, but as an exciting investment.

If you're not risking with your giving, and emotionally engaged and excited about seeing results, then you're just buying insurance of some sort.

And if you don't seem to be reaping what you want, examine your sowing pattern.

Find a cause for your passion and a passion for your money
Remember, money only amplifies, reveals or highlights what's already in your heart. If you were passionate about a particular cause, be it spiritual, social, artistic, medical, cultural, whatever, and prospering in your own pursuits (including your money) then 10% would not be an issue. If your delight and joy found its right-

ful expression, then you'd be giving all you could spare toward it and figuring out how to give more, not figuring out how to afford the minimum.

In a sense, you're already doing it. For instance, having a place to live is a big motivation, and your level of motivation is reflected in how much you spend on, or invest in, housing. Same with the vehicle you drive. And how much care you put into what you eat. And how you treat yourself with what you wear. Unless you're in survival mode, those decisions are already being guided by your true areas and levels of interest.

If you aren't an outstanding giver to a cause,
then it's because you haven't found
an outstanding cause to give to.
Not outstanding to you, at least. If it was, you'd already have thought of ways to change your spending to make room for what you really want – the opportunity to pour more of your time, thought, energy and money into that passion and conviction.

Sharing should transcend the spending/expense paradigm. The real potential lies in *growth* – finding ways to mobilize more effort, time, interest, energy and money and re-directing it into that cause you're passionate about. Why fret over how you'll afford to give $100 a month if you can re-direct your energies into leveraging your income to where you can give $1,000 a month?
Instead of pinching harder, leverage up!

Sharing that sparkles
If you haven't done so yet, go back to that Title / Strategies / Tactics chart we worked on and choose a tactic you can do right away. Before you go on to this next exercise.

I've deliberately focused on you and your relationship with money rather than jump into exhortations to give. Or tell you that complying with appeals to give will fix your finances. That's backwards. I am confident that if you have a healthy money mindset, you'll be open-hearted and open-handed with the God-given abundance you are now beginning to participate in. When you take your rightful place in an abundant, fruitful and generous Creation, you will become a more abundant, fruitful and generous person and sharing will be natural, purposeful and pleasurable. This was part of the reason we did that 'Seed for the Sower' exercise – to dislodge the tax/payroll deduction mindset that we are forced into by church maintenance mentalities, and to educate our mindsets that "as good as it is to receive, giving is even better."[14] You can't do one without the other.

I believe we could go even a step further. Grab a pen.

Tapping into the flow of generosity

God is creative. And he gave us that creative bent when he shaped us in his own image. It's something he likes about us – he likes that about you. And we have the amazing privilege of relating to him in the same delightful, fun, compassionate manner. He wants us to enjoy tapping into his personal delight in sharing, so the Bible says, "God loves a cheerful giver." The 'cheerful' part comes from the New Testament Greek word *nahar*, which means something like...

To sparkle cheerfully, like sunshine reflecting on a flowing river of prosperity.[15]

That's how good it's supposed to feel.

And Paul said God loves it when we feel like that.

There are certain mornings and afternoons I've spent with Charmaine over the years that I still savour – sitting at a waterside table on a bright, sunny day; enjoying time, conversation and food with someone you love. There's laughter, sharing, pleasure, profundity, abundance, contentment, satisfaction. An open sky and warming sunshine glittering right beside you, atop the mesmerizing and comforting flow of deep, moving water... are you there yet? Hold that picture. Use your key and "*I am rich in _____!*"

Lord, I want to flow with that kind of joy in your sparkling generosity, your flowing abundance.

I'm sorry for every time I succumbed to giving out of duty, guilt, coercion, embarrassment, peer pressure, need, routine or hype. I'll trust you to recognize what was willing and well-meant in that mix.

I also let go my judgments of other people's understanding and methods regarding ministry finances, and drawing on the energy of that offense to consider myself superior to them.

And I forgive every person who affected me, or people I love, with their approaches. [Name them, if their faces, names or voices spring to mind.]

I release them now and bless them to enjoy your prosperity – including financially.

I also forgive myself for the times I bought into, submitted to and enabled those methods – I shrug off that burden now. [Go ahead, physically shrug it off.]

Thank-you, Lord, for this renewed freedom for the money flowing through my life.
You have made me rich in _____!

Stay in that frame of mind, and let's ask the Holy Spirit, your tutor, for a new vision for sharing out of abundance, creativity and generosity.

Lord, would you show me, in pictures, words, sensations or memories, your vision for the money that you want to flow through me. How can I sparkle with the river of your abundance? [Just start writing, here or in the back of this book, without correcting, until you sense the flow has finished.]

_____

_____

_____

_____

_____

Now, look back over what you've recorded...
  Picture it vividly...
    Tune into the sound of it...
      Allow yourself the physical sensations and emotions,
        the *feelings*, of living in that certainty...
          and anchor that scenario into your thinking with your key.

Based on what you just saw, heard and felt, ask & answer these questions in a relaxed free flow of ideas and impressions:
  Who am I meant to serve with the money I'll share?

_____

  What problem will I solve?

_____

  What magnitude of money will it involve? (thousands, millions?)

_____

  Where will this need to happen? Do I want to be there myself?

Who else will be involved in accomplishing this?

What other resources will I need to access?

Are there already circumstances or people that are pushing against or leading me away from that goal? What is my opposition?

What's the next, small, simple thing I need to find out, in order to move toward that scenario for my money?

Sow what?
  ◆ Now, based on the above information, where could you either make a purchase or send a financial gift – a place, group or person already somehow related to that scenario?
  ◆ It might relate to a people group, a country, a medical cause, an online store, a ministry, an arts group, a profes- sional organization, a freeware or shareware business, a per- son you know, or don't know...
  ◆ If you need ideas, try taking some of the words you've writ- ten and use them in a Google® search of the internet.
  ◆ Go to their website or get their contact information.
  ◆ Get out your cheque book or credit card and sow!
  ◆ Alternatively, you could buy a relevant gift (something that will help them do what they're doing) of the same value and give it to them. But make it relevant in some way to that spar- kling river of abundance you just connected with.

Write here what you've decided to do with that money:

And when you follow through, pray something like this:
  Lord, I am casting this bread
  into the flow of our shared creativity
  onto the waters of your abundance.

And I LIKE the way it feels!
Because I am rich in _____!

Come back to this spot when you notice something relevant return to you, like an invitation, unexpected money, an introduction to someone, a thank-you arrives, a problem dissolves, you discover a new resource... and write it here:

_____

_____

And of course, express your gratitude and thanks that
"I am rich in _____!"

1 Matthew25. The version in Luke19 is more dramatic and harsh.

2 The talent was the largest measure of weight in use in Jesus' time and culture and weighed about 33 kilograms or 75 pounds. Such calculations are problematic, but at the time of this writing, silver was trading for US$13.50 per Troy ounce (which has nothing to do with the City of Troy). If the talents were gold, they'd now be worth about $730,000 each. The point is that it was a lot of money.

3 Or were you hoping Heaven is one massive, perpetual church service? Or all-inclusive resort?

4 Discussions of the ensuing bloodbath will have to wait.

5 If I say, "Do not think about Winston Churchill." Who is occupying your thoughts?

6 James 4:8

7 Not because we're complying, not because he needs it, but because of what it does in us.

8 www.charmainehicks.com and www.coachcharmaine.com

9 Acts 15:28,29

10 Acts 5

11 There is the occasional case of people holding funds back to ransom and leverage decisions in churches – I'm not suggesting that. I'm saying to figure out where you can be committed.

12 Matthew 23:23

13 Exodus 36:4-7, II Chronicles 24:10-14, 31:4-21, Acts 4:32.

14 Acts 20:35

15 2Cor.9:7 and Strong's Concordance.

Closing (but probably not final) Thoughts

So, back to the opening question: *Does God want you to be rich?* You may have seen the cover story of *TIME* magazine asking that question.[1] Not a bad article, but of course not offering any conclusions. Only that debate and apprehension continue to simmer among Christians. Kind of laughable really, when millions of poor people would gladly switch places with the people pontificating and criticizing.

But I noticed that running through the various points of view there was common ground: life is about living in a way that is significant, purposeful and fulfilling in a whole, complete way – not the naked pursuit of a fat bank account. No one was saying that 'rich' is the same as 'fulfilled'. I think we've all gotten beyond the 'Greed is Good' thing from the '80s.

But I trust that you're now clearer on what the answer to that question looks like for you.

 + Maybe wealth – affluent people have spiritual needs too, and their resources can do a lot to feed, heal, employ and encourage others.
 + Maybe self-imposed simplicity – like Jesus himself, there are times when you need to roll up your sleeves and get in there *mano a mano.*

For either scenario, you'll want to *go in healthy about money* because both entail freedom & responsibility, humility & confidence. Including where it comes down to your ability to engage with people at the other end of the spectrum.

 + For the resource people to connect with the needs of those who struggle and the opportunities to get involved with them.
 + For the field agents to access the support of the rich and influential with confidence and conviction.

It's not about you
In both financial contexts, it's a matter of effectively serving and mobilizing people. You'll be in a better position to reach into the lives of others and encourage them to step out with purpose and direction if you know your own purpose and direction, and money could be an important part of the equation.

I especially hope a lot of people will move out of the middle range of stuckedness, worry and impotence and make for one end or the other of the scale as a result of reading and working with this book. Someone needs to break out and start a business, and someone needs to buy their ticket to Mozambique.

What I'm *not* saying is that Christians should be rich to become self-indulgent consumers of 'lifestyle' & 'convenience' – these usually turn out to be neither. And the results are banal and boring. Christians should know better than to buy into the notion that luxury is the logical end-product of faith. Remember: "riches in Heaven", "excel in generosity", "good & faithful", "what you did for the least of these you did for me."

The key issue in terms of my purposes for this book is this:
> Every Christian should be free
> > of the debilitating prejudices and misperceptions
> > about the nature and effect of money
> > which sabotage their aspirations
> > and bar them from getting on with kingdom stuff.
> If you can't master those,
> > they will continue to thwart you
> > and hold your dreams hostage.

So do something! Be bold! Take risks! It's time to embrace your responsibility and expand your capacity.
Your reservations and inhibitions are crap!

Ah yes, the testimony thing

Perhaps you've noticed that I haven't said a lot about my own experiences with money. This was deliberate. I realize that testimonies can be encouraging, but not for everyone all the time. When Charmaine and I were "going through it" with our finances, glory stories and declarations of victory and breakthrough were only galling. It only gave us vision for how badly things were going, how far we were slipping and how doing the right thing just wasn't helping. (Believe me, our experiences had a lot of people shaking their heads.)

Yes, we were happy for the blessed folk, but also very mindful of those still struggling. Including us. I wouldn't discourage anyone from bearing testimony about healing and breakthrough in their finances – in fact, it's important to share what God has done – but in the context of this book, while someone is still in the thick of getting real about their own issues surrounding money, I thought such stories could be counterproductive. I didn't want to undermine the focus on the reader's own experience by clouding the discussion with other people's conclusions.

Also, too many of those testimonies are about people squeaking out of a jam and into a state of relief – yes, thank God for it, but that's not what I'm going for here. I don't want to settle for a series of rescues, bail-outs and bumbling subsistence. I want people to break free of meagreness, shoot past normality into excitement and have fun with dynamic God-experiences. I want to see crazy success, hilarious giving and exhilarating prospects open up.

Most of all, the joy of seeing people flourish free of self-perpetuating financial impotence and depression – you know that verse about a hope deferred making the heart sick, but a desire fulfilled being a Tree of Life[2]? I'm so tired of seeing people reconciling themselves to that sickness, as if that's 'faithfulness' and the best we can cling to until Kingdom Come.

Having said that, when we start to see stories of people's experiences of financial healing, restoration and flourishment [sic] relating to the processes and benefits of this book, I'll tuck them back here in the closing pages of future printings – if people want to read them, they'll be available but not in their faces while they go through the book.

So I seriously want your stories and feedback
Even if it's just about typos or grammatical transgressions.
Either email me directly at
    david@healingyourfinancialsoul.com
or via the website:
    www.healingyourfinancialsoul.com

Back to us...
Let it suffice that I personally, and Charmaine & I as a couple, have experienced more of the ups & downs than I'd willingly choose. Much of it self-fulfilling stuff in my heart. Some of it still seemingly random. Most of it in 'Christian' contexts. Bottom line: I don't know if I could have learned what I know now some other way, much less written a book for other people about it, but I doubt it. And anyways, here I am now.

I'm sensitive to the dynamic that not everything that happens around us and to us is personal self-fulfillment. But I suspect there's more of it than meets the eye. So given the way the universe has been entangled and designed to respond, it can hardly help but reveal things about God – best to trust him with the random stuff as well.

For sure, our progress gets tested

You've seen it other areas: Learn something and along comes the opposite to prove whether or not what you've just gained is true – a nasty call, a difficult client, a weird reaction from your siblings, a committee collapses in disagreement, something breaks, someone loses something... most of it will come in the form of pressure on relationships, in which case the wisest thing to do is to take a breath, and say to yourself, "I'm going to pass this test..." and do something generous and kind. The test will pass itself.

So what about the broadsides?

In general, things go better if we are proactive about dealing with our faulty wiring. But when the random 'stuff' happens, including in our finances, you might need to consider it part of the process of brokenness. We've been through it, and it's how you learn to bless your enemies. Sometimes after the fact.

If you've been through a period of brokenness in regards to money, let me close with these thoughts. I can't presume to hold up my own experiences in the light of some of the awful financial trials other people have been through – all I know is as much as I've experienced. And one day the Lord pointed out to me a few things about brokenness:

1 - **It hurts** – that's why they call it *broken*-ness.
2 - **It's not fair** – if you deserved it, it'd be sowing & reaping.
3 - **It's universal** – everyone goes through it in some fashion.
4 – **It's kinda necessary** – if we come out the other side of it *with* him, we're left with personal qualities of depth (flexibility, softness, compassion, appreciation and perspective) that simply cannot be won any other way. That wisdom is your entryway to better things and will make you trust-able.

So even the crummy stuff can eventually serve you.
But it's up to you. Bitter or better, you choose.

Have I done all this stuff myself?

Yes, I have worked through all of the book's material myself, either

specifically applying the activations I've designed here, or covered the same ground in other contexts, such as pastoral training, personal ministry and counseling work with others. In some cases I went back and re-did them anyway, just to be sure. And the results for me have been both
  remarkable and subtle
    immediate and gradual
      grand and small-scale
        startling and incremental.

One last encouragement
Keep this book handy and refer to it from time to time. Healing and wellness in your finances will be an organic process which will move at different tempos in different seasons. And spill over into different areas of your life. Part of the dynamic of working through these things is that it's not as contained and compartmentalized as we've cared to think. You will see ripple effects in other areas of your life: career, social, family, physical health and so on. It's all interconnected, so when you make improvements and embrace change in one aspect, such as your finances, expect to see benefits manifest in others areas as well.

Once in a while, flip the book open and just dip in for a few minutes – you'll see stuff that didn't really phase you the last time. Your written responses will reveal dynamics and depths that you didn't fully understand were coming into play back then.

And whatever you do,
    be persistent, consistent and insistent that
      You are rich in _____!

1 September 18, 2006.
2 Proverbs 13:12, upper case my addition.

Appendix
You Can Hear God's Voice!
by Mark Virkler

The age in which we live is so married to rationalism and cognitive, analytical thought that we almost mock when we hear of one actually claiming to be able to hear the voice of God. However, we do not scoff, for several reasons. First, men and women throughout the Bible heard God's voice. Also, there are some highly effective and reputable men and women of God alive today who demonstrate that they hear God's voice. Finally, there is a deep hunger within us all to commune with God, and hear Him speak within our hearts.

As a born-again, Bible-believing Christian, I struggled unsuccessfully for years to hear God's voice. I prayed, fasted, studied my Bible and listened for a voice within, all to no avail. There was no inner voice that I could hear! Then God set me aside for a year to study, read, and experiment in the area of learning to hear His voice. During that time, the Lord taught me four keys that opened the door to two-way prayer. I have discovered that not only do they work for me, but they have worked for many thousands of believers who have been taught to use them, bringing tremendous intimacy to their Christian experience and transforming their very way of living. This will happen to you also as you seek God, utilizing the following four keys. They are all found in Habakkuk 2:1,2. I encourage you to read this passage before going on.

Key #1 – God's voice in our hearts sounds like a flow of spontaneous thoughts. Therefore, when I tune to God, I tune to spontaneity.

The Bible says that the Lord answered me and said...(Hab. 2:2). Habakkuk knew the sound of God's voice. Elijah described it as a still, small voice (I Kings 19:12). I had always listened for an inner audible voice, and surely God can and does speak that way at times. However, I have found that for most of us, most of the time, God's inner voice comes to us as spontaneous thoughts, visions, feelings, or impressions. For example, haven't each of us had the experience of driving down the road and having a thought come to us to pray for a certain person? We generally acknowledge this to be the voice of God calling us to pray for that individual. My question to you is, "What did God's voice sound like as you drove in your car? Was it an inner, audible voice, or was it a spontaneous thought that lit upon your mind?" Most of you would say that God's voice came to you as a spontaneous thought.

So I thought to myself, "Maybe when I listen for God's voice, I should be listening for a flow of spontaneous thoughts. Maybe spirit-level communication is received as spontaneous thoughts, impressions, feelings, and visions." Through experimentation and feedback from thousands of others, I am now convinced that this is so.

The Bible confirms this in many ways. The definition of paga, the Hebrew word for intercession, is "a chance encounter or an accidental intersecting." When God lays people on our hearts for intercession, He does it through paga, a chance-encounter thought, accidentally intersecting our thought processes. There-fore, when I tune to God, I tune to chance-encounter thoughts or spontaneous thoughts. When I am poised quietly before God in prayer, I have found that the flow of spontaneous thoughts that comes is quite definitely from God.

Key #2 – I must learn to still my own thoughts and emotions, so that I can sense God's flow of thoughts and emotions within me.

Habakkuk said, "I will stand on my guard post and station myself on the rampart..." (Hab. 2:1). Habakkuk knew that in order to hear God's quiet, inner, spontaneous thoughts, he had to first go to a quiet place and still his own thoughts and emo-tions. Psalm 46:10 encourages us to be still, and know that He is God. There is a deep inner knowing (spontaneous flow) in our spirits that each of us can experience when we quiet our flesh and our minds.

I have found several simple ways to quiet myself so that I can more readily pick up God's spontaneous flow. Loving God through a quiet worship song is a most effective means for me (note II Kings 3:15). It is as I become still (thoughts, will, and emo-tions) and am poised before God that the divine flow is real-ized. Therefore, after I worship quietly and then become still, I open myself for that spontaneous flow. If thoughts come to me of things I have forgotten to do, I write them down and then dismiss them. If thoughts of guilt or unworthiness come to my mind, I repent thoroughly, receive the washing of the blood of the Lamb, and put on His robe of righteousness, seeing myself spotless before the presence of God (Is. 61:10; Col. 1:22).

As I fix my gaze upon Jesus (Heb. 12:2), becoming quiet in His presence, and sharing with Him what is on my heart, I find that two-way dialogue begins to flow. Spontaneous thoughts flow from the throne of God to me, and I find that I am actually conversing with the King of Kings.

It is very important that you become still and properly focused if you are going to receive the pure word of God. If you are not still, you will simply be receiving your own thoughts. If you are not properly focused on Jesus, you will receive an impure flow, because the intuitive flow comes out of that upon which you have fixed your eyes. Therefore, if you fix your eyes upon Jesus, the intuitive flow comes from Jesus. If you fix your gaze upon some desire of your heart, the intuitive flow comes out of that desire of your heart. To have a pure flow you must first of all become still, and secondly, you must carefully fix your eyes upon Jesus. Again I will say, quietly worshiping the King, and then receiving out of the stillness that follows quite easily accomplish this.

Key #3 – as I pray, I fix the eyes of my heart upon Jesus, seeing in the Spirit the dreams and visions of Almighty God.

We have already alluded to this principle in the previous paragraphs; however, we need to develop it a bit further. Habakkuk said, "I will keep watch to see," and God said, "Record the vision" (Hab. 2:1,2). It is very interesting that Habakkuk was going to actually start looking for vision as he prayed. He was going to open the eyes of his heart, and look into the spirit world to see what God wanted to show him. This is an intriguing idea.

I had never thought of opening the eyes of my heart and looking for vision. However, the more I thought of it, the more I realized this was exactly what God intends for me to do. He gave me eyes in my heart. They are to be used to see in the spirit world the vision and movement of Almighty God. I believe there is an active spirit world functioning all around me. This world is full of angels, demons, the Holy Spirit, the omnipresent God, and His omnipresent Son, Jesus. There is no reason for me not to see it, other than my rational culture, which tells me not to believe it is even there and provides no instruction on how to become open to seeing this spirit world.

The most obvious prerequisite to seeing is that we need to look. Daniel was seeing a vision in his mind and he said, "I was looking...I kept looking...I kept looking" (Dan. 7:2,9,13). Now as I pray, I look for Jesus present with me, and I watch Him as He speaks to me, doing and saying the things that are on His heart. Many Christians will find that if they will only look, they will see. Jesus is Emmanuel, God with us (Matt. 1:23). It is as simple as that. You will see a spontaneous inner vision in a manner similar to receiving spontaneous inner thoughts. You can see Christ present with you in a comfortable setting, because Christ is present with you in a comfortable setting. Actually, you will probably discover that inner vision comes so easily you will have a tendency to reject it, thinking that it is just you. (Doubt is satan's most effective weapon against the Church.) However, if you will persist in recording these visions, your doubt will soon be overcome by faith as you recognize that the content of them could only be birthed in Almighty God.

God continually revealed Himself to His covenant people using dream and vision. He did so from Genesis to Revelation and said that, since the Holy Spirit was poured out in Acts 2, we should expect to receive a continuing flow of dreams and visions (Acts 2:1-4,17). Jesus, our perfect Example, demonstrated this ability of living out of ongoing contact with Almighty God. He said that He did nothing on His own initiative, but only that which He saw the Father doing, and heard the Father saying (Jn. 5:19,20,30). What an incredible way to live!

Is it actually possible for us to live out of the divine initiative as Jesus did? A major purpose of Jesus' death and resurrection was that the veil be torn from top to bottom, giving us access into the immediate presence of God, and we are commanded to draw near (Lk. 23:45; Heb. l0: 19-22). Therefore, even though what I am describing seems a bit unusual to a rational twentieth-century culture, it is demonstrated and described as being a central biblical teaching and experience. It is time to restore to the Church all that belongs to the Church.

Because of their intensely rational nature and existence in an overly-rational culture, some will need more assistance and understanding of these truths before they can move into them. They will find this help in the book Communion With God by the same authors.

Key #4 – Journaling, the writing out of our prayers and God's answers, provides a great new freedom in hearing God's voice.
God told Habakkuk to record the vision and inscribe it on tablets...(Hab. 2:2). It had never crossed my mind to write out my prayers and God's answers as Habakkuk did at God's command. If you begin to search Scripture for this idea, you will find hundreds of chapters demonstrating it (Psalms, many of the prophets, Revelation). Why then hadn't I ever thought of it?

I called the process "journaling," and I began experimenting with it. I discovered it to be a fabulous facilitator to clearly discerning God's inner, spontaneous flow, because as I journaled I was able to write in faith for long periods of time, simply believing it was God. I did not have to test it as I was receiving it (which jams one's receiver), because I knew that when the flow was over I could go back and test and examine it carefully, making sure that it lined up with Scripture.

You will be amazed when you attempt journaling. Doubt may hinder you at first, but throw it off, reminding yourself that it is a biblical concept, and that God is present, speaking to His children. Don't take yourself too seriously. When you do, you become tense and get in the way of the Holy Spirit's movement. It is when we cease our labors and enter His rest that God is free to flow (Heb. 4:10). Therefore, put a smile on your face, sit back comfortably, get out your pen and paper, and turn your attention toward God in praise and worship, seeking His face. As you write out your question to God and become still, fixing your gaze on Jesus, Who is present with you, you will suddenly have a very good thought in response to your question. Don't doubt it, simply write it down. Later, as you read your journaling, you, too, will be blessed to discover that you are indeed dialoguing with God.

Some final notes: No one should attempt this without having first read through at least the New Testament (preferably, the entire Bible), nor should one attempt this unless he is submitted to solid, spiritual leadership. All major directional moves that come through journaling should be submitted before being acted upon.

Used by permission.
For a complete teaching on this topic, order the *Communion With God Study Guide* at www.CWGministries.org
or call 716-652-6990.
Online catalog of 50 books available by Mark & Patti Virkler, as well as 100 college courses through external degree.
Email: cwg@cwgministries.org.

There's also a video feature about Mark and his discovery of how to hear God's voice at:
   http://www.cwgministries.org/huntley.htm

If this book has been a help to you

... and you know someone else who could benefit, you can order copies from our website:
   www.healingyourfinancialsoul.com
where we plan to offer other related materials in the near future, such as:

* an audio version (for those who prefer to listen)
* a video version (for those who like to see who they're listening to)
* a group study guide (for small groups or couple's ministries)
* a corporate business version (imagine if managers and staff got this stuff...)

and more, as time and interest warrant.

I **promise** that you will never see classified ads for a HYFS singing business card holder or HYFS golf shoe scraper.